Believing and Acting

The Pragmatic Turn in Comparative Religion and Ethics

Believing and Acting

The Pragmatic Turn in Comparative
Religion and Ethics

G. Scott Davis

OXFORD
UNIVERSITY PRESS

OXFORD
UNIVERSITY PRESS

Great Clarendon Street, Oxford, OX2 6DP,
United Kingdom

Oxford University Press is a department of the University of Oxford.
It furthers the University's objective of excellence in research, scholarship,
and education by publishing worldwide. Oxford is a registered trade mark of
Oxford University Press in the UK and in certain other countries

© G. Scott Davis 2012

The moral rights of the author have been asserted

First Edition published in 2012

Published in the United States of America by Oxford University Press
198 Madison Avenue, New York, NY 10016, United States of America

British Library Cataloguing in Publication Data
Data available

Library of Congress Control Number: 2011942642

ISBN 978-0-19-958390-4

For Mark

"I turned and knelt on the trail and said 'Thank you, shack.'
Then I added 'Blah,' with a little grin because I knew that
shack and that mountain would understand what that
meant, and turned and went on down the trail back to this
world."

Kerouac, Dharma Bums

Preface

This book has its origins in a Princeton dissertation defended in the fall of 1983. I almost immediately switched areas, but my friends kept remembering it and, starting about seven years ago, began asking for papers that went back to those earlier issues. Papers turned into essays and when Tom Perridge approached me in January of 2009 I thought that I could string them together into a little book. That didn't work for me and so after a year of ineffectual tinkering I started on page one and wrote it straight through. Vestiges of the "precursor" essays remain, but many of those vestiges go all the way back to the original dissertation.

The best thing about the long lapse of time has been a closer acquaintance with history, anthropology, science, and art. In none of those fields am I expert, but it has been helpful to me to be able to weave in issues and examples to illustrate the continuity, as I see it, of interpreting religion with the same issues in the rest of the humanities and social sciences. An earlier version was heavily loaded with even more examples than remain, and my readers owe a debt of gratitude to Lizzie Robottom, Tom's assistant editor, and to Robert Segal, who read the initial draft for the press. Segal also read the original proposal, as did Jeff Stout, and I owe them both a great deal, not only for their help with this book, but for their work and guidance over many years.

The book is, I suppose, a paean to my teachers, living and dead, who belong, at least in my telling, to the tradition of Aristotle, Peirce, and Wittgenstein. Some—Geertz, Douglas, Baxandall—I've known mostly through their works. Others—Pols, Rorty, Stout, Proudfoot—were and are teachers, colleagues, and friends of long standing. Herbert Fingarette, whose works I've been reading since the 1970s, became a virtual friend over a decade ago, when we began an e-mail correspondence that remains one of my great pleasures. He is a brilliant and wonderful person.

The book is dedicated to Murphy, who appears as a character in various chapters. We've been friends for a very long time.

Richmond, Virginia
2 May 2011

Contents

1. Believing and Acting: The allure of method
   in the study of religion — 1

2. Peirce and the Legacy of Pragmatism — 23

3. Ethics, Religion, and the Limits of Empiricism — 49

4. Richard Rorty and the Pragmatic Turn in the Study
   of Religion — 75

5. "Gay Fine Colours": Cognitive science and the study
   of religion — 99

6. The Base of Design: Relativism and fieldwork in
   contemporary anthropology — 123

7. Explaining Innovation: From the history of art to
   comparative ethics and religion — 147

8. From Comparisons to Cases: Pragmatism and the
   politics of virtue — 175

Bibliography — 199
Index — 227

1

Believing and Acting

The allure of method in the study of religion

You don't have to ride the subway long to notice certain regularities. While there is always a crush of people directly beyond the turnstiles, or right around the central stairs, a fair number of riders will immediately and deliberately make their way to a particular spot and wait. If you become a regular you will eventually understand why they wait where they wait, and shortly after that you will begin doing the same thing. You will never exchange any words with your fellow riders, but you will all recognize each other as "regulars," or "locals," members of a community for which riding the subway day in and day out is part of a way of life. This may ultimately connect up with where you sit or stand in the car, the importance of passing through from one car to another, and the ease with which you negotiate the shift from the east side to the west, not to mention the occasional foray into the outer boroughs.

These patterns of acting are closely related to sets of beliefs. If you were initiated by a well-established guide, there might be a core set of practices and beliefs which you learned under his direction though, once you became an independent actor, new complexes of believing and acting developed as part of your routine. Suppose your older brother has preceded you at Columbia. When you fly into Newark he'll lead the way in getting you from the airport to the Port Authority, down through the maze to the westside IRT and then up to 110th or 116th or wherever you need to go. You'll depend on him for a couple of weeks until you make your own friends and develop your own habits and patterns. For quite a while you'll feel more comfortable being a strap-hanger close by the map.

But eventually you will internalize the basics and be able to use the full panoply of available information to get around with ease. You will know which lines are which and where they go. You will have a general sense of where the cars stop at the stations you regularly use and you will know which car to choose if you want the most convenient exit or transfer point for a particular station. After a while you will have a pretty good sense of how long you should allow to get from one point to another at a given time of day. There is no dress code for the subway, but depending on your age and station in life, there will turn out to be certain occasions for which dress, time, and decorum dictate forgoing the subway and taking a cab. Of course, if you're strapped for cash you may have to make concessions. For example, if you live in Washington Heights (perhaps you've made the transition from undergraduate to graduate student and have found a bargain in old Fort George) and are headed for a dinner party with your parents on the east side, you might catch the A train at 190th, ride it to Columbus Circle, and pick up a cab to your final destination. You hope dad will kick in a couple of twenties to help defray the cab trip home.

Human lives incorporate any number of "sub-routines," some more and some less complex than riding the subway. All of these sub-routines contribute to the successful negotiation of the days and years and decades that make up those lives. To the extent that we find each other interesting, we may be intrigued by how people eat, drink, sleep, move around, and do any number of other things at particular times and places. Religion is one of those things. Ethics is another. This is a book about some of the intellectual puzzles that have presented themselves in studying religion and ethics in different places and across various times. It belongs to the genre "theories and methods in the study of religion," but the genre itself is misleading. If we take plate tectonics or quantum electrodynamics as a paradigm of theory in the natural sciences, then there are good reasons to think that religion is not the sort of phenomenon susceptible of theory. Theories in the natural sciences typically take as their subject objects and events in the material world. They attempt either to account for these objects and events in terms of their simpler constituents or show how their subjects interact to produce more complex phenomena. An important goal of these analyses is to produce general accounts of properties and behavior, preferably couched in mathematical form, that can be tested against the experience of the inquirers.

Human activities, whether individual or collective, resist being subsumed under theories of this sort. Economists and psychologists of the last two centuries have occasionally talked as if they could come close to a formal theory, often couched in the mathematics of game theory. But once they have been forced to acknowledge the *ceteris paribus* clauses, the local qualifications, and the unmeasurable probabilities that complicate the situation, their laws and predictions begin to look more like educated, sometimes brilliant, guesses, but not serious contenders for "theories" in the sense promoted by the natural sciences. In part this is true for any complex, nonlinear system, but it is particularly the case when human individuals or groups are in a position freely and rapidly to revise their desires, goals, and strategies and then to act on these revisions.

I'm going to argue that the difficulty in accounting for human phenomena isn't a defect in our rational abilities. Nor does it point to some uncapturable reality in the essence of human experience. It stems from taking ourselves seriously as reasonable agents who act on our beliefs in the hope of securing what we take to be desirable ends. "Religion" functions more like "politics," "literature," and "art," sequestering a particular body of behavior and its products for a specific critical purpose. The population under study doesn't even need to have an analogous term in its conceptual arsenal. The methods available for the student will be whichever ones he thinks may prove useful for his purposes. In any case, he will bear the burden of proof in convincing his peers he has accomplished something worth doing.

It might make more sense to call my genre "approaches to the study of religion." This would at least relieve me of the seeming paradox of endorsing certain "theorists" of religion while arguing all the while for an end to the pursuit of "theory" in the study of religion. For that is what I plan to do. My argument will be that understanding religion requires nothing more than the sensitive and imaginative reading of human phenomena informed by the best available ethnography set in the best available historical narrative. The fruitful arguments to be had are about the details of reading, fieldwork, and narrative, and the best way to understand rival approaches is as suggestions for what we should pay attention to in telling the stories we tell about believing and acting.

The practical upshot of this is that studying approaches to the study of religion is a lot like gardening: judicious pruning and weeding open up the space essential to the flourishing of the field. The tools I plan to use have mostly been furnished by the tradition of American pragmatism, in particular that strand of the tradition identified with C. S. Peirce. My procedure will be to argue that when suggestions stray too far from Peirce's account of inquiry they are likely to lead us down blind alleys into dead ends. In some cases it will prove possible to rein in the excesses of some professed theorist, while retaining his or her helpful insight.

Mary Douglas and Clifford Geertz spent good parts of their careers in a pragmatic rereading of Durkheim and Weber. In other cases—the wide-eyed naiveté of cognitive studies and the postmodern hermeneutics of suspicion—there's not enough to bother and both should probably be uprooted altogether.

I don't expect the reader to believe me on the basis of these remarks alone; the chapters to come will provide the arguments for my position. Nor do I claim to be a trailblazer in the pragmatic approach to the study of religion. I've already mentioned Douglas and Geertz. Wayne Proudfoot and Jeff Stout, among others, have more recently led the way in this pragmatic turn. But I don't think anyone so far has quite seen the opportunity for the new sort of comparativism this turn makes possible. The old comparativism came in two forms, with many variations. On the one hand, there was the serial doxography of the "these guys say this, those guys say that" sort familiar from the heroic age of oriental philology. Max Müller's *Sacred Books of the East* remains an enduring legacy. On the other hand, there was the programatic comparativism that purported to uncover some fundamental truth of human experience: Protestant Christianity is the fullest realization of the encounter with the infinite (Schleiermacher's *On Religion*); religion emerges from the cultural-linguistic urge to capture the reality of the natural world (Müller himself); religion expresses the desire of archaic man to live in the sacred present (Eliade). I doubt any of these has much to tell us because I doubt that there are any fundamental truths about human experience beyond birth and death. Everything in between is local.

The comparativism of the pragmatic turn is perhaps best captured by Quentin Skinner, who writes that "there are no perennial problems in philosophy. There are only individual answers to individual questions, and potentially as many different questions as there are questioners" (2002, 88). This isn't, however, a counsel of despair, for he goes on to conclude that:

> A knowledge of the history of such ideas can show the extent to which those features of our own arrangements which we may be disposed to accept as "timeless" truths may be little more than contingencies of our local history and social structure. To discover from the history of thought that there are in fact no such timeless concepts, but only the various different concepts which have gone with various different societies, is to discover a general truth not merely about the past but about ourselves. [Ibid., 88–89]

What Skinner discovers about politics, and about philosophy generally, holds for students of religion as well, whatever their theological commitments. The non-believer is inclined to sign off with Cronkite's "and that's the way it is"; the believer is disposed to add "just like God intended it."

Either way, the student of religion reinforces our grasp on the contingency of human behavior. Since almost anything might have been otherwise, we must begin by securing the best possible account of why someone or some group said, wrote, or did what was said, written, or done. Thus the first step in comparison will focus on competing scholarly interpretations. Our libraries are filled with often brilliant interpretations of thinkers and events which, having held the field for a generation or more, have relinquished their authority to an upstart rival. Understanding religion and ethics begins with the primary evidence, but reaches maturity in comparing interpretations and testing them repeatedly against each other.

The second step in pragmatic comparison begins with the fruit of interpretive testing. Once we have a rich grasp of the history, we can ask about the issues that arise and the proposals for resolving them when the practices of one group intersect with those of another. This is familiar from the critical history and appreciation of the arts. A stroll through the Metropolitan Museum of Art, for instance, can lead from the Temple of Dendur to a landscape by Cezanne to a contemporary sculptural installation on the Roof Garden. Some people just take in the sights and many don't come at all. But understanding just the rooms dedicated to nineteenth-century European painting requires figuring out what's going on in Courbet's *View of Ornans* and how it compares to Cezanne's *Trees and Houses Near the Jas de Bouffan*, painted just thirty years later. Not everyone is interested in the study necessary to grasp these comparisons, but those who aspire to an academic appreciation of such paintings can be held accountable for a basic grasp of the classic interpreters—Nochlin, Rewald, and Schapiro, for example—and their more recent critics and continuators.

A third step in the comparative project may involve embrace and advocacy, either of the subject for his vision or the student for his subject. Imagine moving downtown to the Museum of Modern Art. One of the great works in its collection is Mondrian's *Broadway Boogie Woogie*, from 1942–43. But how, you might reasonably ask, can the same painter have produced *Truncated View of the Broekzidjer Mill* forty years earlier? At some point an answer will require an account of the different styles Mondrian embraced, from Impressionism through Cubism, and his break from representationalism altogether by the end of the First World War. *Church Facade 6*, a drawing from 1915, has reduced the building to a pattern of verticals and horizontals, with only a few arches along the center vertical. There is perhaps some memory here of the

5

windmill's fan, fence, and door. By 1920 even a hint of objects in the world is banished, as in *Composition with Red, Blue, Black and Yellow-Green*. It will help to know something about the Neo-Plasticism Mondrian developed, in which "the new plastic idea cannot ... take the form of a natural or concrete representation." Rather than a move to cold abstraction, Mondrian is attempting to capture "actual aesthetic relationships" so that the "picture can be a pure reflection of life in its deepest essence" (Chipp 1968, 322). As Schapiro writes, in *Broadway Boogie Woogie* Mondrian returns to his earlier styles in a painting where the "emotion suppressed in his search for an intellectual absolute, was released with a new freedom through his experience of a welcoming American milieu" (Schapiro 1978, 257). This doesn't mean that Mondrian abandoned his quest for the universal. As he wrote in about 1943:

> the first aim in painting should be universal expression ... True Boogie Woogie I conceive as homogeneous in intention with mine in painting: destruction of melody which is the equivalent of destruction of natural appearance; and construction through the continuous opposition of pure means - dynamic rhythm. [Chipp 1968, 364]

The critic himself doesn't need to embrace Mondrian's interpretation of the music to appreciate *Broadway Boogie Woogie*, but if he is going to understand what Mondrian is doing and how it might relate to a contemporary such as Kandinsky, whose lithograph *Abstraction*, from 1923, is also in MOMA's collection, it will be valuable to know what both believed and how their abstractions relate to their commitments.

So far I've been focusing on the sorts of comparisons involved in the advanced academic study of some field of human endeavor, but there is another possible consequence of such studies: advocacy. Schapiro opens his essays as follows:

> Mondrian's abstract paintings appeared to certain of his contemporaries extremely rigid, more a product of theory than of feeling. One thought of the painter as narrow, doctrinaire, in his inflexible commitment to the right angle and the unmixed primary colors. [1978, 233]

In the course of the essay he leads his reader through Mondrian's stylistic changes, his theosophical quest for the truth in painting, up to his final New York paintings. Contrary to the interpretations with which he begins, he shows Mondrian to be constantly experimenting—he takes up Cubism at forty—and relating his own changing work to the European tradition from which he emerged. By the end he gives us a portrait of Mondrian as dynamic, playful, energized late in life by the sights and sounds of New York. Not only does he think we should embrace his interpretation, but it is clear that he believes we should embrace Mondrian, who "was never more free and colorful, and closer to the city spectacle in its double aspect of the architectural as an endless construction of repeated regular units and of the random in the perpetual movement of people, traffic, and flashing lights" (ibid., 258).

The best students love what they study. This is true not only of art historians, but of physicists, philologists, and myrmecologists. J. R. R. Tolkien used his philological skills to populate an entire world. Students of philosophy, government, and religion are, perhaps, a bit more likely than most to edge into advocacy because they study the beliefs and practices that have moved whole populations to transform the world around them. But study and advocacy are not inseparable. In the chapters to come I will argue my positions and I will illustrate what the sort of comparativism I advocate can look like. In particular, the penultimate section of chapter 7 takes up a contemporary debate on the interpretation of Aquinas and the ethics of war, while the concluding section of chapter 8 uses the comparative deployment of rabbinic and Japanese Buddhist materials to get some leverage on a debate about abortion that has often claimed to be driven by arguments drawn from Aquinas. I plan to venture up to the edge of advocacy, if only to show how it might be done, but I plan to leave that argument for another time.

The temptations of theory: a preliminary taxonomy

As tempting as it might be, a full history of theories and methods in the study of religion lies well beyond the ambitions of this book. I want to begin with a look at one or two entries from *Critical Terms for Religious Studies*, an influential recent collection edited by Mark Taylor. The volume comprises twenty-two essays on topics both "familiar" and "strange," in "an effort to raise old questions in new ways and to promote a dialogue between religious studies and important work going on in other areas of the arts, humanities, and social sciences" (Taylor 1998, 18). Among the familiar topics commanding an entry are: "Belief," "God," and "Sacrifice." "Body," "Person," and "Writing" might count as strange. Quite a few—"Conflict," "Culture," "Gender," "Modernity," and "Transgression," for example—seem to speak to "interpreters schooled in postmodernism and poststructuralsm," for whom "the seemingly innocent question 'What is . . . ?' is fraught with ontological and epistemological presuppositions that are deeply problematic" (ibid., 6).

This isn't to say that all, or even the majority, of the essays are plagued by postmodern worries. Jonathan Smith's essay "Religion, Religions, Religious," for example, is a model of how to avoid such worries. He argues that the history of the first term is, "prior to the sixteenth century, irrelevant to contemporary usage" (ibid., 269). He then tells a persuasive story about the way that its use shifted from a "relatively thoughtless language of assimilation" to "virtue, as founded upon reverence of God, and expectations of future rewards and punishments," to "belief as the defining characteristic of religion" (ibid., 270–71). At this point the stage has been set for the worries about "natural religion" that Hume, to cite the most troublesome figure, traces to the human response to anxiety. This generates a debate which turns on whether "the religious" should be "identified with rationality, morality, or feeling" (ibid., 274).

The second term "arose in response to an explosion of data" (ibid., 275). The ages of exploration and empire opened up new vistas onto previously unknown peoples, whose cultures and practices called out for understanding and explanation. Again, Smith sidesteps the worries that make postmoderns wince:

> The most common form of classifying religions, found both in native categories and in scholarly literature, is dualistic and can be reduced, regardless of what differentium is employed, to "theirs" and "ours." [ibid., 276]

From this point it's just a matter of charting the variations on the basic dualism—"Abrahamic/Idolatrous," "high/natural," "world/national"— to the attempts at neutral characterization of Tillich, Smart, and Spiro (ibid., 280–81). Religion, it turns out, is easy to define and those definitions are potentially helpful, as long as we keep in mind that such definitions do nothing more than establish the "disciplinary horizons" necessary to get a discussion going (ibid., 281–82).

Smith writes, as is his wont, in a way that courts misunderstanding. Thus his remark in an earlier essay that "religion is solely the creation of the scholar's study. It is created for the scholar's analytic purposes by his imaginative acts of comparison and generalization" (cited by Taylor ibid., 8), lurks ominously behind the essays on belief, culture, experience, and rationality. Tomoko Masuzawa, for instance, writes of "culture" as "having its prenatal stirring in the eighteenth century," only to be "ushered to life by a series of ground-shifting transformations of the nineteenth century in the ever expanding domain of the West" (ibid., 70). Robert Sharf, discussing "experience," writes that, "by appealing to non-tradition specific notions such as the 'sacred' or the 'holy'...the scholar could legitimize the comparative study of religion even while acknowledging the specifically Western origins of the category itself" (ibid., 96). Both seem to assume that there is something problematic, and perhaps pernicious, in the terms, precisely because they originated in the modern Anglo-European intellectual world. Masuzawa in particular argues that "culture as an object of knowledge and of representation emerged inextricably intertwined with the process of colonialization" (ibid., 89). This is more than Smith's acknowledgment that the period of discovery and empire generated a flood of data. The very ideas of "culture" and "experience" evolved, on her reading, as instruments for the imposition of control, by which the communities that came to be dominated by Anglo-European powers were reinterpreted to the benefit of those powers and their heirs.

The moral of the story is not simply that we should be careful not to allow the comfortable presuppositions of the domineering West to skew our interpretations, but that it is almost impossible for us to avoid reproducing, intellectually, the colonizing moment in our interpretations of the non-Western world without the postmodern therapy of "cultural studies," "museum studies," "colonial and postcolonial studies," or something else of the sort (ibid., 89). Once we have been freed from our oppressive and oppressing intellectual legacy, we will be able to appreciate these other cultures on their own terms. Paul Stoller, in his essay on "rationality," connects this to "embodied rationality," and writes that:

> To accept an embodied rationality, then, is to eject the conceit of control in which mind and body, self and other are considered separate ... To accept an embodied rationality is, like the Songhay spirit medium or diviner, to lend one's body to the world and accept its conplexities, tastes, structures, and smells. [ibid., 252]

If all this means is that we should learn to appreciate the roles that tastes, structures, and smells play in the communities we study, then it's hard to see why anyone would object. But when Masuzawa writes that, "the posthermeneutical moment of cultural studies is also an antihistoricist (and antivulgar materialist) moment" (ibid., 91), or when Stoller writes that, "no matter how deeply we think we have mastered a subject, the world, for the embodied scholar, remains a wondrous place that stirs the imagination and sparks creativity" (ibid., 253), we seem to be warned against making any critical judgments with regard to our subject matter.

A rather different perspective emerges from Ann Taves's recent volume, which she describes as "a building block approach to the study of religion." Taves began her career as an historian of American religion, with a Chicago dissertation on nineteenth-century Catholic religious life, moving from there to a widely praised volume on religious experience and its interpretation in late eighteenth- and nineteenth-century America (Taves 1999; see also Levinson 2002). In her latest book, Taves takes on religious experience as a methodological conundrum in the study of religion. What I'll call the "Romantic" approach to religion, running from the early Schleiermacher to the American Transcendentalists to Otto and Eliade, "placed the experience of the numinous, sacred, or holy at the center of Christianity and, by extension, at the center of all other religions as well" (Taves 2009, 4). I'm not sure that "religious studies," whatever that amounts to, "has focused for the most part on 'high religions' with 'gods' and particularly Christianity" (ibid., 6), but it is true that much ink has been spilt on the methodological question of how we should go about interpreting the claims made for "experience" by the adherents to one or another tradition.

What distinguishes Taves work is an interest in "the growing subfield of the cognitive science of religion" (ibid., 8), This subfield dates at least from McCauley and Lawson's *Rethinking Religion* (1990) and has received its most visible popular exposition in Boyer's *Religion Explained* (2001). Its ultimate parentage can probably be ascribed to Noam Chomsky and its philosophical foundations, such as they are, have been most rigorously pursued by Paul and Patricia Churchland in many publications. Put simply, the Churchlands believe that recent advances in the study of the brain makes it possible, at least in principle, to explain all mental states in terms of physical brain states. Since, they maintain, the brain is a highly evolved organic computational device, these physical states can themselves be explained in terms of complex computer routines. Because Chomsky has argued that the psychological preconditions for generating language are innate, McCauley and Lawson, for instance, have argued that rituals and other religious phenomena are likely to display a structural organization that can be represented in generative form across times, places, and particular cultures.[1]

Taves is nowhere near so ambitious. She begins with the notion that whatever else may be at work in religion, it is about what some people take to be "special." The various categories of specialness can be studied as "experiences deemed religious" (ibid., 8ff.) and it will then be possible

---

[1] It's worth admitting that nothing much turns on the simple-minded genealogy. There are aspects of Chomsky that the Churchlands reject. Chomsky plays a more important role in McCauley and Lawson's earlier work than the later. The "generative approach" of Fredrik Barth doesn't suffer from the evidential opacity I will later attribute to Lawson, McCauley, and their ilk.

to use the psychological approach of "attribution theory" to identify kinds of experience, connect them to the findings of neuroscience, and construct "objects of study" that can be systematically analyzed and compared. This "attributional approach" commends itself by training our academic focus on the individuals and groups who are characterizing particular experiences as "religious." At the same time, it makes it clearer that "experience" is only one component among the various building blocks that can go into the make-up of a particular world. Acknowledging this facilitates the "vertical integration" that would unify the humanities and the natural sciences (ibid., 14, n. 7).

Anybody who feels the need to deny the findings of the sciences in order to protect a cherished belief or attitude is in big trouble. Regularly acting on a false belief is a recipe for frustration. But—except perhaps in Kansas—this isn't the usual problem encountered integrating the humanities and the natural sciences. Instead, we more often find ourselves confronted by remarks such as the following:

> Those who have allowed the "universal acid"...of Darwinism to finally breach the mind–body barrier thus end up living with a kind of dual consciousness... On the one hand, we are convinced that Darwinism is the best account we have for explaining the world around us, and therefore that human beings are merely physical systems. On the other hand, we cannot help but feel the strong pull of human-level truth. [Slingerland 2008, 28]

The rub, of course, lies in the move from Darwinism to "mere physical systems." Slingerland and his sources are way too quick in moving from humans as physical systems to "the idea of the brain as a deterministic, physical system" (ibid., 383; n. 8), to "the conclusion we are 'little robots' all the way down" (ibid., 384). It's worth dwelling for a moment on Darwin himself.

In Darwin, the "theory" is intended to call into question, and ultimately replace, a widely held predecessor, "independent creation."[2] In a nutshell, this long-established doctrine maintained that God envisioned a great chain of being, with individual species created to inhabit each link in the chain. The study of the fossil record, uncovering strange beasts that seemed no longer to exist, suggested to some that certain links ceased to be inhabited, and to a few others that species were regularly transmuted from one form into another, but, as Peter Bowler remarks, "by the 1840s the transmutationist challenge was ebbing...and

---

[2] Butterfield 1949 and Lovejoy 1936 provide classical background to the debate over species, particularly the latter's ch. 8, "The chain of being and some aspects of eighteenth-century biology." For the details of the development of thought about the natural world and its inhabitants, I've found Bowler 1993 exceptionally useful.

the whole movement had been labelled as irreligious and potentially subversive" (1993, 292). The tide seemed to be running against the modification of species from their original form.

Darwin was not alone, much less the first, to buck this tide (see ibid., 293–97). But he was relentless in pursuit of his adversary. Independent creation maintains that each separate species was created exclusively for the particular environment in which it is naturally found. But those of the Galapagos Islands seem so close to those of the South American mainland that the naturalist "feels that he is standing on American land," and this despite the fact that there is "nothing in the conditions of life, in the geological nature of the islands . . . which resembles closely the conditions of the South American coast: in fact there is a considerable dissimilarity in all these respects" (ibid., 293). Why—the implication begs to be drawn—would an all-powerful God recreate an almost identical species for an environment having little or nothing in common with its South American analogue?

One obvious response is to highlight the subtle differences between the Galapagos avians and their South American cousins. But this is to run headlong into the body of Darwin's theory. "On the belief that this is a law of nature," he writes early on, "we can, I think, understand several large classes of facts" (Darwin 2001, 75). In his description of the Galapagos finches, from the *Voyage of the Beagle*, Darwin had already noted that "one might really fancy that from an original paucity of birds in this archipelago, one species had been taken and modified for different ends" (ibid, 71). In *Origin*, he writes that:

> When we see any part or organ developed in a remarkable degree or manner in any species, the fair presumption is that it is of high importance to that species . . . On the view that each species has been independently created, with all its parts as we now see them, I can see no explanation. But on the view that groups of species have descended from other species, and have been modified through natural selection, I think we can obtain some light. [2008, 115–16; ch. V]

Taken togther, we get the standard account: big beaks break big nuts; delicate beaks harvest small seeds.[3]

It's pretty clear what "theory" is doing here. Darwin has an idea about how the world works. Others disagree. Darwin develops his account, with appropriate examples and arguments, to show that it makes more

---

[3] Ruse has a pithy account of the argument, with reference to the detailed work of the Grants, though it is imbedded within one of his many polemical battles, this one against Steven Gould (2006, 116–18). The Grants provide a detailed summary of their work, with bibliography, in Grant and Grant 2003.

sense of more material than its rival. The conclusion, constantly repeated: "Light has been thrown on several facts, which on the theory of independent acts of creation are utterly obscure" (Darwin 2008, 152; ch. VI). Darwin can even conclude, with a pre-emptive shot at his orthodox critics: "When I view all beings not as special creations, but as the lineal descendants of some few beings...they seem to me to become enobled" (ibid., 359; ch. XIV). A true theory is a thing of beauty.

I'm happy to proclaim my Darwinism, but I take this to mean nothing more than a commitment to biology as a natural science, with the addition that the best explanation of the biological creatures we call humans runs along the lines of Darwin's account of evolution by random variation in the struggle for existence. The phrase "along the lines of Darwin's account" is necessary to acknowledge that details of human evolution have been contested, added to, modified—in short have undergone the usual tests of scientific proposals—in a variety of ways since the publication of Darwin's great works. Being, as I am, a godless pagan, I've never taken seriously any of the worries of religious literalists, nor the moral tremors of those who claim, without much by way of argument, that ethics is impossible without at least some god. The flip side of this, however, is that I tend to be embarrassed when such a fine philosopher as Michael Ruse lets his indignation run away with him in responding to the "New Creationists" (see Darwin 2001, 605–12).[4] For me, there's nothing dangerous about Darwin's ideas.

What's dubious, however, is the move from biology to determinism. Determinism, in its many forms, has a long and contentious philosophical history. Many of the arguments are theological and won't concern us here. Some, such as those derived from LaPlace, are mathematical, and simply assume that the ultimate physical account of the world will be represented by a non-probabilistic mathematics.[5] We'll look at that assumption later on. There is no biological research program that *requires* a deterministic, as opposed to a probabilistic, interpretation of

---

[4] The best introduction to Darwin for non-scientists is the Norton Critical Edition edited by Philip Appleman (Darwin 2001). In its current edition, the section on ethics would benefit from something by the "no ethics without god" camp, but the section on religion is very helpful in including selections not only from Christian, but Jewish, Muslim, and Hindu creationists as well. In addition to Appleman's selections from various of Ruse's works, see his *Darwinism and Its Discontents* (Ruse 2006). In this recent volume, Ruse's tone is a bit milder and his discussions of the philosophical implications of the science, as always, are clear and cautious.

[5] The great survey of the development of the mathematical vision of the cosmos remains Koyré's *From the Closed World to the Infinite Universe* (Koyré 1957). LaPlace appears dramatically in the penultimate paragraph of Koyré. His argument for the in principle knowability of everything on deterministic grounds is presented in Gillispie 1972.

nature and nature's laws. It would seem, rather, quite the opposite. As Richard Lewontin puts it, in one of his popular essays:

> Developmental biologists are so fascinated with how an egg turns into a chicken that they have ignored the critical fact that every egg turns into a different chicken and that each chicken's right side is different in an unpredictable way from its left. [Lewontin 2000, 67]

Even a philosopher as sharp as Ruse can make the following leap, necessary to generate Slingerland's robots:

> One would expect that perhaps consciousness started to emerge in a primitive way as animals developed bigger and better brains. Then it was picked up by selection in its own right and developed and refined, perhaps pulling brains along in its wake to provide the material underpinning. [Ruse 2006, 178]

In humans, the only creatures whose consciousness I'm absolutely sure of, being able to think well is directly correlated with having the sort of brain that normally develops in healthy examples of the species. But I don't think that nature, much less some abstract power "selection," is either conscious or capable of picking something up or pulling it along. Nature doesn't act with a purpose; humans, individually and in groups, do. And it's no excuse to say that selection, or the selfish gene, is merely a metaphor. Metaphors aren't arguments; genes aren't selfish. Darwin's legacy is about variations in populations dependent on interactions with other populations in their environment.

But let's get back to Taves. While usually more cautious than Ruse, she too let's her enthusiasm get the best of her, as when she moves from the neuroscience of dreaming to such remarks as "dreams, which typically rework memories, process the memories into emotionally linked sequences below the threshold of dream consciousness" (Taves 2009, 62). Dreams happen; they don't do anything. In reporting my dreams I say things like "First we seemed to be in a restaurant in Princeton; there were lots of smart attractive women. Then there was music, but people kept stepping in front so I couldn't see. And then I seemed to be at a subway station in lower Manhattan, but . . . " I will usually admit that there was a lot of other really interesting stuff going on, but that now I can't remember any of it straight. Events happen in dreams, not unlike they seem to happen in movies, but we understand the mechanisms of cinematics much better than those of dreams. Most neurobiologists probably think that the more we understand those mechanisms, the more we will replace metaphors of reworking and processing with strings of chemical formulae. But that's going to reinforce the difference between the intentional acts of human agents and the biochemical reactions of molecules.

Elsewhere Taves falls into similar traps. In her discussion of sleep paralysis, for example, she discusses researchers who suggest that "the felt-presence experiences associated with sleep paralysis...result from pre-hallucinatory activation of the threat vigilance system" (ibid., 134). The "threat vigilance system" seems somehow connected to the "threat-activation system (TAVS)," which "is similar to what some cognitive scientists of religion refer to as the hyperactive agency detection device (HADD)." This "device," we're told, "has an evolved bias toward the detection of agents in ambiguous situations" (ibid., 135). Like many a psychological acronym, it's hard to know what to make of TAVS and HADD. Taking just the latter, for example, it's obvious that "device" is not to be construed literally. The natural reading is to take HADD as shorthand for the disposition of some (perhaps many?) people, when they find themselves in unfamiliar circumstances, to construe a wide range of stimuli as indications of danger. So, for example, driving down an unfamiliar road in the dark of night, looking for a hidden driveway, I take the glint of my headlight off a polished steel mailbox to be the front bumper of another car bearing down and swerve to avoid a collision. Common enough.

Unfortunately, this reading introduces the vocabulary of "dispositions, construals, beliefs, judgments and actions," all of which involve my thinking x about y. This blurs precisely the boundary between intention and biochemistry that neuroscience was supposed to bridge. It's open, of course, to the researcher to say that "device" really does mean a biochemical mechanism, but that's a move fraught with academic dangers: what does it look like, where is it located, how does it get installed? To answer that these questions are unfair won't do. These are precisely the sorts of question the neuroscientific approach is supposed to answer. If it can't, the researcher must face the accusation that he's just making stuff up.

Bear in mind that I'm *not* saying that there are no neurochemical events happening in my body while I'm driving down the woody lane; of course there are. Some of them have a direct and immediate impact on what I do. There was the time I was driving in South Central LA and a kid pointed what looked like a gun out the window at me. The "fight or flight" reflex, with its attendant cascade of adrenalin, kicked in and I flew. I crossed two lanes of traffic (though not without checking to see they were clear) and made a left turn against the red light. Not my normal behavior, but I didn't want to stop next to them. Here, however, the neurochemical explanation and the intentional, agent-centered explanation, work hand in hand.

We'll return to the claims of cognitive science later on, but for now it will be enough to note two related motives that seem to be driving Taves into the arms of the neuroscientists. One seems to be the desire to take seriously the most recent work in the cognitive psychology of religion. That's fine. But it always remains open to ask how much that work is telling us. Suppose that the most sensitive available machine indicated that my brain was in state S whenever I was subsequently inclined to report that I dreamed of flying unaided among the mountains of California. The brain state doesn't cause my report; that's a function of my memory of the dream. Does the brain state cause the dream? It's not clear how to answer that. But that leaves the dream itself up in the explanatory air. Is the brain state identical to the dream? They seem to have different properties; I'm in one, for example, and the other is in me. In short, it simply isn't clear what explains what.

Taves's second worry seems to concern what are called "functional" arguments or theories of religion. "Functionalist definitions of religion," she writes, "cannot be employed as formulated in a building block approach to religions because they focus on how the scholar thinks religions *function*...rather than on how people put religions together" (ibid., 177). I plan to defend a version of "functionalism" in chapter 3, but its worth at least beginning the argument here. In its most simple-minded form, a functionalist argument goes something like this: X exists because it does Y. Cars, for example, exist because they are an efficient means of transportation. I take it that nobody thinks this is much of an explanation, even if it's true. More to the point, I take it that even Durkheim wouldn't have thought that the following explains much of anything:

> A religion is a unified system of beliefs and practices relative to special things, which beliefs and practices unite into one single moral community [the goal] all those who adhere to them. [Ibid., 176. Italics in original]

But this is the paraphrase Taves takes to characterize Durkheim's functionalism.

Without anticipating too much, and without denying that Durkheim frequently leaves himself open to criticism, I'm going to suggest here that nothing in the basic argument of *Elementary Forms* commits Durkheim to the defects of crude functionalism. While it may not be exactly Taves's sense of a "building block approach," the most coherent reading of *Elementary Forms* would follow the lead of books two and three, looking at the various beliefs held about the world, the community, and the individual, and connecting those to the particular forms of action, group and individual, to see how the whole hangs together.

That Durkheim weaves his own polemical concerns about rival social theories into the exposition should not become a distraction. The fact that Durkheim is in critical dialogue with materialists, idealists, and positivists, should signal, as Mark Cladis points out, that Durkheim is "none of these" (Durkheim 2001, xxxi). But rather than move directly into Durkheim, it's worth looking at yet another recent approach to the "theory" of religion.

Durkheim in Miami

Taylor and his cohort think students of religion should pay more attention than they have to postmodern worries about "truth," "rationality," and the dynamics of "power." Taves thinks those same students should be more deferential to the practices and findings of the neuroscientists. Thomas Tweed wants to bring everybody into the tent. His 2006 volume *Crossing and Dwelling: A theory of religion*, finds something helpful almost everywhere. In chapter 3, "Toward a Theory of Religion," Tweed invokes his "role-specific obligation to reflect on the field's constitutive term by offering a definition of religion, a positioned sighting that highlights movement and relation" (Tweed 2006, 54). He discharges this obligation by surveying the ways in which recent scholars have provided vocabularies for talking about religions, given that "interpreters—even armchair interpreters—never encounter religion-in-general" (ibid., 55). There is, for instance, a predominantly French strain that emphasizes "dynamism and interdependence," invoking "terms such as *field, force,* and *chaos*" (ibid., 57). At the same time, we "should combine the perspectives of, for example, William James and Emile Durkheim," since religions "are always both solitary and social" (ibid., 64). Tweed insists that "we can learn a great deal from recent theories that draw on neuroscience and cognitive science," but we should not lose sight of the fact that mind and culture "are—to use Geertz's apt phrase—'reciprocally constructive'" (ibid., 65). Add a bit of Darwin, Hume, Freud, Weber, and feminism (ibid., 69–72) and you're methodologically good to go.

When we actually look at Tweed's primary motivation, however, "theorizing" collapses into the much less formal, and much more interesting, "reflection on current practice." Thus in his conclusion, Tweed writes that his "theory" does not "aim at explanation or prediction," but "will be useful if it sparks more conversations and generates other accounts—even, or especially, accounts that challenge this one" (ibid., 165–66). Granted, I've left out the exhortations to modesty and political earnestness, but I don't see how they are relevant to his subject matter.

17

If we go back to the beginning of his reflections, it turns out that Tweed "had a sense" that "there seemed to be more to say than other theoretical lexicons allowed me to say...I was looking for a theory of religion that made sense of the religious life of transnational migrants" (ibid., 5). In *Our Lady of the Exile* Tweed concludes with a "theory of diasporic religion" (Tweed 1997, 141), but it's unclear how much work this does. What he is looking for is a way to talk about a community that incorporated Old World Catholicism and the New World tradition of the *orishas* in a social world that was not simply shifted, but displaced from its originating locale. The competing and deforming forces which also merge into something new invite the use of "hydrodynamics" and the language of "surface turbulence or faucet drippings" (2006, 171–72). But Tweed is wise enough to realize that pressing the metaphor risks being "washed away while trying to chart the transfluence of innumerable causal currents" (ibid., 172). Metaphors aren't theories.

In order to tell the story he wants to tell, Tweed brings together William Christian on the continuity between the lived religion of Spanish Catholics from the sixteenth to the twentieth centuries, Robert Thompson on the continuity of New World altars with African tradition, and Jonathan Smith on ritual and diaspora in Judaism. He cites many more scholars, but these three share his central concern to combine what people say about what they do with a larger Durkheimian urge to see how the whole hangs together and makes it possible for one generation to make way for another.[6] Let me put it this way. In the beginning there was Durkheim, whose most important contribution to the study of religion was convincing scholars that it was, for the most part, pointless to speculate about origins. Real insight could be gleaned from exploring how a system of beliefs and practices could maintain enough solidarity among the members of a community to sustain it over multiple generations. Durkheim begat van Gennep, who complained about Durkheim's "bookish ethnography" and "his well-known personal tendency to emphasize the collective element (social) above all

---

[6] This is the sort of cavalier remark likely to cause trouble down the road, so let me make it clear that I am aware of the competing lineages in anthropology. Adam Kuper's *Culture* (1999), with its focus on the American tradition, complements his earlier volume on British social anthropology (Kuper 1973). The *History of Anthropology* series edited by George Stocking, beginning with Stocking 1983, contains many illuminating essays. Nonetheless, it seems to me that Jack Goody is correct to describe the formative perspective of mid-twentieth-century anthropology as broadly Durkheimian (Goody 1995, ch. 7). Students of African art, from Fagg and Bascom to Willett and Thompson, have been particularly important in securing the recognition of the individual agent. Willett has an interesting introduction to the field (Willett 1971, ch. 2). Thompson's early essay on Yoruba art criticism has been particularly influential on my thinking about these matters (see D'Azevedo 1973). Recent issues, theoretical and interpretive, are addressed in Abiodun et al. 1994.

else" (van Gennep 1913, 205–07). But from a distance, van Gennep's insistence on the complexity of fieldwork, his more nuanced understanding of the relation between individual actor and the social order, and his classic work on rites of passage, are best seen as positive developments of the Durkheimian paradigm. Van Gennep, in his turn, begat Mary Douglas and Victor Turner—not only the watershed volumes *Purity and Danger* and *The Ritual Process*, but the detailed fieldwork from which those later generalizations proceeded.[7] This is the line to which Tweed belongs. Talk about "theory" just obscures it. Durkheim, modified to accept van Gennep's insistence on the role of individuals, allows Tweed to do justice to the role of Bishop Román in organizing and perpetuating the devotion at the shrine (see Tweed 2006, 174ff.). So it turns out that what Tweed is really looking for isn't a theory, but the resources to tell a story more complicated than the already convoluted tales that anthropologists tell about isolated cliff-dwellers and highland New Guinea hunters. How to assemble those resources lands us in the middle of a discussion that turns on what's living and what's dangerous in the legacy of Durkheim. We'll get back to that discussion in chapter 3.

Religion without theory: the pragmatic turn

Taylor, Taves, and Tweed all advise us to be more theoretically sensitive to the definitions, tropes, methods, and metaphors that fly around in the study of religion. That's fair enough, but it's a far cry from establishing either an obligation to be theoretical or the need for a theory. By this point, however, Tweed is likely to complain that I'm being unfair. After all, he goes out of his way to distinguish what he's doing from both the "deductive-nomological" approach of the heyday of logical positivism and the more modest "constructivist view of theory," which he characterizes as offering only "contextual understanding of interacting motives" (2006, 7–8). In fact, he is likely to complain, he makes it clear that "on questions about truth, meaning, and interpretation I have been influenced by pragmatism" (ibid., 192, n. 17). But here Tweed risks stepping out of the frying pan right into the fire. For although he identifies himself with the "conservative pragmatism" of Peirce and

---

[7] Lukes surveys the criticisms of van Gennep and others in Lukes 1972. On van Gennep and his exclusion from the French academic world by the circle of Durkheim, see Zumwalt 1982. Jack Goody, reflects on the importance of van Gennep for British anthropologists working in Africa in Goody 1995, particularly at p. 125. Turner 1969 is upfront about the influence of van Gennep, as is Douglas from 1966 on. See, in particular, Douglas 1968, 112–13.

Putnam, he claims that it "only makes sense to talk about reality-for-us . . . it aims for—to use John Dewey's term—"warranted assertability" (ibid., 16). This won't do. Where theory claims too much, warranted assertability claims too little. It is false modesty to claim that scholars, when they set out to interpret their subjects, want anything less than truth. When Roy Rappaport writes that "taboos served to define areas of behavior in which the anger and bitterness generated by death and injury could be expressed, while permitting cooperation in most of the important tasks of living" (1984, 209), he doesn't just mean that that's his opinion; he doesn't even mean that it is warrantedly assertable, based on his research. He means to be taken as speaking the truth, and criticisms of this claim are precisely what doubled the bulk of his second edition.

This brings me, at last, to the heart of my thesis: to make sense of the scholar's enterprise we don't need "theory" but we do need "truth." What masquerades as theory is almost always, as it is in Tweed, reflection on scholarly practice wrapped up in a pithy metaphor. Debates about theory, at least in the study of religion, have typically been contests to lay bare the presuppositions that have informed one or another scholar's professional practice. That, I've hinted above, is at least part of what motivated the dispute between Durkheim and van Gennep. And those presuppositions, when they come into contact with the material under investigation, are what generate the various hypotheses that push scholarship forward.

"Hypothesis" signals my own commitment to pragmatism, and specifically to the pragmatism of C. S. Peirce. In the last of six seminal papers that appeared between November of 1877 and August of 1878, Peirce sketches the relations among empirical formulae, laws, hypotheses, and theories:

> formulae, though very useful as means of describing in general terms the results of observations, do not take any high rank among scientific discoveries . . . We may, however, and do desire to find formulas expressing the relations of physical phenomena which shall contain no more arbitrary numbers than changes in the scales of measurement might require. [1878a, 195]

Peirce, as a practicing scientist, knows that any set of observations can be plotted in one or another form. What the investigator wants to do is discover correlations between observations of one kind and those of another. He gives the relation of "specific gravity as compared with water, and temperature as expressed by the centigrade thermometer" (ibid.); F=ma would do just as well (see Einstein and Infeld 1938, 5–35; Cohen 1985, 164ff.). "When a formula of this kind is discovered," Peirce continues:

it is no longer called an empirical formula, but a law of Nature; and is sooner or later made the basis of an hypothesis which is to explain it . . . and the great triumph of the hypothesis comes when it explains not only the formula, but also the deviations from the formula. In the current language of the physicists, an hypothesis of this importance is called a theory. [1878a, 195]

Peirce means to be taken seriously and I plan to accord him that respect. And because, as I'll argue, the purported formulae for generalizing about the intentional actions of human beings never rise above the level of counterfactuals expressed in relative probabilities, we're never going to get anything like a theory of human behavior in the physicists' sense. Or, to put the same point the other way around, anything that purports to be a theory of human behavior will rapidly be exposed as a vapid generalization.

To eschew theory, however, is not to deny, much less despair of, the acquisition of knowledge in the study of religion. Taves, Tweed, and many of the contributors to Taylor, have made exceptional contributions to the study of religion. But rather than "constructing an object of study," as recommendd by Taves, they tend to evolve in the way identified by Peirce. Something gives someone pause and "the irritation of doubt causes a struggle to attain a state of belief. I shall term that struggle *inquiry*" (Peirce 1877, 114). Consider a favorite article of mine, Robert Sharf's "Zen and Japanese Nationalism." As a student of Chinese and Japanese Buddhism, Sharf comes to feel that the "popular conception of Zen is not only conceptually incoherent, but also a woeful misreading of traditional Zen doctrine, altogether controverted by the lived contingencies of Zen monastic practice" (Sharf 1993, 2). This prompts a set of questions surrounding the origins and maintenance of the popular Western view, which leads Sharf on an exceptionally rich journey through the sources of Buddhist reform in Meiji Japan to the impact of Western intellectual currents on a number of Japanese intellectuals, most notably D. T. Suzuki and Nishida Kitaro (see ibid., 8–24). Suzuki's English writings became enormously influential in America, and a number of Japanese intellectuals, in particular Abe Masao, have continued to champion this particular version of Zen (see ibid., 30–31). All of this leads Sharf to conclude that:

The modern notion of religion as an appropriate cross-cultural object of scholarly investigation emerged directly out of this complex dialogue, in which Western investigators were ever encouraged to find their own romanticized notion of true or essential religion mirrored back to them in their Asian protégés. [Ibid., 43]

This is good stuff. It identifies a worry in the study of Japanese religions, which generates a story about how the Western image was formed, which in itself generates both a revision of the image and further worries about "the secular study of comparative religion in the West" (ibid.). The fact that Sharf can successfully offer a revisionist account of a major moment in the study of religion belies, to my mind, his worries about comparative religion. Tweed's *American Encounter with Buddhism* appeared just before Sharf's article, and Sharf doesn't appear in the preface to the paperback edition (see Tweed 2000). But Sharf's article is reprinted in Lopez 1995 and mentioned in Prebish and Tanaka 1998, which Tweed does cite in his 2000 preface. Thus it has become part of the critical literature. As it produces worries on its own, inquiry will push forward.

Because I think that inquiry in the humanities is continuous with inquiry in the social and natural sciences, and because I think that Peirce is largely right about both the nature of knowledge and the practices that lead to it, the chapters to come lay out Peirce's pragmatism, identify those students of religion who have most clearly turned to this particular form of pragmatism, and chart a path between those approaches to the study of religion that are a good bet to push understanding forward and those that are just rehashing what Imre Lakatos calls "degenerate research programmes" (see Lakatos 1978).

2

Peirce and the Legacy of Pragmatism

The distinctiveness of Peirce's pragmatism has been clear to everyone, including Peirce, since James first popularized the term in the 1890s. My partisanship for Peirce rests on the conviction that he provides the clearest and most credible account of what knowledge is, how we get it, and how we should think of inquiry in light of what we already know. Peirce identified pragmatism with making our ideas clear and illustrated his approach with the example of applying the predicate "hard." Before we think about it, we don't know whether a given thing is hard or soft, but we do have certain expectations. For example, if it should properly be called "hard," we would expect "that it will not be scratched by many other substances. The whole conception of this quality, as of every other, lies in its conceived effects" (Peirce 1878, 132). If, in the process of investigation, we discover that a particular substance, say diamond, is very hard, then we may reasonably assume that diamonds in general are very hard. This would remain true even in the face of the rather odd claim that "all hard bodies remain perfectly soft until they are touched, when their hardness increases with the pressure until they are scratched" (ibid.). Such a claim, since it would have the same results if tested that we currently get, isn't false; it is best thought of as a recommendation—not a terribly good one—for revising the way we talk. That's always an option, for the language-using community is always free to innovate and clean house, but whatever we do, it it essential "to know what we think, to be masters of our own meaning" (ibid., 126). If a property or distinction doesn't have any impact on our possible experience, then it is doing no work. If it is doing no work, then worrying about it can't generate a real doubt.

James, on the other hand, identifies pragmatism with a theory of truth. James identifies truth with usefulness and in so doing creates a host of problems connected to rationality and relativism. They will come up in various places, in various forms, in the discussion that follows. But from the beginning Peirce viewed James's move here as a disaster. Within a few years Peirce announced "the birth of the word 'pragmaticism,' which is ugly enough to be safe from kidnappers" (1905, 335). It didn't work. James's account of pragmatism continued to crowd out much of what was important in Peirce. But I am not going to embark on a full-scale exposition of Peirce's thought. Instead, I'm going to limit myself to his critique of Cartesianism, his account of the relation of knowledge to inquiry, and his nondeterministic paradigm of the sciences.

Peirce's pragmatism and the Cartesian legacy

Peirce's early attack on Cartesian epistemology comes in a series of essays written for the *Journal of Speculative Philosophy* and published in 1868–69. In the first essay, he poses seven questions, each related to some supposed power of the human mind. He first asks whether:

> by the simple contemplation of a cognition, independently of any previous knowledge and without reasoning from signs, we are enabled rightly to judge whether that cognition has been determined by a previous cognition or whether it refers immediately to its object. [1868, 11]

It is not immediately clear, to say the least, what's going on here, but imagine the following. Suppose I look up from the computer and say to myself, "the sky is clear." The expanse of sky outside my window is a lovely blue; I see no clouds; the dogwood on the right is reflecting sunlight off its glossy green leaves and so on. This might seem to be immediately clear and depend on nothing more than the soundness of my vision. A tradition in philosophy has called these immediate awarenesses of the world "intuitions" (ibid., 12). Contrast this with a famous passage from *Inferno*, XV, where Dante and his guide come upon a company of sodomites, one of whom recognizes the poet:

> That spirit having stretched his arm toward me,
> I fixed my eyes upon his baked, brown features,
> so that the scorching of his face could not
> prevent my mind from recognizing him;
> and lowering my face to meet his face,
> I answered him: "Are you here, Ser Brunetto?" [Dante, *Inf.*, XV,
> ll. 25–30]

Here the character Dante encounters a soul who seems to know him. He searches the visage of the soul for familiar clues and, discerning the likeness of Brunetto Latini, he asks for verification. In this example every thought—cognition[1]—prompted by the encounter relies on inference from some previous thought: if he's reaching out he must recognize me; if he recognizes me I must have known him at some time; if I knew him then, I should be able to recognize him now; if it's Brunetto he will confirm it for me.

Cognitions of Dante's sort are common; we use them almost thoughtlessly to negotiate our daily chores. I pull up in front of the house, see that my wife's car is gone from the driveway, and take out my keys, assuming that the door will be locked. Sometimes I'm right, but sometimes I'm wrong. She took her car to be inspected, for instance, and has already returned on foot. Or I get up in the morning and notice that the time display on the radio is blinking and conclude that, sometime overnight, there was a power outage which has now been rectified. So Peirce is asking whether we should acknowledge two kinds of cognitions, those based on inferences from prior knowledge and those that are immediate intuitions of the way the world is.

His answer is "no." Every component of my intuition above should be analyzed in terms of previous knowledge drawn from previous inferences. The relation of "blue sky" to "clear sky" is an inference we're taught to make from an early age. "Shiny green leaves" to "dogwood" is one that inhabitants of the south learn not long after they arrive. And so on. Many of the inferences we make are learned as part of learning to speak. The fact that we think of our intuitions as immediate and certain is of no evidentiary value whatsoever. Dreams often seem as immediate and certain as our waking experience, but they are clearly concocted out of the materials of consciousness. "Besides," Peirce goes on, "even when we wake up, we do not find that the dream differed from reality, except by certain *marks*, darkness and fragmentarinesss" (1868, 14). There is, in short, nothing in the cognition itself that guarantees that my awareness is of the world directly as it is.

The stakes become a bit clearer when we move on to Peirce's second question, about "intuitive self-consciousness" (ibid., 18). This too, for Peirce, is learned. If we look at the development of language in the child, it turns out that about the time he begins to talk:

> he begins to find that what these people about him say is the very best evidence of fact. So much so, that testimony is even a stronger mark of fact

---

[1] Peirce's "cognition" encompasses more than "thought." It is more like "the content of a meaningful intellectual experience." Unfortunately, this involves a lengthy exposition as part of a shifting debate that pretty much covers the history of modern philosophy. Fortunately, a handy sketch of that is available in Ian Hacking (1975).

> than *the facts themselves*, or rather than what must now be thought of as the *appearances* themselves...Ignorance and error are all that distinguish our private selves from the absolute *ego* of pure apperception. [Ibid., 19–20]

The prelinguistic child is indistinguishable from any other mammal in its basic behavior. It acts and reacts to the environment in which it finds itself. As it begins to interact linguistically with others of its kind it acquires the ability to distinguish appearances, the sorts of situations that might earlier have elicited certain reactions, from realities, the constraints that will thwart expectations and lead to adverse results if those inclinations are carried into act.

The experience of thwarted expectations is all that's necessary to motivate the distinction between "true" and "false." Both, now that the child has entered a linguistic environment, are going to be attributes of propositions which purport to state the way the world is. The "true" ones are the ones that connect our expectations to the anticipated outcomes. What is true of the world around us turns out to be true of ourselves as well. Our elders, and then our peers, provide us the language we use to talk about ourselves in just the same way that they provide us the language we use for talking about the rest of our world. Instead of behaving instinctively in response to rumblings from the region of our solar plexus, we learn to say "I'm hungry." Repeated failures to succeed in simple tasks may provoke "I'm tired," "I'm nervous," or any of a number of responses. And each of these, in turn, will be subject to correction and revision. So "I'm hungry," may provoke "You had lunch just 45 minutes ago," which may lead to "My stomach's upset," "Maybe you've caught that bug," "No, I think it was the greasy onion-rings," and so on. Peirce's point is that, "there is no necessity of supposing an intuitive self-consciousness, since self-consciousness may easily be the result of inference" (ibid., 21). No immediate intuitions of the world, no immediate intuitions of the self.

And so with the the remaining questions. Peirce's point is that there is no need to postulate these faculties; that the evidence, when we think about it, is against them; and that to postulate them just gets us into philosophical trouble. Confronted with the claim that we seem naturally to think we have them, he replies that the apparent naturalness is simply a function of early and long familiarity with the inferences and actions we live with every day. The importance of recognizing this comes out in the second essay, "Some Consequences of Four Incapacities." Here Peirce puts his anti-Cartesian motives front and center, writing that, "Descartes is the father of modern philosophy" going on to provide four characteristics of Cartesian philosophy: universal doubt;

the certainty of the individual consciousness; the foundational dependence of knowledge on a single argument; and the inexplicability of fundamental facts of nature. The problem, as Peirce sees it, is that "modern science and modern logic require us to stand upon a very different platform from this" (1868a, 28).

Building upon the conclusions of the first essay, Peirce argues that human beings have the following four "incapacities:"

1. We have no power of Introspection, but all knowledge of the internal world is derived by hypothetical reasoning from our knowledge of external facts.

2. We have no power of Intuition, but every cognition is determined logically by previous cognitions.

3. We have no power of thinking without signs.

4. We have no conception of the absolutely incognizable. (Ibid., 30)

These four incapacities are so tightly woven together that starting with one almost immediately leads on to the others, but for my purposes it will be easiest to begin with the third. To think is an intentional notion; it is always about something. This needn't mean that we can immediately articulate all of our thoughts, for the follow exchange is not only reasonable, but familiar:

> "What are you doing?"
> "I don't know; just thinking."
> "About what?"
> "Nothing in particular."

If the second interlocutor is being candid, then he typically means that lots of things were fleetingly on his mind, but that they didn't add up to a train of thought. The evidence for thought is the ability to string words together in ways that are recognizable by a language community. When individuals whom we take to be language-users are, for whatever reason, unable to express themselves, we attribute to them interpretable strings of words. Those people who attribute thinking to dogs, whales, and non-human primates interpret their behavior as significant. And if we ask of what it is significant, those people produce interpretable strings of words. Thinking is with signs and signs have their life in languages.

Peirce's fourth incapacity follows directly from the need to use signs for thinking. To invoke the uncognizable, or ineffable, implies that you can draw conclusions from claims that have, *ex hypothesi*, no content. But this is nonsense; if you can't say it, you can't think it. The second incapacity is closely related. When put forward as knowledge claims, statements about the intuitively certain or the "absolutely inexplicable, unanalyzable ultimate" (ibid., 29), involve contests of will, not the practice of inquiry. "In the sciences in which men come to agreement," writes Peirce, "when a theory has been broached, it is considered to be on probation until agreement is reached. After it is reached, the question of certainty becomes an idle one, because there is no one left who doubts it" (ibid.). Knowledge claims are the product of groups of language-users, who begin with whatever they have been taught and then exercise critical intelligence to develop new accounts of the world as needed.

Pragmatism as an account of inquiry begins, then, with the suggestion that philosophy "ought to imitate the successful sciences in its methods," embracing the anti-Cartesian position that sound reasoning "should not form a chain which is no stronger than its weakest link, but a cable whose fibres may be ever so slender, provided they are sufficiently numerous and intimately connected" (ibid.). From all this, finally, follows our first incapacity. When Peirce writes that "we have no power of Introspection," he takes the purported power to be some sort of privileged access which the individual has to the content of his experience, mind, or inner states. But if thinking depends on signs, which are learned through interaction with others and which take their applications from our shared experience of the world around us, then the language of our inner reports is "derived from hypothetical reasoning from our knowledge of external facts." We are applying it to the first person, who is usually accorded a measure of authority in certain kinds of reports, but those "inner" reports are possible only because we have learned the manner and application of the appropriate signs in the appropriate contexts.

Here Peirce reflects a strand of argument in the philosophy of language that will eventually comprise not only himself, but Wittgenstein, Davidson, and similar thinkers. Wittgenstein, as Donald Davidson puts it, "says that following the rule (getting things right) is at bottom a matter of doing as others do . . . thought as well as language is necessarily social" (Davidson 1999, 129). He could have said the same about Peirce. In making first-person reports I am bound by the same sorts of constraints that bind my reports of everyday external experience. If I ignore them, I am prevaricating.

Several conclusions follow for knowledge claims generally. First, there is no privileged or neutral position from which to pass judgment on the truth of a claim. If I am limited by my knowledge, presuppositions, attitudes, and expectations, so are my potential critics. But this isn't a failing; it's the human condition. Second, there is no reason to believe that a single method can be expounded by which we can determine whether a claim is justified. Different sorts of claim will require different sorts of justification. Again, this is not a failure but a fact of human experience. How my friend Murphy, who manages the Canadian River Basin Program in New Mexico, justifies a claim about water-use depends on certain technical expectations based on his training as a geologist and his experience doing hydrology in the American Southwest. He can be expected to know and be able to apply concepts and procedures that would be totally opaque to me. How he justifies claims about water-use will have little in common with how I justify the claim that my mother loves me. But both are knowledge claims and, for the pragmatist, depend on patterns of thinking learned in conjunction with others in a world we share.

This leads directly the third of these early papers, which Peirce subtitles, "Further Consequences of Four Incapacities." Peirce opens with a recap of the previous essays. "If," he writes, "as I maintained in an article in the last number of the Journal, every judgment results from inference, to doubt every inference is to doubt everything" (1869, 56). This invites, Peirce admits:

> a sweeping objection to my whole undertaking. It will be said that my deduction of logical principles, being itself an argument, depends for its whole virtue upon the truth of the very principles in question; so that whatever my proof may be, it must take for granted the very things to be proved. [Ibid., 57]

Critics, in short, will argue that, if every judgment depends on inferences, then there can be no non-circular justification of inference itself. It looks like Peirce is using inference in his attack on intuitions only to leave the basic laws of inference completely inexplicable.

Peirce's response comes in three somewhat disproportionate steps. First, he makes the important distinction between doing something well and knowing the general theory of how it works. "A man may reason well," he writes, "without understanding the principles of reasoning, just as he may play billiards well without understanding analytical mechanics" (ibid.). This distinction lies at the heart of pragmatism. If we begin in *medias res*, as reasonably successful negotiators of our day to day problems, we must acknowledge that we understand, and for the most part succeed, in identifying those problems, developing successful responses to them, and passing those solutions on to subsequent generations, who refine them and develop new solutions to whatever new problems might arise.

This is the polar opposite of the Cartesian proposal, which seems to oblige us to give up all of our business until we can set our understanding on a firm foundation. Not only would this be practically impossible, it is irrational. Neither Descartes nor any of his epigones ever managed to offer much of an argument that our intellectual activities depended on a single chain of arguments, inferences, and beliefs or that there was much to fear should one amongst our many beliefs prove false. Suppose that some Copenhagen physicists have put forth an account of nature at the sub-atomic level that runs contrary to my beliefs about how nature works. I can mount an alternative interpretation or, if I can't seem to make much headway with that, I can adjust my beliefs to accommodate the more persuasive theory. The lack of a clear and distinct foundation for my beliefs isn't much of a threat to anything. Having made this key pragmatist point, Peirce uses the bulk of the essay to show that the standard philosophical objections to logic are misplaced. Basic logical expressions are intended to capture what we do with signs (57–59); negation expresses nothing more problematic than what we mean by cats being "other than" dogs (59–60); the syllogism is supposed to be demonstrative, not an act of discovery (60–61) and so on. The important problem, to which he devotes the final half dozen pages, turns on the justification of probable inferences to facts about the world.

In an ordinary deductive argument the major and minor premises are taken as given, so in a strict sense we don't know anything that was not already present in the propositions under discussion. "In the case of probable reasoning," however, "the difficulty is of quite another kind... How magical it is that by examining a part of a class we can know what is true of the whole of the class, and by study of the past can know the future" (ibid., 75). How, in short, do we justify claims about things of which we have no experience? A standard approach is the reply that, "nature is everywhere regular; as things have been, so they will be; as one part of nature is, so is every other" (ibid.). But this just isn't true. The practicing scientist encounters a world of differences. While "it is true that the special laws and regularities are innumerable... nobody thinks of the irregularities, which are infinitely more frequent" (ibid.). Casual readers are likely to remark that researchers have decided that certain values are close enough, but that just begs the question. If scientists are making decisions about what is close enough to count as "regular," then it's not regularity per se, but the choices of the researchers that are at work.

Even worse, if this particular constitution of the world is what gen-erates regularities, it might happen, as Peirce takes Mill to maintain, that we "can imagine a universe without any regularity, so that no probable inference would be valid in it" (ibid., 77). But this causes real problems. If there were no regularities, then there would be no universal proposi-tions, since they take the form "all x are y." But then there would also be no individuals, since identifying them involves noting that "this A is an x." Since no one proposition would be more probable than another, any and every proposition would have a probability of 0.5. If P and not-P are equally probable, there is no good reason to act in one way as opposed to another. The more we press this idea, the more unintelligible it becomes.

We are committed to a world of things and events that act in regular and predictable ways, not because of our judgments, but because of the way things are. "All probable inference, whether induction or hypothesis, is inference from the parts to the whole. It is essentially the same, therefore, as statistical inference" (ibid., 78). This divides into two subordinate questions, one about the general principle and another about the particular occasions of statistical reasoning. For the first, a common-sense realism requires that in the long run, "the validity of induction depends simply upon the fact that the parts make up and constitute the whole" (ibid., 79). If the bag really contains half blue and half gray hats, then in the long run I will distribute half blue and half gray.

The second question asks "why men are not fated always to light upon the small proportions of worthless inductions" (ibid.). On the one hand, any given induction may fail. Over any fixed set of judgments, there is no a priori guarantee that they aren't all defective; we can never be certain that the run has been long enough. Nonetheless, "we know that, by faithfully adhering to that mode of inference, we shall, on the whole, approximate to the truth. Each of us is an insurance company, in short" (ibid., 81). We're intended to take this analogy seriously. Insurance companies flourish because the mathematics employed by actuaries has proved to approximate pretty closely the way the world works. Every now and then an unexpected blip in the cycle of life and death will generate a momentary downturn, but if risk is apportioned over enough policies and a long enough time, those downturns even out into a steady stream of profit. The pursuit of knowledge in general, for Peirce's pragmatism, works the same way. Universal doubt is impossible as a beginning to inquiry; the individual consciousness provides no justification for certainty; rather than a single foundation, knowledge is secured by a variety of contributions from the members of a complex social whole; and if anything is an object of knowledge, then it can be described and incorporated into the fabric of what we know.

Truth, inquiry and the "logic of science"

It seems to me that all the basics of Peirce's pragmatism are at work in the essays of 1868–69, but they are developed more fully, with reference to the history of science, in a series of six papers for *Popular Science Monthly*, collectively known as *Illustrations of the Logic of Science*. Published in 1877–78, this series contains Peirce's most famous and most influential essays.[2] In the first, Peirce distinguishes four ways in which we attain fixation of belief: tenacity, authority, agreeability to reason, and the method of science. Not surprisingly, Peirce holds that the last "is the only one of the four methods which presents any distinction of a right and a wrong way" (1877, 121). The first three depend on the will of the agent, while only the fourth commits the inquirer to subordinating his purposes and prejudices to the outcome of investigation. But it would be a mistake to imagine that Peirce is embracing the old-fashioned high-school version of the "empirical" or "scientific method." As we have already seen, he rejects appeals either to introspection or intuition, thereby cutting off any appeal to direct, immediate, or self-justifying claims. Peirce's ideas are propositional and thus, if they are about the world, they are subject to our ordinary fallibility.

While all thinking goes on in language, the objects of scientific investigation are the facts and phenomena of reality. "Though their characters depend on how we think," he writes in the second installment of this series, "they do not depend on what we think those characters to be" (1878, 136–37). Peirce maintains that genuine science, properly pursued, tends toward a truth independent of what we think, a position summarized in the claim that, "the opinion which is fated to be ultimately agreed to by all who investigate, is what we mean by the truth, and the object represented in this opinion is the real" (ibid., 138–39). But he immediately qualifies this by acknowledging that "our perversity and that of others may indefinitely postpone the settlement of opinion; it might even conceivably cause an arbitrary proposition to be universally accepted as long as the human race should last" (ibid., 139). So, true statements about how the world hangs together are the legitimate object of inquiry, and the set of those true statements, properly understood, will be mutually consistent, but it might just happen that we incinerate ourselves before we discover them all. This acknowledges fallibilism; it doesn't limit inquiry to "warranted assertability."

---

[2] The first two, "The fixation of belief" and "How to make our ideas clear," were almost immediately translated into French and published in the *Revue Philosophique* for 1879. William James locates the origins of pragmatism in the second (see Cohen 1916, 733). Morris Cohen, who compiled the bibliography of Peirce's published work for *The Journal of Philosophy*'s commemorative issue, reprinted the entire series in the first selection of Peirce's work (Peirce 1923), and those same first two papers were canonized in Max Fisch's influential *Classic American Philosophers* (see Fisch 1996). Peirce plays a central role in Cohen 1954, which goes back, in its inception, to the time of Cohen's Peirce anthology. The most detailed history of pragmatism remains Thayer 1968.

Those inquiring into the truth of things formulate hypotheses, make inductions, and fit their findings together systematically in ways that attempt to capture the laws of nature. There is, however, no simple method for moving inevitably from one to the other. Of "synthetic" inferences, induction, which moves from case and result to rule, is much stronger than hypothesis, which moves from a rule and a result to a particular case (1878a, 188). This is so because the hypothesis "supposes something of a different kind from what we have already observed" (ibid., 197), and thus rests on a thinner justificatory base. Nonetheless, inquiry can move from any starting point. Thus:

> When the kinetical theory of gases was first proposed by Daniel Bernoulli, in 1738, it rested only on the law of Boyle, and was therefore pure hypothesis... Now, it has been shown by experiment that, when a gas is allowed to expand without doing work, a very small amount of heat disappears...In this point of view, the kinetical theory of gases appears as a deduction from the mechanical theory of heat. [Ibid.]

The actual progress of inquiry, as opposed to the method imagined by non-scientists, is a constant movement back and forth among hypothesis, experiment, induction, theorizing, and the like.

So far Peirce's pragmatism, unless you are a committed follower of Descartes, throws up few red flags. It dismisses certain positivist and idealized accounts of science in favor of a more complex picture of how inquiry actually gets done. It begins in doubt, which can only be recognized against the backdrop of a web of beliefs most of which must be held true. This isn't a fact of human psychology, but a matter of logic. If the majority of our beliefs were not true, then the simple inferences we make in moving from one moment to the next would be thwarted, making it impossible to understand the connections of our beliefs and the world in which we act. The tension generated by one recalcitrant piece of experience sufficiently illustrates the barrier simple doubt puts up to action. Massive, or global, doubt would paralyze action completely.

At this point some readers might expect to encounter the "pragmatic theory of truth." But Peirce has no such theory. He stands in a distinguished line that runs from Aristotle to Tarski and Davidson, for whom the very idea of a "theory" of truth is confused. For theories are the sorts of things we test to see, ultimately, whether we are justified in holding them true. Davidson locates our urge to define "truth" in our still being "under the spell of the Socratic idea that we must keep asking for the *essence* of an idea...We still fall for the freshman fallacy that demands that we *define* our terms as a prelude to saying anything further with or about them" (Davidson 1996, 34).

Davidson's dismissal of truth theories is likely to leave some readers dissatisfied. Fortunately, there have been a couple of recent attempts to apply to Peirce the strategy that Davidson recommends, which is "to trace the connections between the concept of truth and the human attitudes and acts that give it body" (ibid., 35). Peirce's inquirer, faced with a sufficiently disturbing doubt,[3] sets out to settle it. "Here," writes David Wiggins, "it helps to distinguish very deliberately the roles of inquirer and of philosopher of inquiry. Normally, when we engage as inquirers in some investigation, we do not think, in the abstract, about methodology" (2004, 95). Real doubts, in other words, typically fit into a framework of beliefs which the inquirer is already fitted to investigate. Nonetheless, Wiggins continues:

> if, even as inquirers submit to experience, they do reflect abstractly about their procedures and the rationale of what they do, then, according to Peirce, the thing they are bound to find they have discovered is the ideas of truth, of fact, and of a reality or (as Peirce rewrote some passages of "Fixation" to say) "a Real." [Ibid., 95–96]

Whether inquirers begin with an abstract notion of truth or not, in other words, as they cast around for something that will alleviate the tension of doubt and fix their belief, it turns out that the only thing that fits the bill is truth. What we want—what inquiry demands—is an account of the facts that provides us with the truth, or at least a good reason to believe that the truth cannot be found.

At this point, returning to Peirce, Wiggins introduces an important distinction between a "theory" of truth and:

> some form of words that fastens down and promises in due course to help elucidate, in terms that essentially involve the business of inquiry and the method of "experience," the nature of that property, namely truth, which (unless we are complete strangers to opinion or doubt) is already familiar to any or all of us. [2004, 114]

Most competent adults develop a notion of truth early on, as a result of having knowledge claims go wrong. To clarify the concept, the learned

---

[3] Peirce distinguishes at various places between real and "paper" doubts, typically dismissing the latter as mere philolophical self-indulgence. This seems a reasonable move, even in the absence of a clear way of distinguishing the real from the paper. Thus in a 1913 essay, Peirce refers to the Michaelson-Morley experiment as creating a serious doubt for explaining the speed of light. (Peirce 1913, 467) More mundane, but genuine doubts are of the sort that we might easily Google: did Barry Bonds graduate from USC or Arizona State? Worries about whether or not we all might be brains in vats are, for Peirce, inconsequential (see Misak 2004, 50–52). Distinguishing one from the other will typically involve telling a story about the difference getting it right would make.

father might introduce this famous passage from Aristotle: "To say of what is that it is not, or of what is not that it is, is false, while to say of what is that it is, and of what is not that it is not, is true" (Aristotle *Meta.* IV, 1011b). This, of course, isn't a "theory" of truth; it takes for granted a complex set of practices involved in saying x of y, the notion that something "is," the very broad idea of "anything," and a host of other facts. As Peirce says, "that truth is correspondence of a representation with its object is, as Kant says, merely the nominal definition of it. Truth belongs exclusively to propositions" (1906a, 379).[4] Being a nominal definition doesn't make it wrong. Nominal (Peirce also uses "trivial") definitions are important for orienting the beginner and closing off distracting lines of discussion, but Peirce's goal is to connect our ordinary understanding of "truth" to the practice of scientific inquiry.

Cheryl Misak, following Wiggins, characterizes this as "the provision of a pragmatic elucidation of a concept—an account of the role the concept plays in practical endeavours" (Misak 2004, viii). If, as Peirce intends, we attempt to understand truth in the context of inquiry, then it differs from "warranted assertability" or "what works" as the best available account we have differs from the best available account we could conceivably have. As Misak puts it, Peirce's account of logic, truth, and inquiry "can absorb something like a Tarski-style definition of truth and add that it is much more interesting to notice the relationship between truth and a sufficiently prolonged experience-constrained inquiry" (ibid., 129). This, I take it, is Peirce's point:

> A proposition has a subject (or set of subjects) and a predicate. The subject is a sign; the predicate is a sign; and the proposition is a sign that the predicate is a sign of that of which the subject is a sign. If it be so, it is true. [Peirce 1906, 379]

This intentionally convoluted passage reinforces the fact that truth is exclusively a property of propositions and that propositions are functions of signs. The last sentence simply restates the Aristotelian characterization, though it could just as easily be expanded to read "proposition 'X' is true if and only if X."

Once the criticism of Peirce as conventionalist about truth has been disposed of, it is fairly easy to lay out his account of inquiry. As social

---

[4] The publishing history of this essay illustrates the complexity of Peirce's texts. The editors' headnote to Peirce 1906 indicates that, "many versions of a text titled 'The Basis of Pragmaticism' are extant; they were written over a period of nine months starting in August 1905, and they were all meant to become Peirce's third *Monist* paper." Parts of Peirce 1906a, yet another version, were scattered through the *Collected Papers*, specifically I, 573–74; 5, 448n, and 5, 449–54 (see headnote, p. 371). My debt to Peirce's editors and commentators grows ever greater.

beings we imbibe a complex array of beliefs, habits, expectations and the like from the community around us. As long as things go pretty close to expectation, we rightly take our beliefs for granted, but when our expectations and events collide we develop doubt. The goal of inquiry is to fix belief and thereby eliminate the doubt. While belief can be fixed in a number of ways, the "method of scientific investigation," Peirce insists:

> is the only one of the four methods which presents any distinction of a right and a wrong way. If I adopt the method of tenacity and shut myself out from all influences, whatever I think necessary to doing this is necessary according to that method. So with the method of authority: the state may try to put down heresy by means which, from a scientific point of view, seem very ill-calculated to accomplish its purposes, but the only test *on that method* is what the state thinks, so that it cannot pursue the method wrongly. So with the *a priori* method . . . But with the scientific method the case is different. [Peirce 1877, 121]

It is precisely because the method of science pursues truth that it is subject to error; unlike tenacity, authority, or the *a priori*, science makes itself accountable to the world. We are likely to recognize error—as opposed to disagreement or heresy—because it generates expectations that are at odds with the facts. That, in turn, calls for more scientific investigation. There may be more efficient ways of securing agreement, but not of pursuing the truth.

At the same time, the answers generated by inquiry are shot through with the fallibilism that permeates human judgments. Human error and theoretical innovation—Peirce was much influenced by Lobachevsky and Riemann and approached Simon Newcomb to support funding for his study of the curvature of space (Eisele 1979, 71)—should qualify accepting even deductive inferences. As for the natural sciences, "they always have been and always must be theatres of controversy" (Peirce 1898, 44). In our pursuit of truth, "there is no positive sin against logic in *trying* any theory which may come into our heads, so long as it is adopted in such a sense as to permit the investigation to go on unimpeded and undiscouraged" (ibid., 48). But even when the community of inquirers has settled on a particular hypothesis, it remains subject to future experience. Such "established truths" are merely "propositions into which the economy of endeavor proscribes that for the time being further inquiry shall cease" (ibid., 56). And even if a given hypothesis stands the test of time, we will always be bumping up against new and interesting doubts that will themselves impel us toward the further fixation of belief. This is true of religion as much as science.

Chance, law, and habit

A third important set of essays appeared in *The Monist*, between 1891 and 1893. While the fourth of these "seemed to Peirce's former student Christine Ladd-Franklin to be clear evidence that he was losing his mind" (Brent 1993, 211), Peirce was not straying from his basic principles. By the time the essays appeared in the *Collected Papers*, however, their point had become obscure to contemporary readers. Despite his obvious disdain, Lewis Feuer, one of several young Harvard graduates assigned to review the *Collected Papers*, produces a pretty accurate summary of Peirce's key points:

1. All laws are the products of evolution.
2. The paradigm for law is the habit formation of rational agents.
3. No law of nature is absolute.
4. Chance increases variety while being checked by natural selection.
5. This understanding of natural law can be confirmed experimentally. (See Feuer 1936, 205)

To be a scientist is to be committed to investigating the way the world is, in the hope of discovering the truth. As opposed to the "nominalist," the "realist" of Peirce's stripe thinks that the truths at which he aims are part of the natural world, not merely instrumental generalizations of abstractions from collections of observations. Unlike certain sorts of empiricists, "Peirce refuses to say of any kind of hypothesis that it is not a candidate for a truth-value" (Misak 2004, 96).[5] If it can have a truth value, then it is at least possibly part of the fabric of reality.

Since scientists are looking for truth, and since the evidence for this truth is the experience of the scientific community, there should be some correlation between that experience and the best available hypotheses. This is where Peirce parts company with the mechanists and determinists of his day. Experience simply doesn't jibe with either; no experiments perfectly conform to the formulae of mathematical physics. Some of this must derive from the limits of our senses and instruments, but this can't be the end of it. "We have no right," Peirce insists, "to suppose that the real facts, if they could be had free from error, could be expressed by such a formula at all" (Peirce 1878a, 195). Our evidence

---

[5] This comes out not only in the review of Karl Pearson's *Grammar of Science* (Peirce 1901) but in Peirce's critique of the Poincaré and, in particular, Mach (see Eisele 1979, chs. 11 and 21). All fall into some form of nominalism or conventionalism.

for the laws of nature does not suggest determinism. He repeats this position in the second of the *Monist* papers:

> The principle of universal necessity cannot be defended as being a postulate of reasoning. But then the question immediately arises whether it is not proved to be true, or at least rendered highly probable, by observation of nature. [1892, 303]

It isn't. Practical and scientific observers regularly encounter deviations for the predicted value. "Try to verify any law of nature," he writes, "and you will find that the more precise your observations, the more certain they will be to show irregular departures from the law" (ibid., 304). In fact, he continues, "those observations which are generally adduced in favor of mechanical causation simply prove that there is an element of regularity in nature, and have no bearing whatever upon the question of whether such regularity is exact and universal, or not" (ibid.). Observation yields regularity, not mechanical causation. To be true to the observed facts, those laws of nature should be stated as probabilities. "The determined advocate of exact regularity," he concludes, "will soon find himself driven to *a priori* reasons to support his thesis" (ibid., 305). And as we learned in the previous set of papers, a priori methods of fixing belief run contrary to those of the sciences.

"The next step in the study of cosmology," Peirce writes in the third of the *Monist* essays, "must be to examine the general law of mental action" (Peirce 1892a, 313). Here he explicitly connects his thought to the anti-Cartesian essays of 1868–69. Identifying his understanding of continuity as "*synechism*," according to which "the present is connected with the past by a series of real infinitesimal steps" (ibid., 314), Peirce explicates the notion mathematically, invoking the work of Cantor, Euler, and others. But his real objective is an account of the continuity of the human mind, in space and time, with the rest of the natural world. He asks us to imagine a slime-mold, or amoeba, "or at any rate some similar mass of protoplasm." It can be given a reasonably complete material description and, in a quiet state, it appears inert. But:

> a place upon it is irritated. Just at this point, an active motion is set up, and this gradually spreads to other parts. In this action, no unity nor relation to a nucleus, or other unitary organ can be discerned. It is a mere amorphous continuum of protoplasm, with feeling passing from one part to another. [Ibid., 324]

As with feeling in the simple organism, so, Peirce argues, with ideas in the human mind. What happens in the human mind is the continuous development from particular stimulus to general idea to habit:

Habit is that specialisation of the law of mind whereby a general idea gains the power of exciting reactions. But in order that the general idea should attain all its functionality, it is necessary, also, that it should become suggestible by sensations. [Ibid., 328]

From the regularity of nature, a fact ubiquitously observed, we go up the ladder to the predictable excitability of living matter, to the less predictable, but still regular and intelligible, behavior of the human being. To capture the continuity of the natural world, we need a hypothesis that explains all three, and mechanical determinism doesn't fit. Rather, the evidence suggests a generalization which, if correct, still admits of variation and exception. The best model for this is "habit."

Habits cross the boundary between matter and mind. In the essays of the late 1870s Peirce writes of belief that its "essence . . . is the establishment of a habit, and different beliefs are distinguished by the different modes of action to which they give rise" (1878, 129–30). Since "what the habit is depends on *when* and *how* it causes us to act" (ibid., 131), it naturally gives rise to a set of conditional statements. And since "the identity of a habit depends on how it might lead us to act, not merely under such circumstances as are likely to arise, but under such as might possibly occur, no matter how improbable they may be" (ibid.), this results in a set of counterfactuals indicating what we should expect to happen under certain circumstances, even if those circumstances are never realized.

Habits, expressed as conditionals or counterfactuals, would thus fall within the larger discussion of causes in general. Thus, to say "If it were 5:15, Davis would be listening to the radio," is almost certainly true. My friends know, and are sometimes exasperated by the fact that, I go to great lengths to organize my schedule so that nothing interferes with listening to NPR's afternoon news. If it turned out that I wasn't listening, they would expect some intervening cause to be offered in explanation. And I think "cause" is the right word here, for if someone offered a "reason," say "Davis didn't feel like it," the event would be so unusual that it would illicit dissatisfied incredulity: "What happened!?"

Over a period of twenty-five years, Peirce argued that the paradigm of causal explanation is the invocation of habit, something with which all inquirers are presumably familiar and which they understand to explain the regular and predictable occurrence of sequences of events that are, nonetheless, not necessitated by any mechanism. So, when Peirce subsequently writes that "the one intelligible theory of the universe is that of objective idealism, that matter is effete mind, inveterate habits becoming physical laws" (1891, 293), his point is much less metaphysically freighted than it might appear. Any metaphysical dualism, he implies, is at odds with scientific inquiry because it breaks the world into two mutually inaccessible parts. To begin with matter and attempt to explain the emergence of mind has typically required postulating some point at which, for reasons unclear, the original matter achieves a level of organization and complexity that leads to its acting like a rational agent. So, for example, Gerald Edelman sketches how:

> the reticular nucleus of the thalamus developed enhanced inhibitory circuits by which it connects to the specific nuclei. This allowed the activity of the reticular nucleus to gate or select various combinations of the activity of those specific thalamic nuclei corresponding to different sensory modalities. [2004, 54–55][6]

Edelman tips his hand in the second sentence, where he attributes "selection" to the "activity of the reticular nucleus." We know what it means to select for "normal" shaped bananas, for example. We could even design a machine that did it automatically. But the design would be based on the specific selection parameters that we chose.[7] How selection is accomplished by the reticular nucleus is, at best, unclear. The same can be said for even more incautious remarks such as, "in REM sleep, the brain truly speaks to itself in a special conscious state—one constrained neither by outside sensory input nor by the tasks of motor output" (ibid., 144). Except for the "truly" it would be possible to see this as metaphor. But if "truly" is intended to carry the weight of "literally, not metaphorically," then we're left with the cartoon image of a disembodied brain chattering away in the darkness.

What Peirce is actually suggesting is that we drop the dualism of mind and matter in favor of whatever the best account tells us about the stuff of the universe. Going back to Feuer's sketch of his cosmology, the recommendation would then be to embrace the continuity of the universe's first three minutes, as described by Steven Weinberg, for example, with the last 3.8 billion years of life on this little patch of the universe, as described by Darwin and his successors, including Edelman and those who come after him. If the best of scientific inquiry requires giving up a tradition of

---

[6] I find Edelman's "neuronal Darwinism" helpful for several reasons. First, he acknowledges the intellectual limits of "medical materialism" and is willing to admit that his approach to ridding "the stables of dualism, mysterianism, paranormal projections, and unnecessary appeals to as yet poorly characterized properties," requires him to submit "to the paradoxes of epiphenomenalism" (2004, 145). Second, he nicely lays out the impediments to thinking of the brain as a computer (ibid., 35–39). And third, he is usually more sensitive to the problems of anthropomorphizing neurochemical systems than the "cognitive scientists." But nothing turns on Edelman's being the correct account of the functioning of the brain. Whatever the best neuroscience turns out to be, it will still need to account for the local, innovative, and eccentric facts about rational human activity.

[7] This example derives from an NPR story on EU produce regulations that was run in *All Things Considered*, June 21, 2009. It is accessible at NPR.org through their archives.

mechanistic determinism, so be it. Einstein gave up the mechanistic aspect of earlier physics (see Einstein and Infeld 1938, 120–21).

Suppose that Weinberg is more or less right that sometime less than 20 billion years ago:

> there was an explosion. Not an explosion like those familiar on earth, starting from a definite center and spreading out to engulf more and more of the circumambient air, but an explosion which occurred simultaneously everywhere, filling all space from the beginning, with every particle of matter rushing apart from every other particle. [1993, 5]

This, as Weinberg happily admits, rests on "a good deal of highly speculative theory" (ibid., 148), but for Peirce there is nothing wrong with that. The results of experience, in this case the technically informed experience of the physicist, produce uncertainties which give rise to speculations—call them hypotheses, abductions, or what have you—which are then elaborated and put to the test. And these tests give rise to more of the same. Looking back over the decade and a half since his original writing, Weinberg writes that, "the years since 1977 have seen a sequence of brilliant experiments—most dramatically, the discovery from 1983 to 1984 of the W and Z particles that transmit the weak nuclear forces" (ibid., 190). The emergence of string theory generated new excitement, followed by new puzzles. (Ibid., 191)

On Peirce's account of inquiry, this is precisely what we should expect. The fact that we see much the same at the level of quantum physics as we do in cosmology is, for the pragmatist, reassuring.[8] That the hurdles faced in explaining humans and their behavior are many times greater than those encountered by cosmologists and quantum theorists is also, in its way, reassuring. Edelman, once again, is refreshingly up front about the source of this complexity. "The human brain," he writes:

---

[8] In 1966 Gamow could write that "after the thirty fat years in the beginning of the present century, we are now dragging through the lean and infertile years, and looking for better luck in the years to come. In spite of all the efforts of the old-timers like Pauli, Heisenberg, and others, and those of the younger generation like Feynman, Schwinger, Gell-Mann, and others, theoretical physics has made very little progress during the last three decades" (1966, 161). Less than twenty years later Feynman had become one of the old-timers and was able to produce a popular account of quantum electro-dynamics that took advantage of quarks and other new concepts, with their attendant elaborations and experiments. In typical fashion, he wrote that, "throughout these lectures I have delighted in showing you that the price of gaining such an accurate theory has been the erosion of our common sense" (Feynman 2006, 119). And Feynman was more than willing to acknowledge the "loose ends" hanging out of the then current account. Another twenty years and popular accounts now include figures, notably John Bell, who weren't players in earlier versions of the story (see Polkinghorne 2002 and, especially, Louisa Gilder's imaginative 2008 reconstruction). Each new twist has, in its turn, sent ripples through the technical philosophical community. This is as the Peircean pragmatist would expect.

is the most complicated material object in the known universe... If the cerebral cortex were unfolded (making the gyri, its protrusions, and the sulci, its clefts, disappear) it would have the size and thickness of a large table napkin. It would contain at least 30 billion neurons, or nerve cells, and 1 million billion connections, or synapses. [2004, 15–16]

So the neurochemistry of the human brain depends not only on quantum physical relations that were created in Weinberg's first three minutes, but on the organic chemistry that spawned living organisms here almost 4 billion years ago. Getting from there to the first primates will require connecting that organic chemistry to the latest version of Darwin's *Origin*, and we will still need to fill in 65 million years of human evolution to get to the present. Even then, a complete theory, while it won't be required—*pace* Laplace—to predict what I have for dinner, will need to account for how it is that creatures like me make the sorts of choices they make and then integrate them into comprehensive plans for the near and distant future. Anything less would be a failure. To put it in terms of our earlier discussion, anytime we make a true statement, we've captured a bit of reality. If we believe what we say, and if we're justified in believing it, then we know something about reality.

The legacy of Peirce's pragmatism

Peirce died in 1914, but he hardly vanished as a force in American philosophy. Well before the publication and digestion of the *Collected Papers*, which appeared between 1931 and 1958, he had become a major presence in American philosophy. In 1916, the *Journal of Philosophy* brought out a commemorative issue, with essays by Royce, Dewey and others, and a "tentative bibliography" compiled by Royce's student Morris Raphael Cohen.[9] Cohen's preliminary comments indicate a full familiarity with Peirce's fallibilism, understanding of probability, and doctrine of chance. In 1923 Cohen edited the first, and in many ways still the best, short anthology of Peirce's writings. It was this anthology that introduced Peirce to Frank Ramsey and through him, in all likelihood, to the later Wittgenstein.[10] In the later 1920s Cohen was instrumental in raising the money that made it possible for Harvard to edit

[9] Cohen identifies himself unabashedly with Royce in his 1916 essay, but is somewhat reticent about his Harvard influences in his autobiography. See Cohen 1949, section XVII. Hollinger makes the Royce connection in more detail in 1975, 53ff.

[10] I can find no reference by Wittgenstein to Peirce, though Ramsey was using Cohen's anthology when Wittgenstein returned to Cambridge. By this time, Ramsey had turned to probability, in a series of essays much influenced by his reading of Peirce. In January of 1929,

and publish Peirce's *Collected Papers*. More importantly, it is largely through Cohen that Peirce achieves a major role in Anglo-American philosophy of science.

Gerald Holton describes Peirce's "process of abductive inference" as:

> powered by the unashamed proposal of forward-looking hypotheses that are scrutinized, and made corrigible by experience and disciplined thought—not only by its originator, but by the community of scientists. [Holton 1984, 172]

Holton goes on to add that, "this attitude, verging on the outrageous when first proposed, has since become an element of the implicit lore and tool kit of most scientists" (ibid., 173). Cohen displays the legacy of Peirce in numerous places. In a discussion of causality in physics, for example, he writes that:

> We need not here press the hypothesis of C. S. Peirce that there is a domain of radical indeterminism, that besides the variations due to errors of observation there are variations due to the fact that our physical laws do not express with absolute accuracy the actual behaviour of things. [Cohen 1953, 222]

Reasonableness, as encountered in all forms of inquiry, doesn't depend on certainty, or the determinism that certainty desires, but only the self-critical practices that make up "the daily procedure of scientific investigation" (ibid.).

Cohen transmits the legacy of Peirce to his most influential student, Ernest Nagel. Nagel studied at City College while Cohen was compiling his Peirce anthology. A decade later, Nagel wrote one of the most important early reviews of the first volumes of the *Collected Papers* (Nagel 1933). The next year Cohen and Nagel published *An Introduction to Logic and Scientific Method*, long a respected text in the field. And the year after that Nagel travelled to Europe to report on the state of analytic philosophy in England and Central Europe. There's a lot to be gleaned from Nagel's two long articles, but here I'm only interested in the role Peirce plays in his account of analytic philosophy. Reporting on Cambridge, for example, he begins with a long appreciation of Moore before turning to Wittgenstein.[11] Having been denied access to Wittgenstein's lectures, Nagel is forced to base his report on "certain notes on his

Wittgenstein began meeting with Ramsey "several times a week . . . for many hours at a time" (Monk 1990, 259).

[11] A footnote pleads lack of space as the excuse for omitting "comment on the Peircean-pragmatic turn which the discussions of induction and probability have taken in the cases of Braithwaite and the late Frank Ramsey" (Nagel 1936, 10, n. 1).

lectures which are in circulation" (Nagel 1936, 17).[12] He notes that Wittgenstein has apparently disowned the *Tractatus* and now sees "the perennial problems of philosophy...as a disease which it is the task of sound philosophy to cure" (ibid.). This cure is to be achieved through the clarification of problematic expressions in order to overcome the tendency to proliferate problematic entities. "Much of this," it strikes Nagel, "reads like a page from Peirce" (ibid., 18).[13]

For an important strand of Anglo-American philosophy of science, Peirce will turn out to be the natural intermediary between the progressively more unsustainable verificationism of the early positivists and the gnomic utterances of the later Wittgenstein. As Nagel subsequently writes of the Vienna Circle, commemorating the centenary of Peirce's birth, "many of its recent views have been taken for granted for some time by American colleagues, largely because the latter have come to intellectual maturity under the influence of Peirce" (1940, 70). Nagel's view is born out, either directly or indirectly, in the work of Hanson, Kuhn, the later Popper, and van Fraassen. But perhaps the freshest and most Peirce-like move in recent Anglo-American philosophy of science is by a philosopher who goes out of his way not to identify himself with pragmatism, or any other "-ism:" Arthur Fine.[14] Most of Fine's early work was on logic and the analysis of quantum physics. In the mid-1970s he began working on the unpublished Einstein papers and in *The Shaky Game* he lets a series of essays on the details of Einstein's response to quantum mechanics flow into the debate between "realist" and "antirealist" approaches to the philosophy of science. Not only do his essays on Einstein trace "the conceptual odyssey of a single person... that integrates over time Einstein's various works and thoughts on the conceptual issues that relate to quantum mechanics" (1996, 7), they illustrate how cutting-edge science works. Any philosophy of science

---

[12] These are almost certainly what later became known as the *Blue Book*, since the discussions of Augustine on time, kinds of number, and the status of psychological states all occur therein (e.g. *BB*, 26, 28–29, 46ff.). For the composition and circulation of the *Blue Book*, see Monk 1990, 336ff.

[13] Unless Ramsey had remarked on it in conversation, this may well be the first time the connection between Peirce and the later Wittgenstein was made explicit. Wisdom might have made it, but as best as I can tell he never refers to Peirce. It is left to Renford Bambrough to draw the connections between Peirce and Wisdom (Bambrough 1979). He goes on to speculate on Ramsey's role in passing some of Peirce on to Wittgenstein in his 1981. An early and interesting development of the relation between Peirce's thought and Wittgenstein's is Rorty 1961.

[14] In his recent essays, Fine is willing to discuss the relation between his position and some pragmatists, particularly Dewey (notably Fine 2001, 2007). Peirce doesn't seem to figure, except in the ease with which he embraces "abduction" as central to the practice of science (Fine 1984a, 15).

that would render this irrational or "unscientific" has a lot of explaining to do, and the available approaches, Fine argues, don't measure up. This leads him to offer the "natural ontological attitude" (NOA) as a way of side-stepping the whole debate, "for it opts out of the game of inventing factors whose possession would *make* a practice "scientific" (or "pseudo-scientific," or "nonscientific") (ibid., 9).

NOA maintains that we don't need a theory of truth, a theory of rationality, or a demarcation principle distinguishing science from its pretenders. Einstein got along without them; we can too. What we're left with is common sense informed by the ongoing practice of critical science. Thus:

> When NOA counsels us to accept the results of science as true, I take it that we are to treat truth in the usual referential way, so that a sentence (or statement) is true just in case the entities referred to stand in the referred-to relation . . . As a scientist, say, within the context of the tradition in which he works, the NOAer, of course, will believe in the existence of those entities to which his theories refer. But should the tradition change, say, in the manner of the conceptual revolutions that Kuhn dubs "paradigm shifts," then nothing in NOA dictates that the change be assimilated as being progressive. [1984a, 130]

Our everyday sense of truth, in short, is fully at home with the possibility of radical change. Once upon a time we believed in one sort of thing; now we believe in another. If this is sometimes how science goes, then understanding it is a test of any plausible attitude to science. Fine doesn't seem much interested in Peirce, but the NOA is closer to Peirce's account of science than any of the intervening positions. The exciting thing about Fine's work is the way in which he juxtaposes two parallel stories, one about the scientists and the other about the philosophers, to show how the one constantly frustrates the authoritarian goals of the other, leading us back, finally, to a received wisdom that was first made articulate by Peirce.

From the natural sciences to the social sciences

What is less well known is that Peirce figured in an important early account of the philosophy of the social sciences by one of the founders of sociology, Emile Durkheim. In 1913, Durkheim offered a set of lectures on pragmatism, which were published from student notes in 1954 (see Lukes 1972, 485–96). A complete translation appeared in 1983. In his preface to the French edition of Durkheim's lectures, Armand Cuvillier writes that they "both complement and, so to speak, are a continuation of the theory of knowledge mapped out in *The Elementary Forms of the Religious Life"* (Durkheim 1983, xiii). In that volume, which appeared just the year before the lectures, Durkheim elaborates a theory of knowledge based in the social history of a community and argues that such an approach to epistemology has the benefit of being faithful to the limits of the evidence, accounting, on the one hand, for the relation between religious belief and practices, and, on the other, for the constraints of the social order on the individual, and, finally, laying the groundwork for the development of logic and the practice of science (see Cladis's introduction to Durkheim 2001, xxiv–xxxiii). In an important sense, *Elementary Forms* is a case study in comparative epistemology. "The social realm," Durkheim writes early on, "is a natural realm that differs from others only in its greater complexity" (1995, 17). As part of nature, human societies can be studied scientifically the same way as any other phenomenon. But the facts of this social realm are historical, variable, and subject to change. "Hence," he continues:

> the rationalism that is immanent in a sociological theory of knowledge stands between empiricism and classical apriorism. For the first, the categories are purely artificial constructs; for the second, on the other hand, they are naturally given; for us, they are works of art, in a sense, but an art that imitates nature ever more perfectly. [Ibid., n. 22]

The ways in which a society divides up and interprets its world are neither arbitrary nor universal. They are the products of the individual community, but those products themselves are directed toward accommodating the community to the demands of the world around them. In explaining categories in terms of their origins in the social order, the sociological approach:

> leaves reason with its specific power, but accounts for that power and does so without leaving the observable world ... The categories cease to be regarded as primary and unanalyzable facts; and yet they remain of such complexity that analyses as simplistic as those with which empiricism contented itself cannot possibly be right. [Ibid., 18]

The student of society wants to capture the way a particular community understands itself and then to make whatever cautious generalizations seem justified. The claims he makes are grounded in observation and hope to capture the truth about human society.

For Durkheim, James "is the true father of pragmatism" (Durkheim 1983, 7). This pragmatism appeared "in America, between 1895 and 1900" (ibid., 8), and is exemplified not only by James, but by Dewey in America and, since 1902, by Schiller at Oxford (ibid., 9). First and foremost:

It is as a *theory of truth* that pragmatism is of particular interest, and it is from that point of view that we shall study it. We shall discuss pragmatism as a *theory of the universe* only in so far as is be necessary to understand it as a theory of truth. [Ibid., 11]

This is the crucial move, because Durkheim is willing to grant that the pragmatic attack on "the dogmatic conception of truth," by which he means a view of truth as "the transcription of external reality... outside individual minds" (ibid., 12), is for the most part compelling. The goal of "rationalist" philosophy is to capture this truth in a system; "empiricism" in the English sense merely replaces the system of the rationalist with that of the cosmologists. "According to the pragmatists," Durkheim concludes, "the final difficulty presented by the dogmatic conception is that... when one does not understand that there is a reason for the diversity of judgment and opinions, one runs the risk of ending up in intolerance" (ibid., 20). The goal is to "soften" truth, making it "into something that can be analysed and explained" (ibid.). At this point, pragmatism makes one with sociology, because both apply "the historical point of view to the order of things human," and both conclude that "man is a product of history and hence becoming; there is nothing in him that is either given or defined in advance" (ibid.).

Since the attack on the "dogmatic conception" is nothing more than Peirce's fallibilism looking forward, perhaps, to Dewey's emphasis on the emerging social sciences, there would seem to be nothing much to choose between pragmatism and sociology. This is why James's theory of truth is important. Once Durkheim has focussed on "the proposition that *the useful is the true*" (ibid., 72), he can deploy the sorts of argument familiar in the analytic tradition to condemn James's pragmatism as arbitrary; "Pragmatism can call anything it pleases 'ideal truth.' Therefore, its method is arbitrary and leads to a purely verbal definition with no objective reality" (ibid.). Durkheim realizes that here he is agreeing with Peirce, but Peirce's pragmatism, when contrasted with that of James and those who come after him:

is simply the attitude or general cast to be adopted by the mind when faced with problems... This is Peirce's pragmatism, which tries above all to get rid of verbal discussions and useless problems, and is marked by a characteristic choice of questions and its manner of dealing with them. [Ibid., 11]

So Peirce's pragmatism gives us nothing helpful. It is either based on the untenable theory of truth put forward by James or it's what French sociology is already doing.

This, as I read Durkheim, is all that his "rationalism" amounts to. And this reading explains the threat he sees in James. "Pragmatism," writes

Durkheim, "is in a better position than any other doctrine to make us see the need for a reform of traditional rationalism" (1983, 1). In its diagnostic role, that is, pragmatism has identified the centrality of the social and historical component to the pursuit of knowledge. But it seems clear from *Elementary Forms* that Durkheim thinks of himself as having achieved already this necessary reform. Thus Peirce's pragmatism, with its emphasis on history and community, captures what Durkheim thinks he has already done. It is James's pragmatism, centered on an anti-rationalist theory of truth, that goes beyond reform to radical transformation. Consequently, "if pragmatism were valid, we should have to embark upon a complete reversal of this whole tradition" (ibid.). But that would be to give up the commitment to truth that is central to the scientific project. It is ironic that Durkheim should treat as passé the epistemological project that Holton rightly recognized as "verging on the outrageous." In doing so he obscured what could have become the philosophical underpinnings for more nuanced and historically sensitive sociology.

If Peirce's legacy remained attenuated in the social sciences, it was almost invisible in ethics and the philosophy of religion. These areas fell by the wayside in much of mainstream Anglo-American philosophy in the first half of the twentieth century. Thus the "pragmatic turn" will come to appear very dramatic in ethics and philosophy of religion. This will be the topic of the next chapter.

3

Ethics, Religion, and the Limits of Empiricism

When Herbert Fingarette began graduate work, in 1947, the program at UCLA was young. The first masters degrees had been granted in 1934 and the first doctorates in 1942. The department had a long-standing link to American pragmatism, primarily through Charles Rieber and John Boodin, who had worked with James and Royce. By the 1940s they had been succeeded by Donald Piatt, who studied at Chicago, in the generation after Dewey. The arrival of Hans Reichenbach in 1938, however, established an eminent link with the positivist tradition that would define the department for the next two generations.[1] As far as ethics was concerned, "the fashionable issues of the day in professional philosophy were purely intellectual . . . I came to see what I was doing as eternal prolegomena, a systematic evasion of moral concern, ever setting the table but never a bite to eat" (Fingarette 1991, xxi).

Something of the "eternal prolegomena" against which Fingarette chafed can be gathered from *Readings in Ethical Theory*, the anthology that Alan Donagan has called "unrivaled as a sourcebook for Anglo-American ethics in the first half of the century" (Donagan 2003, 150). The anthology is refreshingly upfront in its intention "to provide a

---

[1] Biographical information on Fingarette comes from Bockover 1991. That on UCLA's Philosophy Department and its faculty come from the *University of California Digital Archive*, easily accessed online. Both are brief and incomplete. There is an interesting characterization of UCLA, and of the development of American philosophy generally in the last half of the twentieth century, in Putnam 1997. Putnam is, I believe, correct in minimizing the impact of positivism narrowly construed. What Fingarette will be sensitive to is the focus on those issues central to positivism in the department generally: logic and mathematics, philosophy of language, and philosophy of science. In the period after the death of Reichenbach, Putnam's teacher, the program, at one time or another, included Carnap, Montague, Church, David Kaplan (Carnap's last graduate student), and David Lewis. In any case, Putnam agrees with Fingarette about ethics. Prior to Rawls, he writes, "the field had been rather in the doldrums" (Putnam 1997, 189).

49

balanced and first-hand account of the theoretical controversies that have developed in ethics since the publication in 1903 of Moore's *Principia Ethica*" (Sellars and Hospers 1952, ix). In a historical arc that runs from Moore and the naturalistic fallacy, through the development of intuitionism, emotivism, moral psychology and the problem of justification, pragmatism appears as the "naturalistic rejoinder" between intuitionism and emotivism. Philosophers still wrote on issues of immediate concern, but normative ethics and political philosophy were looked on with some professional suspicion. Fingarette, recently returned from wartime duty at the Pentagon, formulated a dissertation proposal to test his "Pragmatic thesis that value judgments could be based on knowledge, rather than being inherently subjective or 'emotive' as the Logical Positivists of the day would have it" (1991, xxi). To do so he focussed on the literature of psychoanalysis. The dissertation, deposited in 1949, laid the foundations for a wide-ranging pragmatic critique of empiricism and meta-ethics in American moral thought.

Ethics and the limits of empiricism

Invoking "empiricism" is always dangerous. On the one hand, we all consider ourselves empiricists; we pride ourselves on taking a good hard look at how things lie in the world before judging claims, formulating policies, and acting on our beliefs. That broad sense of empiricism isn't my topic here. It's hard to imagine how anybody could be against it. My topic, however, is a particular philosophical stance that claims to be able to distinguish legitimate statements from spurious, counterfeit, and pseudo-meaningful utterances masquerading as statements. A. J. Ayer, in the 1936 preface to *Language, Truth and Logic*, happily announces that, "the views which are put forward in this treatise derive from the doctrines of Bertrand Russell and Wittgenstein, which are themselves the logical outcome of the empiricism of Berkeley and David Hume" (Ayer 1946, 31). A particularly robust statement of the empiricist stance, a few years earlier than Ayer's, comes from Otto Neurath:

> The "moral sciences," the "psychical world," the world of the "categorical imperative," the realm of *Einfuhlung* (empathy), the realm of *Verstehen* ("the 'understanding' characteristic of the historian")—these are more or less interpenetrating, often mutually substitutable, expressions. Some authors prefer one group of meaningless phrases, some another, some combine and accumulate them... It is the duty of the practitioners of unified science to take a determined position against such distinctions; this is not a matter for their arbitrary choice. [Neurath 1931, 295–96]

If the concepts and distinctions that characterize ethics, history, and the like are all equally meaningless, then the distinctions they pretend to describe cannot be real. There cannot even be cognitive disagreements between them. To engage in the enterprise of social science, as something distinct from and not reducible to the physical sciences, is an exercise in self-delusion.

Normative concepts, from this perspective, are "pseudo-concepts" (Ayer 1946, 107). They serve to express feelings and imperatives; they signal what we care about and what we want others to do when they impinge on things we care about. We absorb our moral language from the communities in which we are reared, but beyond that there are no facts of the matter. The existence of moral disagreement *appears* to be about the facts:

> But if our opponent happens to have undergone a different process of moral "conditioning" from ourselves...then we abandon the attempt to convince him by argument. We say that it is impossible to argue with him because he has a distorted or undeveloped moral sense. [Ibid., 111]

Ethics, and with it religion and related areas, "is nothing more than a department of psychology and sociology" (ibid., 112). But the relevant sorts of psychology and sociology themselves are both physicalist and reductive. Fingarette refers to this sort of ethics as "subjective" or "emotive." Reichenbach called it a "volitional ethics," in which, "the use of such expressions as 'he should not lie', or 'lying is morally bad', represents a pseudo-objective mode of speech; what is expressed is actually an attitude of the speaker" (Reichenbach 1951, 288). For empiricists of this sort, "prolegomena," the investigation of the terms used in talk about ethics, is all there is. Such, at least, is the stance of C. L. Stevenson's seminal paper "The Emotive Meaning of Ethical Terms." This is the attitude Fingarette confronted when he began his dissertation.

Fingarette's earliest articles stem directly from the dissertation and illustrate his pragmatist alternative to contemporary ethical theory. The essay on "unconscious behavior" illustrates the approach of the dissertation. He begins by stating the following theses with regard to "unconscious behavior," "repression," and "defense mechanism," which he takes to be key concepts of psychoanalysis:

1. The usual "empirical" or "operational" interpretations of these concepts to date have in fact been misinterpretations.

2. Actual psychoanalytic usage is continuous with (reasonably develops out of) good, common, and sensible English.

3. Actual psychoanalytic usage can be interpreted literally (i.e. not metaphorically or animistically).

4. Actual psychoanalytic usage is in principle with an operationalist and/or an empirically oriented introspectionist approach to human psychology. [1950, 509]

All four are directed against a common mid-century reading of psycho-analysis, of which Fingarette gives Arthur Pap as an example:

> "Didn't the psychologist tell me, the other day, that my feeling of contempt towards young men of my own age is not 'really' a feeling of superiority, as I thought, but on the contrary a feeling of inferiority, which I try to overcom-pensate (in plain English: cover up) by my superior attitude!" Well, if this is what your psychologist told you, then he unnecessarily confused you by using language improperly... It would be absurd to deny the existence of those very feelings which the psychological theory tries to explain. [Ibid., 513]

As Pap sees it, to discern in yourself a feeling of superiority simply is to have the feeling. To deny this is, "according to Pap, nonsense. Hence it must mean that there *is* really a feeling of superiority but that *it is caused by other unknown processes*" (ibid.). This is the claim Fingarette is rejecting.

Why? If Pap were right, then the perceived feeling would be the real feeling and the psychoanalyst would be appealing to some unknown biological mechanism to explain it. Freud, at least occasionally, saw his enterprise in these terms (see Wollheim 1971, ch. 2). But this is not, as Fingarette sees it, the stance that should be adopted by the theoretically sophisticated psychoanalyst. It relies on a materialist prejudice that is neither experimentally established nor theoretically necessary. Both the layman and the psychoanalyst begin from the observation that, in human behavior, there often seems to be more going on than the indi-vidual actor is aware of; we see it in casual remarks, physical expressions, and habits, not just pathological behavior. "Hence," writes Fingarette, "when the psychoanalyst agrees with the layman that human behavior is not always really what it seems, he means this literally" (ibid., 514).

While the layman may be content to notice this and let it go, the psychoanalyst attempts to press further and determine whether there are regular patterns to these sorts of behavior. For him, "'real behavior at *tp*' is a (rather complicated) construct and not a way of referring simply to the publicly observable and/or introspectable behavior at *tp*" (ibid.). How can people be mistaken about their feelings? Fingarette draws an analogy with color reports. My mother, for example, regularly gets in the car and remarks, "Oh darn, I don't match! I thought this shirt was black, but it's navy!" This worries her because she fears that other people will catch her out, and this means she believes that the cloth typically exhibits its blueness to herself and others under the proper light. Fingarette writes that for these judgments to be correct:

> The cloth must be such that under specific standard conditions it usually appears navy blue colored. The standard conditions are often recognized "intuitively" and as a result of slowly acquired habit and belief instead of being checked against a systematically formulated set of specifications. [Ibid., 515]

If the standard conditions are met, as they are in the case of my mother, then we infer that there is some further condition—her preference for low, indirect lighting, perhaps—that regularly leads her to make this mistake.

Though they may differ in the evidence they consult, "in significant lay and psychoanalytic usage, the standards are not arbitrary, at least in the sense that they arise out of a previous background of inquiry and observation into actual situations of a relevant kind" (ibid., 517). What distinguishes the psychoanalyst from the layman is greater access to background history and clinical reports, prior research into the ways in which individuals can be led into mistaken judgments about their feelings and beliefs—"the concept of defense mechanism along with its specific forms such as repression, projection, and so forth"—and the various other hypotheses his field has developed "in the context of a systematic attempt to predict and control human behavior" (ibid., 518). In short, psychoanalysis, whatever our ultimate judgments about its claims and methods, is a perfectly intelligible field of inquiry focussed on developing a comprehensive account of what both professional and ordinary observers recognize as "unconscious behavior." Because that behavior is driven by unconscious mechanisms, and seems to be at odds with our ordinary account of actions in terms of beliefs and conscious choices, it is important, whatever its final form, for a complete account of our lives together.

If this first article argues the intellectual legitimacy of psychoanalytic inquiry, the second affirms the legitimacy of ethics as a cognitive inquiry in its own right. Pragmatists and logical empiricists have "divergent views," writes Fingarette, on the question "in what sense, if any, are evaluations cognitive?" Despite attempts at rapprochement:

> there are certain misinterpretations of the pragmatist viewpoint which are used at times by logical empiricists as a basis for criticism of the pragmatist theory... it implies that at least part of the confusion arises from the failure to understand the pragmatist theory of value. [1951, 625]

The confusion stems from interpreting Dewey to hold that ethical statements involve hypotheses and predictions (ibid., 627). Fingarette admits that Dewey occasionally writes as if ethics and scientific inquiry are continuous, but to see them as identical generates the following problem:

> if ethical methodology were to end with scientific methodology, those involved in an ethical dispute might come to agreement as to which predictions were correct, but they would stop there. The question would still remain open as to what attitude they should adopt in the light of these predictions. [Ibid.]

This reproduces precisely the emotivist understanding of ethics that Fingarette sets out to overcome. But this account of Dewey is mistaken. Ethics, "is distinctive methodologically by virtue of the fact that it affirms commitments, norms, conditions to be met, and thus plays a role distinct from that of the matter-of-fact proposition" (ibid., 629). Why has this distinction proved so confusing?

As in "Unconscious Behavior," the key lies in recognizing the role of inquiry in the investigations under scrutiny. Broadly construed, "inquiry is the process directed toward the controlled existential reconstruction of a situation so as to make determinate what was, prior to inquiry, indeterminate," and the propositions generated by inquiry— he's quoting Dewey here—"are to be differentiated and identified on the ground of the function of their content as means...'"—means, of course, of promoting inquiry and instituting 'final resolutions' of the problematic situation" (ibid., 630). If psychoanalysis is continuous with the common-sense interpretation of human behavior, ethics turns out to be continuous with our common-sense account of judgment:

> When the judge declares, "Objection overruled," his statement expresses a proposition, and a judgment. The sentence states a ruling as to what needs to be done at this point; it symbolizes the resulting and contemporary partial reconstruction of the court situation. [Ibid., 631]

Scientific findings and judgments are both "phases of inquiry" and as such are about values. "There is no methodological distinction between value-judgments and other judgments" (ibid., 632); they both signal that *this* finding, on the basis of knowledge and inquiry, sets the baseline and we will proceed from here.

"Value propositions and judgments," Fingarette goes on, "are not matter-of-fact declarations but they are grounded in, supported by, matter-of-fact propositions in a manner describable in terms of the total process of inquiry" (ibid., 634). Here again, the legal process illuminates the issue. A finding of "guilty" gives the defendant a legal status, justifying all sorts of subsequent actions. It is, we hope, based on a rigorous investigation of the facts, but it is also governed by the judge's charge to the jury. It doesn't just register the jury's collective belief that he did it, but it certifies that, cognizant of its sworn duty, the jury assessed the evidence and delivered its verdict. That things occasionally go wrong doesn't change the role of juries in our social and intellectual life.

"You're guilty," "my mother loves me," "Leila is a better violinist than Randy," are all judgments about the way certain parts of the world hang together. The first is a verdict, the second is somewhere between a report and judgment, and the third is an evaluation. But all three are "cognitive" in a perfectly ordinary sense. They are statements capable of being true or false. They also invoke norms, "the norm and the declaration of it being justified by the process and goal of inquiry" (ibid., 635). People can disagree about them, but that in itself shows them to be cognitive. The "emotivist" account of ethics that appealed to so many logical empiricists, Fingarette concludes, "is not only a distortion of the pragmatist view, but it is logically arbitrary and psychologically inadequate" (ibid.).

Becoming responsible

Throughout the 1950s Fingarette continued to write on psychoanalysis and psychoanalytic concepts. At the same time, he discovered that he "was spontaneously using metaphors, idioms, images, and paradoxes that were inescapably reminiscent of mysticism, of Eastern doctrines such as Karma, and of the enlightenment disciplines of Buddhism" (Fingarette 1991, xxii). The pragmatic strain, while less explicit, remains. Early on in *The Self in Transformation*, the book which brought together this early work, he writes that, "the reader may or may not notice hovering in the background from time to time such figures as Dewey, Russell, the later Wittgenstein, or G. E. Moore" (1963, 8). The connection to Wittgenstein in particular comes out early, when Fingarette invokes, "the analogy between the meaning-systems which give structure to experience and the rules, strategies, and piece-names in a game" (ibid., 22). The game analogy allows Fingarette to explicate therapy in terms of "digressions in a game where we turn our attention to the rules, strategy, or data instead of to the making of moves in the game" (ibid., 24). The therapist attempts to identify and then disentangle the different activities that make up an individual life and illustrate the ways that certain moves the client wishes to make are pathological; they are "pathological" in the sense of making no sense, and thus destroying both the integrity and the good to be achieved in a particular endeavor.

The language of game-playing depends heavily on our common sense talk about reality and the facts of our experience. We don't need a theory of truth to determine whether or not Sandoval hit a homer, for instance. We need an umpire properly positioned, knowledgeable of the rules, and upright in his professional conduct. We don't have to ask whether or not Sandoval wanted to hit a home run; why else would he swing like that? And nobody cares whether anyone thinks baseball is worth watching. If you don't want to watch, do something else. The therapist's client, for whatever reason, is finding it difficult to function, to play successfully, in his social world. He wants, perhaps desperately, to play the game, but there is something that thwarts him.

It is here that the "empiricist self" becomes a problem. As Fingarette will later put it, for the empiricist of the positivist sort "it is mistakenly assumed that rationality is the sufficient condition for responsibility" (Fingarette 2004, 3–4). This just isn't true. Responsibility requires that we acknowledge certain facts about the world and our place in it, *and* that we care about things being the way they should be. The "should" here does not express an individual emotive response to our environment, but judgments about the propriety of our interactions with others in that environment. Sometimes individuals simply don't learn to care, which goes hand in hand with the failure to accept responsibility. Nonetheless, lack of explicit acceptance is not an excuse for socially unacceptable behavior (ibid., 5–6). Fingarette doesn't deny that some sorts of problematic behavior are biologically based, while other sorts are generated by early, pre-rational, conditioning. "There is no way," he grants, "to completely undo sexuality, aggressiveness, or other biologically rooted impulses" (ibid., 15). But this doesn't eliminate responsibility. Because they "can be significantly modified, and often in a wide variety of ways," the individual who has been offered help can be held responsible for persisting in bad behavior (ibid.). Once we locate acts in the logical space of understanding, deliberation, and choice we are committed to the language of responsibility. To excuse the responsible agent is no less irresponsible than allowing a cheat to subvert the integrity of the game.

What seems to have caught Fingarette's imagination is the set of parallels that hold among parent, therapist, and spiritual advisor. The therapist, like the pragmatist, looks for the successful development of a mature self which can take responsibility for life. "The classical therapeutic aim," Fingarette writes, "is to transmute his feelings, desires, and actions through understanding" (1963, 27). The game analogy is not merely a useful pedagogical metaphor: it models the possible forms of social discourse. Without stipulating anything specific about the rules, principles, or piece-names of a particular game, the therapist can say that if you attempt to play this game you are committed not to private interpretations, but to the publicly shared expectations of all serious players. Refusal to submit to those expectations will be pathological in one way or another, if only because your ability to navigate the world depends on "the fact that human beings do reliably, constantly, and publicly grasp meanings by observing the behavior and speech of other human beings" (ibid.). If behavior and speech don't cohere, conflict of one sort or another is inevitable. The fact that most of us carry out our daily chores, interacting with other people who look like, and talk like, we do, is the only evidence we need to conclude that we share a meaningful social life.

A large part of what it means to be "well-adjusted" lies in the ability to understand the meanings of, and take part in, the various aspects of our day-to-day life. The mature agent has accepted responsibility for the values that he shares with the other members of the community. The anxiety that sends a client to the therapist "is meaninglessness" (ibid., 86). Whatever its particular etiology, this anxiety is always connected to the inability, perhaps even the refusal, to acknowledge that "we create our values. We cannot use the prior self and its world to justify them, but we can live by them" (ibid., 101). This is where classic literary and religious texts come in; they illustrate the process of becoming responsible.

Part two of *Transformation* begins with the notion of "blame," particularly as found in Aristotle's remark that, "the man who is angry at the right things and with the right people, and further, as he ought, when he ought, and as long as he ought, is praised" (Fingarette 1963, 116). Central to normal blame, as Fingarette puts it, is a fundamental realism. "This triggering of blame when there is actual wrongdoing," he writes, "is not only consistent with the healthy ego's reality-orientation, it helps, within limits to be mentioned later, to reinforce this reality-orientation" (ibid., 126). The integration of the ego and the superego depends upon an adequate grasp of the reality of the environment, both natural and social. Not just any old condition, *pace* Ayer, will do. The parenting process itself has to be constrained by reality.

"In an important sense," Fingarette continues, "the question as to the justification for blaming is akin to that of justifying the taking of an opponent's piece in chess" (ibid., 140). Just as a surgeon, whatever his motives, should be moved by genuine therapeutic goals in recommending an operation, so the blamer should not be "accidentally" justified in his blaming (ibid., 141). Otherwise, the child will perceive itself as a victim. Resentment and other potentially neurotic responses may then be cultivated, with the result that the individual will never be able to acknowledge genuine guilt and accept responsibility (see ibid., 142). Blame, to function properly in the creation of responsibility, should be spontaneous, based in the fact of wrongdoing, and directed toward the good of the individual and the community.

At least one problem with this, particularly from the positivist perspective, is the difficulty of identifying a good of both the individual and the community that is not merely the expression of local preferences. Fingarette is aware of this problem, particularly the contemporary confrontation of secular freedoms and traditional moral and religious constraints. To resolve the problem he undertakes:

> to show that (1) there is a moral outlook with respect to guilt and responsibility which is compatible with the data and theories of psychoanalysis but that (2) this moral outlook is different from the anticonscience, hedonistic one suggested above. [Ibid., 147]

The central move in the argument is to insist that, paradoxical as it may seem, "the patient *must* accept responsibility for traits and actions of his which are the inevitable results of events over which he had no control and of actions which he did not consciously will" (ibid., 163). This seems paradoxical because it runs counter to a key component of our notion of responsibility. Overcoming it motivates Fingarette's turn to religious texts, here a variety of Hindu and Buddhist texts on *karma*.

Fingarette argues that the doctrine of karma, forcing the individual to take responsibility for the fact that multiple unknown and unchosen selves are responsible for how we are currently situated, ultimately sets the stage for embracing responsibility. It expresses, in cosmic terms, the goal of psychoanalytic therapy. "We become responsible agents," writes Fingarette, "when we can face the moral continuity of the familiar, conscious self with other strange, 'alien' psychic entities—our 'other selves'" (ibid., 180). Multiple lives, embraced as lived, are closely related to "the play of children," which, as psychology has made very clear, "is not play in the trivial sense of that word" (ibid., 190). This, in turn, is closely related to the alternative worlds created in art. Children at play are regularly reincarnated as characters in incommensurable worlds, where they can work out the consequences of embracing alternative forms of life. The doctrine of karma, and the sense of time and place as illusion, makes it possible for the adult to do what children do all the time, to ask which is the real self? "The living of many lives enables the Self to work through, existentially and creatively, various moral tendencies potential in its nature" (ibid., 198).

In the pathological case, where some unwanted self appears to take over, the therapist tries to get inside the world of his patient to see how it works. He becomes a sort of midwife for the patient, detaching the unwanted self from the patient in order to hold it up for inspection. Fingarette goes on to draw an analogy with coming to appreciate a work of art:

> As in therapy, there is no way of decisively grasping this *esthetic* unity of a work of art by means of intellectual or descriptive analysis...Much as we may wish we had more helpful terminology to express the point, we cannot deny that, in some sense of the words, it is essential to get at the "inner life" of the art work in order to see its point, its meaning, its *integrity* as a work. [Ibid., 277–78]

The therapist, like the artist and his audience, tries to get inside the world of his patient to see how it works. In this both therapist and artist, as well as the religious aspirant, see the human world in terms of a brotherhood of individuals sharing the problems of responsibility in a complex world. The great religious traditions provide a comprehensive vision of what responsibility demands.

The secular as sacred

In the course of his career, Fingarette ranges over Hinduism and Buddhism, the mysticism of Meister Eckhardt, classical Greek drama, and the book of Job, to mention just some of the highlights. But it has been his reading of Confucius that has had the greatest impact on comparative ethics and the study of religion, particularly the emphasis on tradition. "Why," Fingarette asks, should Confucius "have finally given primary emphasis to tradition?" (1972, 62). The answer lies in the need to establish, in the Chinese states of the fifth and fourth centuries BC, a commitment to authority sufficient to withstand what Herlee Creel describes as "a regular pattern... of almost continuous warfare between the great peripheral states" (1960, 16). As Fingarette puts it:

> If ever there was an area beset with intracultural conflict of every kind from genteel doctrinal dispute to Machiavellian politics, plain murder and brutal warfare, surely Lu and its neighboring states were such a one. It was a time of great turmoil—including an intense *consciousness* of turmoil. [1972, 59]

Confucius' awareness of pervasive turmoil, as Fingarette reconstructs it, motivates a deep analysis of authority. There are, roughly speaking, three ways of establishing authority: "By effective command, by common agreement and by inheritance through accepted tradition" (ibid., 62). In any historical community all three will play a part, but the most stable by far is tradition. It is not necessary to restrict ourselves to Chinese history to see the limits of command. A reading of Tacitus, the history of feudal Europe, or the struggles for power in the post-Lenin Soviet Union illustrate the subversive dynamics of rule by command. "Common agreement," the social contract of mainstream political theory, is subject to the changing perception of individual and subgroup interests. If agreement itself is the foundation for authority, changed circumstances become both a motive and a justification for changing the inherited order. Sometimes this might be a good thing, but not always. The defects of command and consensus, taken together, direct the political and moral theorist toward some form of authority which can legitimately command both solidarity and sacrifice, even at the risk of personal loss.

A tradition is an inheritance; "one has traditions," writes Fingarette, "one does not choose or create them upon need" (ibid., p. 64). The inheritance must be felt as a desirable obligation, which makes life both meaningful and distinctly better than that of those who do no share in it, even if those outsiders are materially better off. There are two components to the creation of a tradition. On the one hand there is narrative. As with the various games that shape day-to-day life, the specifics of the narrative are open. It is only necessary that it be parallel to the physical realities of life:

> This parallel world may be told of as concurrent with the present but going on in a different realm (Heaven, Mount Olympus). Or it may be presented as a narrative of events here near our home on earth but prior to our times; or it may be a narrative of events presented as both in an earlier time and in some other realm. [Ibid., 65–66]

Whether we call a tradition "religious" or "secular" makes little difference. Crucial is the shared recognition of a set of stories or events which have made us who we are. Those stories act as a template for interpreting our lives and for constructing other stories that solidify our sense of a shared history. Thus the Passover Seder identifies today's unleavened bread with that of the forefathers. The four questions set up the narrative of the delivery from Egypt. The traditional "next year in Jerusalem!" identifies the present with a narrative of loss which contains the promise of restoration.[2] The narrative, the *haggadah*, must be situated and enacted in the appropriate ritual context. Simply reading the *haggadah*

---

[2] Glatzer notes that "Jews in Israel say next year in Jerusalem rebuilt" (1969, 85).

in class, even with props and stage setting, isn't to perform a Seder. It is playacting, however instructional. A "real" Seder must be performed by the right people, in the right way, at the right time. When it is, then it becomes part of the fabric of a Jewish life. And what is true of Jewish ritual is true of Chinese, native Australian, or contemporary American democratic ritual. In the most general sense, for Fingarette, Confucius "perceived humanity through the imagery of ceremony and hence of tradition" (ibid., 67).

For the Positivism against which Fingarette originally rebelled, "value judgments" are "inherently subjective or 'emotive'" (Bockover 1991, xxi). This makes it impossible to connect ethics non-arbitrarily to the world. This thesis in moral theory is "supported by a 'formalistic' analysis of science, language and 'knowledge'... that denies the ultimate irreducibility of such notions as, e.g., 'the ceremonial act' and argues instead for a behavioral or physicalist approach to human conduct" (Fingarette 1966, 64 n. 11; 1972, 14 n. 9). The pragmatists and the late Wittgenstein maintain the centrality of social and cultural action in explaining what it means to be human. "No purely physical motion," Fingarette insists, "is a promise; no word alone, independent of ceremonial context, circumstances and roles can be a promise" (1972, 14). The human world is a ceremonial world and ceremony only becomes meaningful in the context of a tradition. Sharing a tradition depends on accepting responsibility for the ceremonial life. "Distinctively human powers," by which Fingarette means abilities to act shaped by ceremonies directed to more than merely animal ends, "have, characteristically, a magical quality" (ibid., 6). *Li*, "holy ritual," or "sacred ceremony," requires an apprenticeship of committed labor. It requires knowledge of the fine details of the human world, as well as judicious timing and elegant restraint:

> The (spiritually) noble man is one who has labored at the alchemy of fusing social forms (*li*) and raw personal existence in such a way that they [are] transmuted into a way of being which realizes *te*, the distinctively human virtue or power. [Ibid., 7]

"Magic," in this context, is the ability to achieve my will effortlessly. Thus, in Fingarette's example, if I ask a student to bring me a book she will, almost without thinking, do so. Should I have to ask twice, I'm probably deficient in *te*, for "to govern by *te* is to be like the North Polar Star; it remains in place while all the other stars revolve in homage about it" (ibid., 4, quoting *Analects* 2:1). The individual who has mastered *li* and acts with *te* achieves without effort everything worth achieving.

There is, for Fingarette, no single perspective on life, responsibility, and death, that answers all possible questions. "In the eyes of the Lord," he writes, "Job's presumption that the cosmos was understandable from a single perspective, though the orthodox perspective of the time, amounted to trivializing the awesome and dazzling infinity of Existence" (1996, 89). Nonetheless, "there are routine and tensionless times precisely because there are situations where the perspectives happen to harmonize, or at least don't clash" (ibid.). The genius of Confucius was his vision of a ceremonial world in which harmony could be maximized. Unlike many of the other religious traditions whose texts Fingarette considers, Confucius pursued this harmony with a minimal commitment to deities or complex constraints—e.g. Torah and Dharma—on the responsibilities of human agents. But he was doing, nonetheless, what those other traditions do, namely shaping individuals to take a responsible role in the communities from which they emerge.

Mary Douglas and the assault on psychologism

Looking back on *Purity and Danger*, Mary Douglas sees her enterprise not simply as an attempt to account for the phenomena of pollution and taboo, but as a critical assault on a pernicious psychological theory. "Innatism," she writes, "is a theory of mind which sets the psychologists on the search for universal categories hardwired in the human psyche... I wrote *Purity and Danger* with the express intention of replacing psychologistic ideas about such universal tendencies" (Douglas 1999, ix). This may puzzle many, who know the book primarily through its rereading of Leviticus. But that famous chapter is merely an example of the critical leverage which anthropology furnishes "to the reading of ancient texts" (ibid.). Douglas aspires to much more. In the three decades after *Purity and Danger* she lays out an account of religion and society that makes it possible to connect the texts that inspire Fingarette to types of society interpreted along basically Durkheimian lines. In 1986 Douglas writes that *How Institutions Think* "is the first book I should have written after writing on African fieldwork. Instead I wrote *Purity and Danger*" (Douglas 1986, ix). If *Purity and Danger* is an assault on psychological innateness, *How Institutions Think* lays out the sociological alternative, connecting the solidarity necessary for any institution to sustain itself with the ways in which "thinking depends upon institutions" (ibid., 8). To do this Douglas must respond to two key criticisms of the Durkheimian approach: the alleged inadequacy of functional explanations and "the rational basis for collective action" (ibid., 18).[3] I want to begin with collective action.

Life is hard. It was hard in the sixteenth-century Outback and it's hard in twentieth-century Richmond. In order to make it through the day people need to rely on others to pull their weight and play by the rules. In August of 2010, Steve Slater, a Jet Blue flight attendant, captured international headlines for berating a noncompliant passenger and then deploying the emergency slide to exit the situation. The failure of one individual to play by the rules led Mr. Slater to abrogate his professional responsibilities. Many commentators wonder why it doesn't happen more often. Fingarette's three ways of securing collective action won't help, for the simple reason that it presupposes what it is intended to explain. Confucius couldn't contemplate strategies for securing collective action if he did not already have something like "collective action" as a desideratum guiding his contemplation.

Not only that, but we also have to assume that Confucius is broadly aware of the basic threats to such action. Douglas points to several, but a look at the "free-rider" problem will highlight the issues. Consider the California grunion run. During the spring and summer these little fish ride the waves as far up the beach as possible, where the females dig in to deposit their eggs and the males flop around inseminating them. Devotees scoop them up by hand—the only method allowed—and then repair to a pre-established site to fry up a mess of grunion. Suppose I am a fan of fried grunion, but am a bit squeamish about slopping around in the surf and scooping wriggling little fish into a bucket. I might dress the part, but show up late and mingle with my friends as they're heading back from the beach, thereby enjoying the fry without the unpleasantness. Or suppose that I don't want to hoof it up Nob Hill. Contrary to the rules, I swing on to the traffic side while the cable car is in motion and the conductor is in the car dealing with tourists. By the time he notices me we're up to California, where I jump off and continue on my way. In both cases I am a free-rider, enjoying the benefit of other people's toil and treasure without making a contribution of my own.

Contrary to philosophical wisdom, free-rider problems aren't of much interest for moral theory. In a safe and wealthy society they are an annoyance; in a poor society they won't be tolerated. But they are a

---

[3] Douglas actually calls her approach the "Durkheim-Fleck program," using the work of the Polish biologist Ludwik Fleck to link Durkheim's emphasis on early social anthropology to the emerging sociology of science in mid-twentieth-century thought. Most American readers have come across Fleck through an early reference in Kuhn 1970. The work itself, along with Kuhn's reflections on it, is now available as Fleck 1979.

problem for theories of collective action. Once other members of the population become aware of the success of the free-rider, they have an incentive to do the same. As more people ride for free, the cost of maintaining the cable cars, for example, rises for the rest. This is just unfair, and as the cost rises the sustaining group has more and more reason to quit. "The anthropological evidence from small-scale societies," writes Douglas, "supports the widest extension of Mancur Olson's main thesis that individuals are easily deterred from contributing to the collective good" (Douglas 1986, 29). If the obstacles are so great, how can you generate and sustain collective action?

Several strategies won't work, at least not for the Peircean inquirer. There is no substantive evidence for an "anarchic utopian community" (ibid.) to which cooperation came naturally. Nor do individual psychic urges for satisfaction help; "if they work sometimes and sometimes do not, the question is just pushed back into the form of asking what switches on the public-spirited emotional attitudes" (ibid., 31). Nor will it do any good to invoke the power of the community or society or culture. Those are all variations on the worst sort of functionalist mysticism, where something that plainly doesn't have a mind imposes itself on the individual agents that do. Thus, writes Douglas:

> Given the poverty of alternative explanations, it behooves us to look more carefully for a form of functionalist argument that avoids these pitfalls and yet meets the needs of the Durkheim-Fleck idea of a social group that generates its own view of the world, developing a thought style that sustains the pattern of interaction. [Ibid., 32]

Notice the three components here. The social group doesn't simply generate regular forms of behavior; it must generate a view of the world. This view of the world, or set of beliefs, connects to a style of thought, by which the individual members of the group formulate various statements. And, finally, these ways of thinking and talking must contribute to ways of behaving with each other that make it possible to pass on a recognizable version of the social group to a next generation.

Before addressing Douglas's chastened functionalism, it's worth looking at the standard philosophical objections. Evans-Pritchard writes of Durkheim that, "heightened emotion...can hardly be an adequate causal explanation...The argument, like so many sociological arguments, is a circular one" (Evans-Pritchard 1965, 68). Hans Penner applies a similar critique to Douglas herself, writing of *Purity and Danger* that:

> The thesis of the book may be summed up as follows. Anomaly creates disturbances of a high level in undifferentiated societies. Such disturbances must be reduced or removed in order for the society to function adequately.

> Classification systems, taxonomies, and taboos function to reduce anomalies
> in a society and thus to create solidarity by reducing disturbances created by
> anomalies. [Penner 1989, 249–50]

Both Evans-Pritchard and Penner object to the form of the analysis. If
the presuppositions underlying the explanation of history and ethnography are themselves suspect, then it is unclear how they can offer any
help at all to comparative ethics or the study of religion. What to do?
Penner's argument is, on the face of it, stronger than Evans-Pritchard's
because it deploys the critique of functional analysis found in the work
of Carl Hempel. In fact, it follows Hempel so closely that we might as
well turn to the original.

Hempel takes his task to be one of comparative methodology, specifically contrasting the "nomological explanations" that characterize the
physical sciences with the functional explanations thought to be essential "in psychology and the social and historical disciplines—and, according to some, even in biology" (Hempel 1965, 297). As an example of
nomological—law-based—explanation, Hempel offers the following:

> In a beaker filled to the brim with water at room temperature, there floats a
> chunk of ice which partly extends above the surface. As the ice gradually
> melts, one might expect the water in the beaker to overflow. Actually the
> water level remains unchanged. How is this to be explained? [Ibid., 298]

The explanation, of course, is supplied by Archimedes' law that a body
in water displaces an equal weight of liquid. Since the weight of the ice is
equal to its melted weight, there is no change in water level. Similar
invocations of general physical laws, combined with statements of
particular fact, form the premises which yield the explanation of
other surprising physical phenomena (ibid., 299).

Functional analyses, which figure so prominently in the social
sciences, appear to offer explanations of another sort, explaining a
certain phenomenon in terms of its role in a particular system. Hempel
has several complaints against such explanations, but the most devas-
tating is the claim that, merely in terms of their logic, they are fallacious.
Specifically, functional analyses commit the logical sin of affirming the
consequent. Consider the following (sadly counterfactual) proposition:

> "If I were in San Francisco I would be in California."

This is obviously true. But now imagine I call a friend, who notices the
unusual number and asks where I am. I say:

> "I'm in California"

and he, knowing my innermost desires, responds:

"You're in San Francisco!"

Oh that it were true, and it certainly *might* be true, but alas, I answer back:

"No, I'm in Van Nuys."

My friend has, fallaciously, affirmed the consequent. Hempel suggests that functional analyses typically do the same thing and he offers the following example, where i = "trait," c = "context," n = "necessary condition," s = "system," and t = "time:"

(a) At t, s functions adequately in a setting of kind c (characterized by specific internal and external conditions).

(b) s functions adequately in a setting of kind c only if a certain necessary condition, n, is satisfied.

(c) If trait i were present in s then, as an effect, condition n would be satisfied.

(d) (Hence), at t trait i is present in s. (Ibid., 310)

The fallacy comes in (c), which is not strong enough to license the move from (b) to (d). This will be clearer if we flesh out the basic argument. So imagine a friend passes by my house and observes my children busily cleaning their rooms. He might say to himself:

"Those two would only be working so diligently if a parent had threatened them with grave consequences. Their mother must have threatened to suspend their allowances."

This, of course, *might* be true, but as an argument it is defective. In fact, this one is doubly defective because *I* might have made the threat, which threat *might* have been to confiscate their computers. At the more general level of sociological and anthropological theorizing it is usually not so easy to see where the fallacy occurs. Malinowski and Radcliffe-Brown, in some of their more unguarded dicta, may well be guilty. At the very least, we should agree that *if* a functional analysis commits the fallacy in question, *then* it is defective as an explanation.[4]

In a helpful review article, Robert Segal fills in much of the discussion since Hempel's original. In particular he notes that Robert Cummins has challenged two key assumptions in the philosophical debate:

---

[4] I develop this discussion in a different direction, with detailed discussion of *Purity and Danger* and *Natural Symbols*, in Davis 2008a. In particular, I develop a response to Helm 1971.

(A) The point of functional characterization in science is to explain the presence of the item (organ, mechanism, process or whatever) that is functionally characterized.

(B) For something to perform its function is for it to have certain effects on a containing system, which effects contribute to the performance of some activity of, or the maintenance of some condition in, that containing system. [Segal 2010, 347–48]

By dropping these conditions, Cummins "disentangles function from cause" (ibid., 349). The objective becomes accounting for the workings of the whole. Applied to religion, this would amount to identifying what I earlier called "sub-routines" and identifying how they work together to achieve or thwart the health of the whole. Seen this way, writes Segal, "the conclusion would be that religion, like the beating heart, is part of a system that as a whole is capable of providing meaningfulness" (ibid., 352). The irony here is that Segal articulates with clarity a point Douglas had been attempting to make since at least 1966, when she attributed her own "structural approach" to Evans-Pritchard's *Nuer*, which achieved "a political analysis of a system in which . . . the weight of authority and the strains of political functioning were dispersed through the whole structure of the body politic" (Douglas 1966, vii–viii). Her route was simply more devious in its cruising than the one identified by Segal.

Douglas herself accepts the criticisms of Jon Elster and others, and agrees that functional arguments, to be credible, must meet Elster's five conditions:

1. Y is an effect of X.
2. Y is beneficial for Z.
3. Y is unintended by actions producing X.
4. Y or the causal relation between X and Y is unrecognized by actors in Z.
5. Y maintains X by a causal feedback loop passing through Z. (Douglas 1986, 33)

The first condition is necessary to rule out accidental conjunctions. The second distinguishes function from pathology. This isn't to say that societies don't develop potentially self-destructive forms of belief and behavior; chapter 9 of *Purity and Danger* illustrates the phenomenon in detail. But "self-defeating" structures develop when the ways in which differing goods come to be pursued find themselves at loggerheads (e.g. Douglas 1986, 150–54). The third condition simply distinguishes patterns that emerge as by-products of social action from those which are intentionally built into the system. The United States, for instance, holds elections for President every fourth year. The purpose is to maintain a legitimate chief executive. But given that all of this is directly established in article II, section 1 of the Constitution of the United States, it would be absurd to call this a functional explanation.

The last two constraints are the most interesting. To be a successful functional argument, the function identified, or the causal relation between the behavioral pattern and the function, must be unrecognized by the active individuals of the group. Suppose I show up with a new watch. If Murphy comments, "Nice watch! Rolex?" I would say, "No. Omega." The conversation might then proceed as follows:

"Why the fancy watch? Showing off your big raise?"
"No. I inherited a little and I decided to replace the one that was stolen back in '75. It reminds me of my father."

I have identified the effect and explained its obvious benefit, but the effect is intended by my action and recognized as such. I might, of course, have said:

"Yeah, it was a big raise and I want those jerks in the office to see how much more important I am than they are."

Not an intention I would admit to in public, to be sure, but a recognizable intention and so explained. My colleagues might not see it and respond the way I intend them, but then the situation would be explained by my intended but unrecognized manipulation of them—not, properly speaking, a functional explanation. This would be true even if I bought a fake Omega, not knowing it was a fake. In that case the street-corner capitalist would be taking advantage of my base intention. If I did know it was fake, then my intention would properly be described as "fooling them into believing I bought a fancy watch" for whatever reason. It is only when all the relevant actors fail to recognize the explaining function, and the function is made part of the regular working of the institution or behavioral pattern (condition 5), that you have a genuine and successful functional argument.

At this point Douglas makes a bold move, deploying the early work of David Lewis. "Minimally," she writes, "an institution is only a convention." Conventions are social creations with which we are reasonably familiar. We act on them all the time. For instance, to avoid dissent and distraction, my high-school friends and I agreed that whoever drove got to choose the music. This made it possible to control one of our members, who would punch in a new station at the end of every song, even if he eventually came back to the original station; it also gave him an incentive to drive. This can be generalized as follows:

> A convention arises when all parties have a common interest in there being a rule to insure coordination, none has a conflicting interest, and none will deviate lest the desired coordination is lost (Lewis, 1969). Thus, by definition, a convention is to that extent self-policing. [Ibid., 46]

All of us who drive in this country rely on the convention of driving on the right. A law is just a convention with teeth and a contract is a convention backed by the teeth of the law. Any institution, from a baseball league to a reading group, depends on a shared commitment to a shared activity. It depends on the agreements of the participants and is enforced by the whole against its members. When there is pressure to change or innovate, a particular practice may be altered to the extent that it is acceptable to the participants. When too few of the members find it worthwhile to continue the activity, the institution folds.

An important feature of this account brings us back to Fingarette. Once put into place a convention may continue to function even if the original members lose sight of, or were never privy to, the initial discussion or agreements. This makes it possible to grasp how it could be that in contemporary policing arguments might arise and steps be taken that would not have been consistent in the original situation. It also explains why, particularly with well-established and entrenched institutions, "we have always done it that way" is both a reasonable explanation and a reasonable response to suggested innovations. If the members of a group can be brought to value a particular practice or institution for itself, then they have good reasons for maintaining it, regardless of its origins or their knowledge of its origins. What was at one point a simple behavioral habit or an explicit convention continues to provide a benefit and is retained by a "causal feedback loop," despite the fact that the causal relation is now unrecognized and thus unintended by the current practitioners.

At the same time, "we have always done it that way" may prove an inadequate pedagogical tool. Thus it is not in the least surprising that, when "we've always done it that way" isn't sufficient, someone adds, "and that's the way God told us to do it." Douglas puts it more generally:

> Before it can perform its entropy-reducing work, the incipient institution needs some stabilizing principle to stop its premature demise. That stabilizing principle is the naturalization of social classifications... by which the formal structure of a crucial set of social relations is found in the physical

world, or in the supernatural world, or in eternity, anywhere, so long as it is not seen as a socially contrived arrangement. [Ibid., 48]

As long as a convention is mere convention, and recognized as such, it is subject to criticism, revision, or even rejection. Identifying a practice with the way the world, or at least our particular part of the world, is puts a break on such criticism. This is the work done by the texts that Fingarette explores. The fact that substantial groups repeatedly return to them both to explain the present and to train the next generation illustrates their authority. From a Durkheimian perspective, all of this helps us account for the willingness of group members to act in consort, observing both the positive and negative cults, despite the often severe sacrifices demanded of them. It may even, sometimes, explain why those sacrifices themselves are seen as essential to both group and individual success.

It's not, I think, necessary to follow Douglas through the further development of *How Institutions Think*; we have enough to reconstruct the conceptual order of things. Collective action is essential to the survival of this particular species. At some point on the evolutionary time-line, this collective action was greatly facilitated by the emergence of language. Language makes possible the sorts of robust counterfactuals that figure into conventions, resolving coordination problems, and formulating long-term plans. As these forms of linguistic behavior become embodied in regular practices, we have the prerequisites for institutions, which think, in the sense of conferring identity, classifying, and facilitating life-and-death decisions, not through some "overmind," but by creating the space in which sharing, disagreement, and coercion—to mention just three crucial activities—take place. "Our social interaction," Douglas writes, "consists very much in telling one another what right thinking is and passing blame on wrong thinking. This is indeed how we build the institutions, squeezing each other's ideas into a common shape" (ibid., 91). When we chastise a colleague or a rival by saying "Nobody takes so-and-so seriously anymore," or "Everybody knows that," we are engaged in institution building. There is an in-group that becomes the Church or the State or the Team, and there is an out-group composed of everyone else we can think of. These groups engage in their own classificatory practices, which are always both descriptive and normative. And there are always ongoing pressures from individuals and subgroups that make those classifications subject to change.

The more an outcome matters, the more pressure there will be for individuals and subgroups to draw the lines in ways that favor their desired outcome. The various versions of Douglas's "grid/group" system are attempts to illustrate how certain types of group construct norms of classification that perpetuate their own beliefs and desires.[5] But for our purposes, it will be enough to sketch how a recent volume on the Hebrew Bible sheds light on Douglas. Karel van der Toorn's *Scribal Culture* describes an institution that exists to maintain and protect a "scribal curriculum," which "could be viewed as a laboratory from which the canon was issued" (van der Toorn 2007, 245). On van der Toorn's admittedly speculative reconstruction, "Ezra the scribe took the first step toward its creation . . . Ezra promulgated the Torah of Moses as the law of the land" (ibid., 248). This impetus itself, according to van der Toorn, was imposed as part of imperial government by Persia and was not unique to Israel. Once constituted as an official elite, the scribes had a variety of reasons to maintain their control and outsiders their own reasons for wanting to influence the scribes. The result, over the following centuries, was the Hebrew Bible.

How does this relate to Douglas and Fingarette? If the scribes are the gatekeepers of the canon, however pressured they might be, they are in charge of the texts that will shape the self-understandings, not to mention the careers, of those who are trained up by them. That both Leviticus and Job found a place in the canon does not necessarily show that every Israelite or member of the Jewish diaspora maintained a cosmology or moral code that unified every aspect of those two radically different texts, but Leviticus and Job did provide authoritative parts of the vocabulary in which the giving of reasons and the formulation of arguments would subsequently take place. Thus for Douglas and Fingarette to mine those texts for insight into the cosmologies and moral worlds that inform them is a promising path of inquiry. And what is true for Ancient Israel is likely, in turn, to prove fruitful for other ancient literate cultures such as that of Confucian China.

---

[5] While it is one of the most enduring contributions that Douglas made to the literature, a detailed exposition of the development of grid and group would take us too far afield. Spickard 1989 is a useful introduction, though he doesn't fully appreciate that the "beginnings" of the approach are laid out in the last half of *Purity and Danger*, before she takes up the vocabulary of "grid" and "group" (but see Spickard 1989, 158, n. 9). In a later article, Spickard appreciates the importance of *How Institutions Think* in responding to critics of Durkheim. He shows nicely how "Douglas's sociology adds to our awareness of the ways belief both justifies and attacks social life" (Spickard 1991, 158). This solves the problem diagnosed by van Gennep, while avoiding the pitfalls of "rational choice theory."

History, empiricism, and pragmatism

Anthropology is the quintessential form of empirical inquiry in the study of human behavior. Its emphasis on what goes on in the communities under study helps to insulate it against economic "rationalism" and the game theoretic abstractions that often plague politics, economics, and sociology.[6] But even in anthropology, it will be necessary to explain some aspects of communal practice in terms of the past, if only because the agents themselves do so. When the objects of our study are far removed from us in time, history is all we have and the ethnography must be reconstructed from what remains, both material and literary. Acknowledging this fact is the start of credible inquiry.

History is also a legitimate form of empirical inquiry in the study of human activity. John Arnold, in his smart little book, forthrightly admits that "every historical account has gaps, problems, contradictions, areas of uncertainty" (Arnold 2000, 12). But all of these are true of quantum physics, plate tectonics, and any other scientific endeavor. Historians, like their colleagues in the natural sciences, "always *attempt* to get it 'right.' We try to stick to what we think the evidence actually says, to search out all the available material, to understand fully what is happening, and we never fabricate 'the facts'" (ibid.). Like every other form of inquiry, at least in Peirce's sense, history is about discovering the truth. And like every other form of inquiry, the claims asserted will be fallible, subject to critical revision or rejection. No surprises here.

Douglas spent fair chunks of the 1970s, '80s, and '90s searching for the philosophical firepower to dislodge the psychological and sociological universalists from their positions of authority. It should come as no surprise that, at various times, she found help in the works of Wittgenstein, Quine, Kuhn and, above all, Nelson Goodman. Douglas invokes the full spectrum of Goodman's work, from *Fact, Fiction, and Forecast* to *Ways of Worldmaking*, but one example should illustrate how she uses him well enough. In an essay from 1993, Douglas writes that:

> Goodman distinguishes two processes of justification. One is authentication of an individual object, achieved by answering questions about its history. The other is a form of sampling, answering the question of whether it is a true member of its class. [1993, 295]

---

[6] This is the central point of Douglas and Ney 1998. The "missing persons" of their title are the other sorts of human types that inhabit actual societies along with "homo oeconimicus," a creature rare in its pure form, but ubiquitous in economic and political theory.

Drawing a connection between Goodman's discussion of art and the practices of both science and anthropology, Douglas argues that justification, in either case, is not a simple matter of direct intuition. The history of an object is judged in terms of a community's accepted standards of relevance, evidence, and the like. So is the sampling. And so is justifying a pressure gauge by looking at the dial face. Without knowing the proper ways of going on, the dial is mute. Knowing how to go on, in its turn, means having learned the appropriate moves in the particular practice. "Mentioning the pressure gauge," writes Douglas, "reminds us that these regular checking processes are among the so-called 'linguistic habits' that justify the choice of a predicate" (ibid., 298). In fact, she continues, all of our category-talk depends on linguistic habits which are scrutinized, commented on, and corrected by the other members of the community.

Douglas is recasting the argument of *Purity and Danger* in Goodman's terms, supplementing the account of institutions offered in *How Institutions Think*. This allows her to update and further the argument against psychological innatism. Goodman provides an alternative in which "hypotheses have to be brought into agreement with acceptable rules, and rules into agreement with acceptable claims, and knowledge with the testing of claims" (ibid., 289). This is the account of Peirce, which Durkheim dismissed, emerging after almost a century as a credible philosophical perspective on the social sciences. It is tempting to call this "pragmatic empiricism," distinguishing it from the empiricism of Hume and the logical positivists. But this is a temptation we should resist. "Empiricism" has become so heavily freighted with rhetorical baggage that we will be better off dropping it and its attendant dogmas and just calling Peirce's account of rational inquiry "pragmatism," plain and simple. In this we will be following Richard Rorty.

4

Richard Rorty and the Pragmatic Turn in the Study of Religion

Peirce was never far off the radar of American philosophy. Nonetheless, as Cheryl Misak writes, "Richard Rorty single-handedly brought into being a renaissance for pragmatism." Specifically, "when Rorty's *Philosophy and the Mirror of Nature* appeared ... comet-like, in 1979, there were very few pragmatists or students of American philosophy in major American universities" (Misak 2010, 27). *Philosophy and the Mirror of Nature* provoked a torrent of response, pro and con.[1] This doesn't mean that Rorty's readers have always read him well. Understanding the pragmatic turn requires understanding Rorty's project as an evolving whole. Just before he died, Rorty wrote that, "the only two articles I published in the sixties that I still like are one on Peirce and Wittgenstein ... and another on Whitehead and Sellars" (Rorty 2010, 11). We might as well start there.

"Pragmatism," writes Rorty in his first major publication, "is getting respectable again." One reason for this is the impetus provided by Wittgenstein, for, as Rorty argues, "Peirce's thought envisaged, and repudiated in advance, the stages in the development of empiricism which logical positivism represented." In this it embodies "a group of insights and a philosophical mood much like those we find in the *Philosophical Investigations*" (Rorty 1961, 197–98). Rorty seems to have been among the first since Nagel to see the connection between Peirce and Wittgenstein. In particular, Rorty charts the way in which the

---

[1] From the forest of commentary the following should be enough to give a reader the lay of the land: Malachowski ed. 1990 includes many of the heaviest philosophical hitters in a volume explicitly given over to *Philosophy and the Mirror of Nature*. Brandom ed. 2000 offers another take by major philosophers. Misak ed. 2007 adds several other important philosophers to the mix, including Rorty's favorite philosopher of science, Arthur Fine. Michael Williams's introduction to Princeton University Press's thirtieth anniversary edition has some valuable reflections by one of Rorty's most distinguished students.

various reductionisms rejected by both trace "back to 'the Protean metaphysical urge to transcend language'" (ibid., 198). He focuses on Peirce's example of giving. "Can you replace the three-place predicate 'giving' with a set of two-place or one-place predicates?" (ibid., 200). No. You can get a description of what a camera would record, but not the act of A giving x to B. "This example makes clearer," writes Rorty:

> what Peirce meant by describing nominalists as people who try to reduce Thirds to Seconds. It should also suggest that these "nominalists"—who for Peirce included just about everyone from Descartes to J. S. Mill, with the possible exception of Kant—are the intellectual ancestors of the "reductionists" whose downfall Mr. Urmson takes to be "the beginnings of contemporary philosophy." [Ibid., 201 citing Urmson 1956, 161]

If nominalism were correct, then science would be impossible, for we would not be entitled to talk about laws as genuinely instantiated in the world. "Science" would simply record our conventions to use a certain kind of language when talking about correlated perceptions. Inquiry, on this model, would not pursue the truth about the way the world works, but merely catalogue the ways that people had chosen to talk about it. "But Peirce," Rorty continues:

> looking at the universe as perfused with habits as well as with signs, explains the convenience of naming certain batches—of slicing up nature in certain ways, and thereby developing certain habits of expectation—by reference to the fact that nature has already sliced itself up by developing habits on its own. [Ibid., 211]

Peirce's pragmatism is designed to cut off the nominalist tendency to relativism and retain the traditional connection of scientific inquiry to telling a true story about the world. Scientists are not mere fact collectors, though they depend on reliable collections of facts; they want to formulate laws that capture, in as finely grained a way possible, those habits of action manifested by the world and all the things in it. In the case of dumb matter, these habits are so routinized that they can be captured, for the most part, by classical physics within some range of probability. The classical approach gets shaky at the cosmically large and the microcosmically small, and becomes pointless when trained on the self-critical actions and beliefs of human agents.

This is where Peirce connects most straightforwardly to Wittgenstein. "Wittgenstein's 'master argument' against all forms of reductionism," writes Rorty:

> is clearest in his insistence on the vagueness of rules (and, a fortiori, of concepts). If a rule were perfectly definite and nonvague—if it left nothing

to the discretion of its applier—then the applier would need a rule to determine the application of this rule, and so ad infinitum. [Ibid., 214]

This should sound familiar. It makes the same move used by Peirce in his critique of Cartesian intuitions, and Rorty rightly identifies it as such. Recall Peirce's conclusion that "there is no necessity of supposing an intuitive self-consciousness, since self-consciousness may easily be the result of inference" (Peirce 1868, 21). No belief, no matter how seemingly self-evident, justifies itself. Even the "Ah, bacon!" response triggered by the smell of succulent meat, sizzling in the kitchen, is learned as part of the body of inferences and actions that take us from bed to breakfast. As Rorty puts it, "whenever we try to resolve the indeterminacy which is in doubt by an appeal to intuition, we let ourselves in for being forced to postulate a superintuition" (Rorty 1961, 215). The "superintuition" signals the desire to transcend language or, to put it in Peirce's terms, to reduce Thirdness to Firstness and Secondness.

Explanation and understanding always take place in terms of bits and pieces of language that mutually support one another. But this sort of circle, or regress, is "harmless;" what else could explain a remark except another remark? The "superintuition" is not harmless because it attempts to seduce us into thinking that we've explained something when we haven't. In the context of following a rule, it is the equivalent of shouting "why can't you see it!" when a pupil is having trouble. But "intuition," as Wittgenstein puts it, is "an unnecessary shuffle. If you have to have an intuition in order to develop the series 1 2 3 4 . . . you must also have one in order to develop the series 2 2 2 2 . . . " (*PI*, 213–14). Everything humans do involving concepts—obeying the law, playing the game, speaking the language etc.—involves Peircean Thirdness, and Wittgenstein and Peirce agree that these activities depend on the practices of communities. "How," Wittgenstein asks:

"am I able to obey a rule?"—if this is not a question about causes, then it is about the justification for my following the rule in the way I do.
If I have exhausted the justifications I have reached bedrock, and my spade is turned. Then I am inclined to say: "This is simply what I do." [Ibid., 217]

Questions about causes demand one sort of answer; questions about practices demand another. For both Wittgenstein and Peirce many of the most intransigent puzzles in philosophy have their origins in the temptation to reduce the one to the other.

Rorty concludes with the thought that "drawing historical parallels, in the fashion illustrated by this paper, can be mischievous if done in a 'reductionist' spirit—treating one mode of philosophizing as merely a confused approach to what some other mode has made plain" (1961, 223). Wittgenstein is not a deeper, richer Peirce, or vice versa. But both saw a similar confusion in the thought of their day and developed strategies for overcoming it. The history illuminates the larger philosophical issues at stake and we can and should learn from it. So too with the linguistic turn. "Among contemporary realistic philosophers," Rorty begins, "there is a tendency to see the history of philosophy from Descartes to Wittgenstein as one continuous process of garnering the wages of sin" (1962, 307). Descartes erected a barrier between the real world and the mental world of the thinking subject. Kant turned that wall into a city, fully articulated but with no access to the real, noumenal, world. Epistemology replaced metaphysics, to be replaced in its turn by the analysis of knowledge claims, as opposed to knowledge, leading finally to "the total confusion of the theoretic and instrumental orders, and the consequent replacement of philosophic controversy by ideological conflict" (Rorty 1962, 307).[2]

The irony, according to Rorty, "is that something very much like a rediscovery of realism *has* taken place among linguistic analysts," in particular "among the so-called 'ordinary-language' analysts" (ibid., 308). On Rorty's reconstruction, what classical realists think of as the "linguistic consensus" (see Pols 1992, ch. 3). turns out to be internally split between what he calls the " 'ideal-language' theory, or, indifferently, the 'pragmatist' theory about categories," and the "*ordinary*-language theory of categories" (Rorty, 1962, 310). Both agree that language cannot be "transcended" and both agree that "philosophical problems are indeed problems about what language works best" (ibid., 311). Both also agree that the way to understand, and eradicate, persistent philosophical problems is by investigating what our language requires us to say about the world.

---

[2] It's hard to convey the combative stance taken by classical realists toward the "linguistic turn," but something of it is exemplified in the career of my first philosophy professor, Edward Pols. Mr. Pols, as we invariably referred to him, received his Ph.D. at Harvard in 1948 for a dissertation on Whitehead. Learned in philosophy, literature, and the sciences, Pols developed his own accounts of mind, action and knowledge in ways intended to do justice both to the findings of science and to the experience of conscious agency. In one of his earliest publications, a long and literate review of Wittgenstein's *Investigations* and a number of related works, he concludes that Wittgenstein's admirers "tell us that there was something of Socrates in their leader... Let us, in no polemical spirit, rejoice for him and for them. But we others may see in him something else as well: the fatigue of two world wars and a long philosophical delusion" (Pols 1958, 251). In a footnote to his third book he directs his reader to Rorty 1967 for an introduction to linguistic philosophy, adding that they can consult his 1958 piece "for a less friendly one" (Pols 1975, 355 n. 7). Toward the end of his distinguished career Mr. Pols was still battling the "linguistic consensus," opposed as he took it to be to his own radical realism (see Pols 1992, ch. 3).

The paradigm of the ideal-language approach is Peirce. "More consistently and candidly than any other systematic philosopher," writes Rorty, "Peirce carried out the program of reversing the usual relationship between signs and what they signify." By looking at language, or the subdivision of language at issue, we attempt to discover what it shows us about the preconditions of making sense. Peirce helpfully illustrates how "the intimate historical association of 'ideal-language' philosophy with reductionist empiricism is no more than an historical accident" (ibid., 316). The empiricism of an ideal-language sort such as Carnap's, to put it in Peirce's terms, is one more attempt to evade the demand for Thirdness.

If Peirce is the heroic figure of ideal-language philosophizing, the later Wittgenstein is the champion of the ordinary. "The job of dissolving philosophical problems can be accomplished," from this perspective, "by simply refusing to accept questions posed in philosophical jargon . . . They are to be restated in such a way that each word is used, in Wittgenstein's phrase, as it is 'in the language-game which is its original home'" (ibid., 318). By adopting Wittgenstein's strategy it's possible either to prevent puzzles from getting started or, by dividing and conquering, to coax an already puzzled colleague back onto firmer ground. And this facilitates the return to realism. For once we begin to focus on the specifics of an area of inquiry, we wind up with "an epistemology and a metaphysics which sound remarkably like Aristotle's" (ibid., 319).[3]

At this stage in his thinking, Rorty sees himself as a proponent of Aristotelian, by which he means common-sense, realism against positivists, on the one hand, and metaphysicians on the other. Peirce, on the ideal, and Wittgenstein on the ordinary language side illustrate the linguistic turn in its purist forms, untainted by any epistemological bias. The essay on Whitehead picks up on the anti-metaphysical aspect of Rorty's realism. That it was written for a volume dedicated to the "clarification, criticism, and theoretical development of some of the central philosophical ideas and insights of Alfred North Whitehead" (Kline 1963, xi), probably insured that it would get less notice than Rorty's other papers, but it's here that he begins to exploit the full resources of Wilfrid Sellars.

The "subjectivist principle" of Rorty's title is Whitehead's term for the position that "the whole universe consists of elements disclosed in the

---

[3] Needless to say, this isn't the metaphysically top-heavy Aristotle of the neo-Thomists and an earlier generation of British Aristotle scholars. In the American context what Rorty has in mind is best exemplified by J. H. Randall's *Aristotle*, a book Rorty admired. In the foreword to that volume, Randall writes that he "has come to Aristotle, not from the problems of medieval philosophy, but from the problems of philosophers like . . . Charles S. Peirce, George Herbert Mead, and John Dewey" (Randall 1960, iv).

analysis of the experience of subjects" (Rorty 1963, 135). Coupling this with the view, which Rorty attributes to Locke and his followers, that human experience is of the properties of substances, not the substances themselves, leads to the seeming paradox that we can never know anything about the stuff of the world, only the consequences of our interactions with it. Whitehead joins with Berkeley in finding this absurd, but develops his own metaphysics of process as a way of capturing our knowledge of reality. The unique "actual entities" that make up the world undergo "objectification" in which "the 'now' of a present actual entity A becomes, for the later actual entities which prehend A, a mere 'time t'" (ibid., 141). Followers of Whitehead, as Rorty puts it, see the positivists as doing nothing more than offering an alternative metaphysics which is too impoverished to do justice to the evidence of history and experience.

The motivation for metaphysics lies in Whitehead's insistence that "an account of knowledge which preserves the realism of common sense must postulate the existence of entities which are describable neither in ordinary language nor in an extension of ordinary language" (ibid., 146). If Whitehead is right about this, then "most of contemporary analytic philosophy is headed straight for a dead end" (ibid.). Here's where Sellars comes in. "Whitehead has assumed too quickly," writes Rorty, "that, so to speak, there is really one language-game which is played in ordinary language—that of describing substances by reporting their properties—and that all ordinary uses of language somehow 'reduce' to this" (ibid., 147). But this is wrong. It neglects "the principle form in which, in ordinary language, we report and discuss our knowledge: the form 'S knows—,' where the blank is filled by the name of a *fact*, rather than the name of either a substance or a property of a substance" (ibid., 148). Here a "fact" is not an "object" or a "complex of objects," but either "what is named by that-clauses, or...the sort of thing which we know" (ibid., 149). Semantics gets us everything we need.

In such articles as "Being and Being Known," Sellars extends "to mental words the familiar distinction drawn by C. S. Peirce between word *tokens* and word *types*" (1960, 44). Embracing Peirce is the first step toward using semantics to explicate the relation between one form of language and another. Specifically, in an earlier piece, Sellars writes "the grammar of epistemological predicates large in order better to see it," and discovers that:

> a reconstruction of the pragmatics of common sense and the scientific
> outlook points to conformation rules requiring a story to contain sentences

which are confirmed but not verified. In this sense the ideal of our language is a realistic language. [1948, 454–56]

If what we believe are claims about the facts, then what we know are facts. If facts are "named by that-clauses," then whatever our best account of such clauses turns out to be is going to give us the best account of knowledge. This turns out to be a variation on the topic of meaning, not in the existential sense, but in the sense of:

> such formulae as "When '...' is uttered, then in general such-and-such is the case" ... The analysis of 'S is thinking that...,' therefore, can be built around "S is disposed to utter '...' under appropriate conditions, and '...' means that—." [Rorty 1963, 150]

The semantic strategy explicates what seem to be problems of knowledge in terms of unproblematic features of talking. Our knowledge is knowledge of facts, which are intimately connected to, but distinct from, the ordinary stuff that populates the world. The fact that my mother loves me is not an object in the world, but then neither is the fact that fixing her air conditioner this summer cost over 600 dollars. Discovering these facts involves a whole lot of interaction with my mother and the world we share. Saying what I know involves using a particular language to say specific things at a specific time. But what I know about are the creatures of the world and their activities. Knowledge is "perspectival," in the sense of being what a particular subject knows, but the semantic approach shows us that whatever the perspective, "knowledge is about objects distinct from and independent of the experiencing subject" (ibid., 153).

Rorty may refer to his analysis here as "a vulgarized version of a view which Sellars has presented ... over the past fifteen years" (ibid., 155 n. 17), but both see themselves as developing a project that originates with Peirce. It is parallel to another project. About this time Donald Davidson, as he puts it, "became obsessed with the problem of giving a satisfactory semantics for indirect discourse, belief sentences, and other sentences involving intentionality" (Davidson 1999, 34). It doesn't seem Rorty knew much about Davidson's work before the latter left Stanford for Princeton. Davidson doesn't appear in the bibliography of *The Linguistic Turn*. "But in 1971," writes Rorty, "my philosophical views were shaken up, and began to be transformed. That was the year in which Donald Davidson let me see the text of his 1970 Locke Lectures" (1999a, 575). What was it that drew Rorty to Davidson in the early 1970s?

Davidson's original project was to develop an analysis of intentional language, language, as he notes above, that involves beliefs, desires, intentions, and other opaque situations. "Opaque," in this context, refers to our inability to preserve truth by substituting one term for another, even when both terms refer to the same object or set of objects. In math, it doesn't matter, beyond questions of convenience, how you describe something as long as it's equivalent to whatever you're replacing. For example, the diameter of a circle is twice the radius, so it doesn't matter whether you use "r" or "½d" in calculating the area of a circle. Not so with beliefs. Suppose Jack happens to be the tallest guy in the room. I might know that Sue is married to Jack without ever having been introduced to Jack himself. So I could truthfully say "Sue is married to Jack" while not being able to say that "Sue is married to the tallest guy in the room," even if I were looking straight at him. Davidson's initial motivation was to master this problem, in the hope that it would then be possible to use formal methods to study systems much closer to complete natural languages. It's not clear, however, that he had any interest in the epistemological problems that engaged Rorty, even though "that clauses" were at the center of both. Nonetheless, in his Locke Lectures Davidson was drawn from indirect discourse to the problem of relativitism. Relativism had been a matter of serious debate in the philosophy of science since at least the appearance of Kuhn's *Structure of Scientific Revolutions*. Kuhn's account of the development of scientific inquiry seemed to challenge the status of the natural sciences as the paradigms of progressive rationality.[4] In the common parlance of the times, moving from one theory to another required that we choose between competing "conceptual schemes." Davidson, "persuaded by Wilfred Sellars of the absurdity of an unconceptualized 'given', and by Quine of the impossibility of cleanly separating the aspect of our thinking that constitutes the conceptual framework from its empirical context" (Davidson 1999, 51), proceeds to see what sense can be made of such schemes.

For Davidson, conceptual schemes only make sense if we presuppose a "dualism of scheme and content," but this dualism is itself "a dogma of empiricism . . . The third, and perhaps the last, for if we give it up it is not clear that there is anything distinctive left to call empiricism" (Davidson

---

[4] Kuhn never thought that he was denying the rationality of science or committing himself to any problematic form of relativism. For his last recorded thoughts on the matter see the essays and interview reprinted in Kuhn 2000, particularly pp. 305–14. For the mainstream response and a comprehensive, if conservative, account of changes in the philosophy of science in the period, see Suppe 1977.

1974, 189). This is the move that excited Rorty. In his earliest essays Rorty uses the linguistic turn to defend common sense realism against both positivists and metaphysicians. Peirce, Wittgenstein, and Sellars help us see that both camps are not only misguided, but unnecessary. Common-sense realism doesn't need empiricism as its philosophical underpinning; nor does it need metaphysics to give depth and unity to the ordinary findings of the natural sciences. Now Davidson, armed with rigorous formal methods, shows that, by "giving up the dualism of scheme and world, we do not give up the world, but re-establish unmediated touch with the familiar objects whose antics make our sentences and opinions true or false" (ibid., 198). He has, working from Quine, Tarski, and Sellars, arrived at exactly the conclusion Rorty had reached, over the preceding decade, with the help of Peirce, Wittgenstein, and Sellars. But all of this will come to be obscured by *Philosophy and the Mirror of Nature*.

Professionalized philosophy and the disciplinary matrix

There was a story going around Princeton in the 1970s that every five years Gilbert Harman dumped everything on his office bookshelves. Impoverished grad students would muse over what gems might be found if they lasted until the next such apocalypse. Robert Brandom tells a more plausible tale, remarking that Harman "was of the opinion that there is just no point in reading anything written more than five years ago ... anything that hasn't been addressed in that length of time probably isn't important enough to bother with" (Brandom 2008, 201). On either version, the prevailing impression was that the cutting edge of philosophy had little, if anything, to do with its history. Rorty's views were heading in the opposite direction. "In the course of the nineteen-sixties," he writes, "I became more and more struck by the fact that Wittgenstein's debunking approach to philosophical problems could ... easily be applied to what my Princeton colleagues thought of as the 'principal problems of analytic philosophy'" (Rorty 2010, 12–13). In addition to his defense of common sense realism, he "began to construct a historical narrative about the development of modern philosophy designed to support Wittgenstein's suggestion" (ibid., 13). These two projects stand in tension in the work of the 1970s.

On the one hand there are the essays that continue the earlier project. These, like most of the essays from the '60s, Rorty seems to have given up on. But this may, in large part, be because they cover the same issues dealt with in parts one and two of *Philosophy and the Mirror of Nature*.

Another set of essays, such as his review of Hacking's *Why Does Language Matter to Philosophy?*, treat of technical matters but end with hints at an alternative to the academic status quo. Thus he writes that:

> It may be that what Hacking calls the death of meaning at the hands of Quine, Wittgenstein, Davidson, and Feyerabend, brings with it the death of philosophy as a discipline with a method of its own ... There may remain only philosophy as kibitzing—philosophy in the style of Aristotle, Dewey, and the later Wittgenstein. [1977, 432]

This strand of Rorty's thinking occupies many of the articles that make up *The Consequences of Pragmatism*.

In "Professionalized Philosophy and Transcendentalist Culture," for example, Rorty writes:

> The period since the Second World War has been one of professionalization ... At the beginning of the professionalizing period, philosophers attempted halfheartedly to define their activity in relation to mathematics and the natural sciences. In fact, however, this period has been marked by a withdrawal from the rest of the academy and from culture—an insistence on philosophy's autonomy. [1976b, 61–62]

In the process, philosophy jettisoned the self-image fostered by Dewey, for whom the new social sciences provided the instruments and information that philosophers could then bring to bear on social problems. Dewey and his circle, "kept political morality alive among the intellectuals ... Having sat at their feet, a whole generation grew up confident that America would show the world how to escape both Gradgrind capitalism and revolutionary bloodshed" (ibid., 63). But in its professionalized form, philosophy lost contact with, "the common moral consciousness. Philosophers' contact with colleagues in the social sciences became as minimal and incidental as their contacts with colleagues in literature" (ibid., 64). Professional philosophy thus divorced itself from "highbrow literary culture." This is a culture that sees its origins in Goethe, Carlyle, and Emerson, and engages in cultural activities as part of becoming the kind of person worth becoming. This, Rorty writes, is Santayana's "transcendentalism proper ... the justification of the intellectual who has no wish to be a scientist or a professional, who does not think that intellectual honesty requires what Kuhn calls a 'disciplinary matrix'" (ibid., 66–67). Susan Sontag, for example, eschewed an academic career to reflect on literature, politics, and the visual arts. William Buckley wrote on sailing, in addition to politics. Garry Wills has maintained an academic career, but not in the field for which he trained. This "splendidly aristocratic posture ... the side of

Emerson that resembled Whitman rather than the side that resembled Royce," as Rorty puts it, stands above any merely professional training (ibid., 68). It turns on a sense of confronting the eternal verities that give meaning and purpose to life, the sort of broad philosophizing that makes professional philosophers uneasy.

What philosophy had been before the Second World War—what Sidney Hook called "the theory and practice of enlarging human freedom in a precarious and tragic world by the arts of intelligent social control" (ibid., 69–70)—may have ceased to matter to professional philosophers, but there is no reason it shouldn't matter to society as a whole. And there is no reason that professional philosophy should attempt to squelch it. But, Rorty's point, it's important to be honest about what everyone is doing. Insofar as philosophy is "concerned with developing a disciplinary matrix," we need to treat its results one way; if it aspires to rejoin a larger cultural dialogue, we should probably treat them in another. This sets the table for *Philosophy and the Mirror of Nature*.

Those of us who worked through one or another mimeo version as grad students were all about the disciplinary matrix. Rorty fosters that reading when he writes that "this book is a survey of some recent developments in philosophy, especially analytic philosophy, from the point of view of the anti-Cartesian and anti-Kantian revolution" (1979, 7). The agents of this revolution are Sellars, Quine, Davidson, Ryle, Malcolm, Kuhn, and Putnam. Their visionary inspiration might be Wittgenstein, Heidegger, or Dewey, all of whom "are in agreement that the notion of knowledge as accurate representation made possible by special mental processes, and intelligible through a general theory of representation, needs to be abandoned" (ibid., 6). But whatever the original inspiration, the subsections of the first two parts of the book were read as Rorty vs. Nagel on philosophy of mind, Harman on epistemology, and Putnam and Dummett on philosophy of language. The weapons in these battles are provided by Sellars, Kuhn, and Davidson.

Rorty's peers, however, were much more attuned to the alternative metaphilosophical story Rorty tells in part three. A symposium on the book organized within months of its appearance sets the tone. Jaegwon Kim worries that in demolishing the "philosophical tradition that originated with the Greeks and was shaped by Descartes, Locke, and Kant," Rorty ends by "renouncing philosophy itself as an area of cognitive inquiry. In its place Rorty would put hermeneutics, that is, philosophy as an activity whose aim is 'edification,' not the discovery of truth" (Kim 1980, 589). A major strain in the interpretation of Rorty is already developing in Kim's last sentence, where the "discovery of truth" is juxtaposed to "'edification.'" The scare quotes translate pretty easily into "mere." But worrying about this strand of the debate is, for students of religion, a waste of time. We should, instead, read *Philosophy and the Mirror of Nature* for Rorty's take on the then current disciplinary matrix, for, as Robert Schwartz writes, the book "challenges the basic premises of several problems that play a prominent role in current philosophical discussion. If he is right, many of these projects are not worth the intellectual effort put into them" (Schwartz 1983, 67).

Rorty's synthesis of Sellars, Quine, and Davidson turns on three familiar pragmatic theses: logic is a normative science; categories are historically specified; and our use of intentional language is fundamentally anomalous. Logic originates in the practical purposes of the human community. As Peirce puts it in his Harvard lectures of 1903:

> Logic is the criticism of conscious thought, altogether analogous to moral self-control; and just as self-control never can be absolute but always must leave something uncontrolled and unchecked to act by primary impulse, so logical criticism never can be absolute but always must leave something uncriticized and unchecked. [Peirce 1903, 169]

Logic and ethics both involve reflection of how we do things and how we think we should do things. In *Mirror*, Rorty identifies this move with Quine's attack on the analytic-synthetic distinction. "Thus for Quine," he writes, "a necessary truth is just a statement such that nobody has given us any interesting alternatives which would lead us to question it" (1979, 175). This shouldn't be taken, to revert to Peirce, as the claim that "logical criticism is mere feeling," for that "would be like arguing in the other case that the only ground of morality is mere impulse" (Peirce 1903, 169). Logic and morality, as Fingarette puts it, are about the world, but they are also about norms.

This last point should be enough to deflate the worries of critics such as Susan Haack, who describes Rorty's position as "vulgar pragmatism" and contrasts it with the scientific rigor of Peirce. "The question at issue" is, she writes, "does Rorty have any arguments that establish that it makes no sense to suppose that criteria of justification need, or could have, objective grounding?" (Haack 1995, 129). This is a bad reading of Rorty and a bad reading of Peirce. Criteria of justification are grounded in the most objective of activities, namely how we actually do things and how we think we should do things. As Peirce put it, "the very origin of the conception of reality shows that this conception essentially involves the notion of a COMMUNITY, without definite limits, and capable of an indefinite increase of knowledge" (1868a, 52; the caps are Peirce's). Haack is confusing "objectivity," which we have in abundance, with "infallibility," which we cannot have in inquiry about the world around us. Rorty, Quine, and Peirce are not obliged to give up the familiar claim that when we say we know something we are claiming a justified true belief; all they maintain is that there is no distinctively philosophical account of truth or justification that can transform the everyday reasons we give on behalf of our beliefs into "objectivity" in the sense of a "view from nowhere."

Logic as normative leads almost immediately into the historical specificity of the categories. This might seem odd, given that Peirce views his account of Firstness, Secondness, and Thirdness as a singular achievement, but what I mean by "categories" here is the sortal function of the symbols we are taught to use by our cultures. Here I'm just pointing to a common feature of a great many of our words; they facilitate sorting the components of our environment into different sorts, kinds, categories, and types. Being able to make a wide variety of distinctions, and to act on the basis of those distinctions, is essential to solving the coordination problems that make cooperation necessary. Thus any social animal has to have the basic hardware necessary to make and act on similar discriminations. The human animal has developed the ability to formulate, criticize, and reformulate the language of kinds and thus to reconceive the relevant problems and reorganize the structure and goals of its various societies. This is what led Durkheim to argue that society is the source of logic and science (Durkheim 1995, 433ff.). It is what led Douglas to reject innatism. Kinds, however natural, are not things, like the roses you might put on the table. But neither do they seem, at first blush, to be social conventions, the product of a particular linguistic development.

Critics of Rorty such as Hilary Putnam have repeatedly accused him of relativistic incoherence. "Rorty's real worry," writes Putnam, "is this: How can one say that sentences are 'made true' by objects if objects aren't 'what they are independent of my way of talking'?" (Putnam 1993, 301). Rorty's strategy, when confronted with such critics, is to embrace and qualify. "The conviction that science differed from softer discourse in having 'objective reference' to things 'out there,'" he writes:

> was bolstered in pre-Quinean days by the thought that even if there were no such things as Aristotelian essences that could become immaterially present in the intellect, there certainly were points of contact with the world in the presentations of sense . . . The horror which greeted Quine's overthrow of the dogmas, and Kuhn's and Feyerabend's examples of the 'theory-ladenness' of observation, was a result of the fear that there might be no such touchstone. [Rorty 1979, 269]

Kuhn and Feyerabend—and their Peirce-inflected precursor Hanson—were able to make their case against the incorrigibility of observations because Quine had successfully made the case against the second dogma of empiricism, "*reductionism*: the belief that each meaningful statement is equivalent to some logical construct upon terms which refer to immediate experience" (Quine 1951, 20). If all that Rorty is doing amounts to following Quine's rejection of reductionism, then Putnam, like Haack, sees a problem where none exists.

In a review of Putnam, Rorty cites Bernard Williams's worry "that science does not really discover a world that is already there, but (more or less) invents it," only to counter that Williams "runs the Goodman-Putnam claim that there is no Way the World Is together with the strawman claim that there were no dinosaurs or atoms before we 'invented' them" (Rorty 1993a, 56–57). Only the former is of interest because nobody, at least not Rorty, believes that human beings invented dinosaurs or atoms. Humans did invent "dinosaurs" and "atoms" as terms for talking about the world, and those words figure into a number of sometimes competing views of how the world hangs together. It was the history of those accounts that provoked Kuhn and Feyerabend, not some philosophical relativism. When the rhetoric is cleared away, Rorty thinks, Putnam and he disagree on both the need for, and credibility of, "the Apel-Habermas notion of a 'universal validity claim,' something like the nonlocal and nontransient rightness with which religion and realist philosophy provided us" (ibid., 62). But this urge is symptomatic of the first dogma of empiricism, "a belief in some fundamental cleavage between truths which are *analytic*, or grounded in meanings independently of matters of fact, and truths which are *synthetic*, or grounded in fact" (Quine 1951, 20). Once this belief falls, then any claim to universal validity is subject to Peirce's fallibilism, which should lead us to wonder what about it is "universal."

If logic is normative and kind terms are historical, then the mental will turn out to be contingent. To put this in its starkest terms, it is not simply that we learn to identify certain sensations and apply to them the term "red," for example, but that what counts as red is circumscribed not by sense experience but by legitimate moves in our linguistic community. This is the point where Rorty typically invokes Sellars's critique of "the myth of the given," but, as Rorty recognizes in his early paper, much of Sellars's thought is grounded in Peirce. This occasionally percolates to the surface, as when Sellars writes that "reflection on the nature of perceptual experience would lead us to the idea that the receptivity or secondness (Peirce) involved in visual perception has three distinguishable aspects" (Sellars 1968, 15). For the sense-data theorist these three aspects would be the "purely physical," the "primary mental," and "rich conceptual," of which Sellars acknowledges that his:

> objection to this analysis is not to the idea that some such trichotomy is involved... But is it genuinely necessary to impose non-conceptual representations *as states of conscience* between the 'physical' impact of the sensory stimulus and the conceptual representations (guarded or daring) which find verbal expression, actually or potentially, in perceptual statements? [Ibid., 15–16]

Rather than a non-conceptual representation, what makes it possible to move from the physical to the conceptual is the learned practice of reporting, in standard conditions, the specifics of my visual experience. As Sellars puts it:

> the ability to recognize that something *looks green*, presupposes the concept of *being green*, and... the latter concept involves the ability to tell what colours objects have by looking at them—which, in turn, involves knowing in what circumstances to place an object if one wishes to ascertain its colour by looking at it. [Sellars 1956, 146]

In Peirce's language, this ability emerges in the process of taking on habits.

Peirce identifies Firstness, when discussing psychology, as "feeling," Secondness as "reaction-sensation," and Thirdness as "general conception," which arises with habit formation. (Peirce 1891, 290–91) "When we think," he continues, "we are conscious that a connection between feelings is determined by a general rule, we are aware of being governed by a habit. Intellectual power is nothing but facility in taking habits and in following them" (ibid., 291). To the extent that a feeling is of something, that is bears any cognitive significance, it depends on the existence of a habit of responding to particular stimuli with particular words. In this sense the use of the word is a precondition for the experience.

This is an argument familiar from Wittgenstein. It is closely connected to the historicity of categories. And it follows from Peirce's arguments that "all knowledge of the internal world is derived by hypothetical reasoning from knowledge of external facts," and that "we have no power of thinking without signs" (Peirce 1868, 30). In fact, Peirce continues, "I will now go so far as to say that we have no images even in the actual perception" (ibid., 49). There is no microscopic image in the back of the eye, and nothing there to perceive it with in any case. The light, depending on its wavelength, initiates a series of chemical events that ultimately result in the transmission of signals to the brain. In normal members of the species this triggers a variety of reactions. In mature humans this is more than likely to include verbal behavior.

This is the common-sense realism, which takes the findings of the sciences seriously, that Rorty embraced from the beginning. The papers from the early 1960s make that explicit; the responses to his critics, particularly from the '90s to the end of his life, reaffirm it. "If, with Davidson," Rorty writes in a review of Michael Williams:

> we take "true" as a primitive predicate, we will not be tempted to think that there is a a topic called "knowledge," the name of the result of the compresence of justified belief with truth . . . There is a human activity called "justifying beliefs" that can be studied historically and sociologically, but this activity does not have a goal called Truth or, therefore, a goal called Knowledge. [Rorty 1998b, 163]

The last part of this is the sort of thing that gets Rorty in trouble, but we need to take the capital letters seriously. They are shorthand for "a philosophical theory of truth" and "a philosophical theory of knowledge." The common-sense uses of "truth" and "knowledge" abide. As Williams writes a decade later, "Rorty is not an *epistemological skeptic* but rather a *skeptic about epistemology* . . . What leads to skepticism is not inadequate epistemlogy but the very idea that knowledge, justification, and truth are objects of theory" (Williams 2009, xxvii).

Pragmatism and the study of religion

I prefaced the last section by saying that *Philosophy and the Mirror of Nature* obscured the convergence of Rorty's critical enterprise with that of Davidson. Nonetheless, we have arrived, beginning with Peirce and invoking Quine and Sellars, at just the point where Davidson takes off in his Locke Lectures. But rather than pursue those issues just yet, we should ask what impact Rorty's critical, as opposed to his metaphilosophical, conclusions might have on the study of religion. As luck would have it, that too was obscured by the metaphilosophical debate. While Rorty was preparing his assault on Nagel, Harman, and the early Putnam, Wayne Proudfoot was developing an account of religious experience that would set the pragmatist standard for the study of religion. But by the time that *Religious Experience* appeared in 1985, Proudfoot felt it necessary to pit Rorty's pragmatism, in which the "concept of inquiry is rendered as conversation, and literature is viewed as the center of culture," against "the interest of Peirce, James, Dewey, and Quine in scientific inquiry" (Proudfoot 1985, 71).

Proudfoot's project is to investigate the claims of religious experience. The book is laid out as a very tight argument in six chapters, beginning with Schleiermacher's account of religion as the expression of some pre-intellectual experience. Subsequent thinkers in this tradition "have followed Schleiermacher in viewing religious language as expressive and consequently not subject to the critical questions and requests for justification which are appropriately applied to language that is employed to make assertions" (Proudfoot 1985, 26). While it is true that we have to take seriously the hermeneutic demands that must be met in understanding any sort of linguistic product, it is simply illegitimate to assert that the claims of religion are not subject to investigation. "The claim that an experience is unmediated by concepts and beliefs," writes Proudfoot, "is itself a hypothesis that must be assessed. Peirce sets out to do just that" (ibid., 62). Proudfoot deploys the arguments sketched earlier against the claims of unmediated experiential knowledge, uses this critique to argue against the Humean account of emotions and in favor of an alternative that sees emotions as dependent on a learned cognitive background which provides the rules for identifying a particular emotional state. At this point he turns to the analysis of mysticism.

"Reports of mystical experience," writes Proudfoot, "have been of special interest . . . These reports seem to point to an experience, or to a family of related experiences, that can be differentiated from the interpretations placed on it in various religious traditions" (ibid., 120). Students of comparative mysticism have attempted to identify a "core experience" that unifies mystics across cultures. Central to this experience is its "ineffability" (ibid., 124ff.). The mystical experience is supposed to convey direct and certain knowledge of great importance, but it cannot be stated in ordinary human language. William James attempts to finesse this claim by arguing that mystical experiences are "absolutely authoritative over the individuals to whom they come," but that "no authority emanates from them which should make it a duty for those who stand outside of them to accept their revelations uncritically" (ibid., 152; James 1902, 422–23). Some critics, notably Steven Katz, see this as a protective ruse, "serving only to cloak experiences from investigators and render comparative study impossible" (ibid., 125), but Proudfoot takes a much more interesting tack, similar to Rorty's use of Sellars, and argues that ineffability is itself a grammatical rule that serves "to constitute an experience rather than to describe, express, or analyze it" (ibid.). That is, in learning to speak the language of a particular religious community, a speaker is trained to exclude any sort of differentiating description from anything that can be a candidate for religious experience. "The meaning and connotations of these terms," writes

Proudfoot, "shape the ways people understand themselves and their experience" (ibid., 127). To learn the language of such a community is to develop the habit of denying that any of the ordinary predicates by which we distinguish, say, the experience of drinking a fine palomino sherry from that associated with an auslese riesling. The result is an experience to which we are not allowed to attach the predicates associated with any of our senses. At the same time, even those traditions that allow some predicates to be used of God—e.g. "God is Great," "God is that than which a greater cannot be conceived"—insist that those predicates be so general that they don't allow any test. Thus the following exchange:

> "God is great."
> "Greater than Superman?"
> "Superman doesn't exist."
> "Better than Superman if he did exist?"
> "I don't know."

is ruled out. The mature thinker has learned that whatever else might be true, God is greater than anything that can be imagined, so he habitually refuses to engage in adolescent comparisons. The experience, thus, is isolated from any mundane experience of the sort that could turn out to be corrigible. That is, as Proudfoot puts it, whatever the phrase, it serves "to identify God as a religious object in such a way as to preclude all determinate attributions and thus to guarantee, in advance, ineffability" (ibid., 131).

As a rule within the discourse of a particular tradition, the ineffability of the mystical experience will be circumscribed and modified by the rest of the language of the tradition. Richard Zaehner exploits this to highlight the incommensurability of various mysticisms. Comparing nature mysticism to the Indian Samkhya system, Zaehner writes that, "nature mysticism is explicable in terms of the Samkhya system only if *purusa* is eliminated altogether" (1957, 109). Elsewhere he writes that:

> if Sankara had been told of the experiences of Christian and Muslim mystics he would merely have seen in them a laudable exercise in devotion to an imaginary being carried to extreme and incomprehensible lengths, for in Christian mysticism he would have seen merely a variant of what he himself knew in India as *bhakti*, the devotion rendered to personal gods, conceived of in human form, and often as incarnations of the supreme spirit. [Ibid., 176]

Neither Muslims nor Christians can coherently accept this as a veridical account of their experiences, thus it would seem incumbent on them to reject Sankara's tradition.

Whatever the duties of the faithful believer, Proudfoot's pragmatic student of religion can acknowledge the structure of a given religious language without feeling the need to adopt the same language himself. Instead, he can use the resources provided by history, philology, and ethnography to explicate the beliefs of individuals and religious communities present and past. This will always be subject to normative judgments on the part of the student, if only because:

> even when we have sorted out the concepts and assumptions available to people in different traditions . . . we must still decide which experiences we will describe as religious. What are our criteria for identifying an experience as religious? We cannot expect this issue to be settled by empirical considerations alone. *Religious* and *religious experience* are our terms. [Proudfoot 1985, 186]

There is no neutral viewpoint and judgments can be challenged on various grounds. Does the Confucian tradition count as a religion, given the minimal part played by the gods? Interesting debates may emerge from such questions, revealing previously unnoticed aspect of Chinese experience.

For Proudfoot, the student of religion is constrained only by the need to avoid "descriptive reduction," the sort of thing Zaehner attributes to Sankara. Because he assimilates Christian and Muslim practice to a form of Hinduism, he fails to take into account the ways they would describe their experience. For them the religious experience, even when ineffable, is an experience of the one true God, creator and judge of a single universe that has a single arc of history guided solely by God's providential order. Such reduction, writes Proudfoot, is "unacceptable. To describe an experience in nonreligious terms when the subject himself describes it in religious terms is to misidentify the experience" (ibid., 196). It is, in fact, no explication at all because it fails to get to the point, which is why the believer described the experience as a religious experience.

D. Z. Phillips, according to Proudfoot, is an illuminating example of this failure. Discussing E. B. Tylor, Phillips writes that:

> Talk about the soul is a way of talking about people, a way of talking which, perhaps, is not so familiar as it used to be . . . He speaks as if the question of whether people have souls is a hypothetical question, an assumption, and in his view one which is empirically false and without foundation. [Ibid., 203, citing Phillips 1976, 39]

Maybe some people have, sometimes, used talk about souls as just a way of talking about people, but that certainly is not the way it was used by most medieval Europeans, regardless of their allegiances. It might be said by Buddhists, but not by many Hindus. In short, Phillips fails to allow believers to speak and in so doing blocks the road to inquiry.

Once we achieve descriptive adequacy, explanatory reduction is a legitimate enterprise. It is just the enterprise of explanation. This doesn't mean that it is easy. All explanations of human phenomena, especially when they involve many people over many generations, are extremely complex. If explanations of non-human natural phenomena are subject to revision and sometimes rejection, we should expect explanations of human behavior to be even more so. But Proudfoot is hardly guilty, as William Barnard suggests, of attempting "to prematurely limit the field of religious studies . . . to the normative parameters of a particular cluster of Western philosophical and social scientific methodologies and perspectives" (Barnard 1992, 254). As Proudfoot says in response:

> my book defends and exemplifies the value of a plurality of approaches to the study of religion . . . accounts of such experiences should draw on history, literature, and the arts, philosophy, theology, the social sciences, the natural sciences, and whatever relevant sources can be found. Nothing is off limits. [Proudfoot 1993, 800–801]

Here are the by now familiar components of the pragmatic turn: the rejection of foundationalism; the rejection of the myth of the given; and the methodological pluralism necessary to reconstruct the community of discourse required to interpret the intentional language of participants.

What seems to be "off limits" for Barnard is the very idea of questioning the first person authority of experiential reports. He writes in the original critique that "this claim that the external observer is in actuality often a better judge of what a person is *really* experiencing is not only presumptuous, it is also simply wrong" (Barnard 1992, 236). In his rejoinder to Proudfoot, Barnard initially modifies his attack, writing that:

> If emotions do not possess a 'nucleus' that can be felt only first-hand, if emotions indeed are simply cognitions superimposed upon a physiological substratum according the 'logic' of the social context, then Proudfoot might well be correct in his conclusion. [Barnard 1993, 805]

But he rapidly returns to his original position, "that a person can indeed feel emotions, and that, therefore, each individual is the final authority on what he or she is feeling" (ibid.). He adds, by way of expansion, that "emotions can be confusing and complicated . . . Nonetheless, the 'thatness' of the anger itself is mine. I can feel it in ways that no one else should dispute." [Ibid., 806]

This is confused. Proudfoot doesn't deny that individuals feel emotions. The issue is how we come to acquire and recognize emotions in ourselves and others. Peirce's answer, like that subsequently suggested by Wittgenstein and others, is that there are no pre-labeled internal events that we learn from direct introspection. We learn the language of emotions as part of acquiring the full spectrum of linguistic habits that allow us to interact with our neighbors. In the process of language acquisition we learn to pick out and differentiate emotions in others and in ourselves. Under most circumstances, first-person reports of emotions carry an asymmetric authority for much the same reason that we are typically inclined to believe most of what people tell us. If we didn't, their behavior would be uninterpretable.

But this doesn't make any and every report privileged. So it's hard to know what Barnard means when he goes on to write that:

> If religious experiences are viewed as "constituted by concepts and beliefs" ...then this makes it possible for Proudfoot to argue that the mystic's first-person "experience" could simply be the result of mistaken attributions of religious causality onto a purely physiological occurrence. [Ibid.]

Proudfoot is committed to taking seriously the mystic's report to have had an experience of the divine, but he is hardly obliged to accept it as true, particularly since, if the report carries the property of ineffability there is nothing that the mystic can offer as a reason for Proudfoot to accept it as true.

Barnard confuses the obligation to seek descriptive adequacy with the legitimate pursuit of explanatory reduction. For the believer, description and explanation are pretty much one and the same. Why should this be true for observers? Perhaps Barnard believes the "thatness" he invokes earlier should carry extra weight, in much the way that Thomas Nagel maintains that "there is something that it is like to be a bat" (Nagel 1979, 168). The problem here, of course, is that without putting words in its mouth, it's hard to know what that "something" might be; and as soon as we give it words, it's no longer recognizable as a bat. Nagel and Barnard are committed to the "anti-Wittgensteinian and anti-Peircian view that there are aspects of experience which escape language, and thus escape contextualization" (Rorty 1991a, 97, n. 7). Since they escape language, such aspects of experiences can hardly be offered as reasons to believe anything. They remain the objects of Nagel's intuition and, as such, it is not clear what an argument one way or another might look like.

"Sense-data," "thatness," and "what it's like to be something non-human" persist as articles of faith in some approaches to the study of religion. In the same issue that contains the exchange between Proudfoot and Barnard, Robert Forman defends mystical knowledge as grounded in "the pure consciousness event (PCE)." As examples, he provides a 1972 experience of his own, "several months into a nine-month meditation retreat on a neo-Advaitan path" (Forman 1993, 708), and another from "an advanced female practitioner of the Transcendental Meditation technique," who remarks that, "it was like if you have a blackboard filled with figures, and then somebody, without your knowing it, wipes it clean, and then you start writing on it again" (ibid., 709). Forman maintains that "the acquaintance which I have with being conscious is *sui generis*" (ibid., 722) and goes on to admit that:

> My acquaintance with being conscious is, strictly speaking, "nonsense." It is not "sense" if by sense we understand the mechanism or faculty of receiving mental impressions through the action of the sense organs of the body or something which is mentally grasped or conceptually known. [Ibid., 733]

This would seem to fit Proudfoot's description of a rule of grammar learned as part of the discourse of a religious community. That Forman and the TM adept would use similar language is not surprising, given the South Asian origins of their traditions. And they can be the objects of study as members of their traditions.

Thus, when Forman goes on to say that this strict nonsense "is emphatically not nonsense in the sense of being twaddle . . . this is the nonsense which *is* us!" (ibid.) it should be taken as the pronouncement of a spiritual master. It is on a par with St. Bernard writing that "because the knowledge of truth itself comes in three stages, I shall distinguish them briefly if I can . . . we seek truth in ourselves, in our neighbors, and for its own sake" (Bernard of Clairvaux 1987, 106). We can use any and all available resources—literary, historical, social scientific or whatnot—to explicate what they are saying and explain why we think they are saying it. Our efforts will be judged by the usual standards of doing history. But we are not obliged to believe what they say.

Conclusion: the pragmatic turn in the study of religion

Students of religion should take from Rorty's critique of twentieth-century philosophical empiricism, and from such fellow pragmatists as Proudfoot, three lessons, which can be applied to any grand theory about religion:

1. the incoherence of scientistic foundationalism;
2. the fluidity of norms and descriptions;
3. the limits of historical predictability.

When Wittgenstein writes that "a *picture* held us captive" (*PI*, 115), he is referring to the general form of the proposition dissected in his *Tractatus*, but elsewhere he extends this to the ways modern thinkers have been seduced into believing that the natural sciences hold a privileged place in the interpretation of human experience and that all of our experience is, at least in principle, reducible to some scientific account. But if, by "science," we mean something like the language of modern physics, extended to include molecular biology and the medical sciences, then this is simply a metaphysical delusion. Rorty takes from Davidson the view that there is no way to separate meaning, truth, and belief in interpreting language. Since languages are learned locally, and learners are held to the standards of a particular community, at a particular time, there is no way to eliminate the intentional component in language. Phrases beginning "I like," "I believe," "I want," etc. all involve descriptions of the world formulated by the speaker, according to his or her particular norms and judgments. Thus there will not be any way to formulate covering laws of sufficient generality to satisfy our ordinary constraints on "scientific" theories. Even when indexed to time and place, languages and the actions based on them are always subject to critical innovation and debate. Thus the covering laws for the various forms of human behavior will take the form:

> Human beings at time T, in place P, when confronted with circumstances C, will do X, unless they choose not to.

I take it that this isn't a recognizable form of science. Any general account of a human institution, including the various practices that we include under religion, will not only be irredeemably speculative but generally pointless.

The standing possibility for critical innovation and debate means that norms generally, and the descriptions based on them, are always subject to revision. That norms are fluid doesn't, of course, mean that they are arbitrary. There will usually be a story to tell leading from a given point, say the Catholic liturgy as practiced in Brandenburg in 1485, to the sorts of church services held there in 1701. This story would include Luther's critique of the Catholic Church, the family history of the Hohenzollerns, and much more besides. And it would be persuasive to the extent that it marshaled the available evidence into a compelling story. What is true of religion will be true of the arts—consider just the various stories that would take us from Courbet, through Cezanne's many versions of Mont Sainte-Victoire, to Picasso's *Demoiselles d-Avignon*—or any other aspect of human behavior we might want to discuss. As long as human beings retain those habits of innovation and judgment that distinguish them from even their closest simian siblings, explanations will have to take into account their ability to criticize and revise their standards.

Finally, there is no way to be sure that the stories we tell about the past will apply in the future. Occasionally a brilliant interpreter will hand us a critical tool that brings out certain similarities—I'm thinking of Mary Douglas on pollution, Victor Turner on the "liminal," and Clifford Geertz on the force and scope of cultural patterns, but we all have our own heroes—and make certain kinds of comparison possible. But those comparisons will always be provisional and relative to the interpretive ends of the current debate.

5

"Gay Fine Colours"

Cognitive science and the study of religion

Back in chapter 1 Ann Taves tempted us with the prospect of insights into the study of religion if only we would consider the emerging cognitive science of religion. She's certainly not alone. At the twentieth world congress of the International Association for the History of Religions, in August of 2010, a surprising number of sessions were dedicated to the International Association for the Cognitive Science of Religion, the EXREL Project, and MINDlab. The website for EXREL, housed at Oxford, where Harvey Whitehouse serves as project coordinator, describes the project as:

> a three-year interdisciplinary research initiative that seeks to understand both what is universal and cross-culturally variant in religious traditions as well as the cognitive mechanisms that undergird religious thinking and behavior. EXREL is large-scale and ambitious in scope, integrating the world's leading centres for psychological, biological, anthropological, and historical research on religion. [*Project Overview*]

With the exception of biology, this seems more or less continuous with the traditional approaches to the study of religion, but if we turn to the "four principal objectives," the level of ambition becomes clear:

1. To characterize precisely the main elements of the universal religious repertoire and the extent of its variation
2. To establish the principal causes of the universal religious repertoire
3. To account for variations in the degree of elaboration (and emphasis) of each element of the repertoire in different religious traditions, contemporaneously and historically

4. To develop models for simulating future courses of transformation in specified religious systems [Ibid.]

Here it seems that the introduction of biology was not a mere addition to the scholarly tool kit, but the linchpin for the project as a whole. For our expanded knowledge of the scope and complexity of religions, garnered over three centuries of philological, historical, and ethnographic research, provides little evidence for non-banal elements of any "universal religious repertoire." Religions deal with life and death, social relations, and the relations of humans to the rest of the cosmos. If we've learned anything from Fingarette, Douglas, and Proudfoot, it's that once we get down to details the best we have are rules of thumb for exactly how things are going to develop.

Motivating the cognitivist impulse

Taves, however, exploits the debate between Proudfoot and Barnard to raise issues about what she calls Proudfoot's contextualist-attributional approach. What Barnard finds "not only presumptuous . . . [but] also simply wrong" (Barnard 1992, 236), I imagine, is the suspicion that Proudfoot will, in discussing the context, beliefs, and social location of Barnard's own adolescent experience, refuse to find it probative. Taves reproduces Barnard's account:

> I was returning home from school . . . Suddenly, without warning, something shifted inside. I felt lifted outside of myself, as if I had been expanded beyond my previous sense of self. In that exhilarating and yet deeply peaceful moment, I felt as if I had been shaken awake. In a single, "timeless" gestalt, I had a direct and powerful experience that I was not just that young teenage boy but, rather, that I was a surging, ecstatic, boundless state of consciousness. [Taves 209, 172]

"From Barnard's perspective," writes Taves:

> the key difficulty with Proudfoot's contextualist-attributional theory is that he had "an experience without any real religious preparation, that possessed inherently 'mystical' qualities" . . . Barnard wants us to recognize (1) that his previous theological views were not sufficient to account for the experience, and (2) that "mystical experiences are actually dynamic . . . processes of awareness" that may challenge our expectations and give rise to novelties that we may not be able to capture in words. [Ibid., 97]

Taves seems to be confusing a couple of points here. Proudfoot will admit that he doesn't have a knockdown argument against the existence of "surging, ecstatic, boundless states of consciousness;" I'm not sure what such an argument would look like. But he does have an argument against treating such retrospective claims as decisive evidence for one "viable interpretive structure" as opposed to another (ibid.). Taves and Barnard both assert that "Barnard's previous views could not adequately explain the novelty of his experience, which suggests that a thoroughgoing constructivist view is not adequate" (ibid., 97–98). But this doesn't follow. First, we don't have adequate evidence for Barnard's previous views or for his initial response to the situation. Second, we don't know what counts as an adequate explanation of any purportedly novel experience.

This last may sound like a high-school debater's strategy, but I intend it seriously. Nothing in Sellars's critique of the myth of the given should be interpreted as precluding novel experiences, and any account of experience that rules out novelty is ipso facto inadequate. But rejecting the myth of the given does mean rejecting the idea that there is some thing, the "experience," which stands between me and the events I'm trying to understand. Take any notable first—culinary, sexual, academic, it doesn't matter—and try to imagine conveying its importance to someone else. We all do more or less what Barnard does. We set the context, we paint a picture of the surroundings, including the people we're with and our hopes and expectations, and then we focus in on the details. But there is no thing that is *the* experience of sex or somnambulism or Sauternes. In describing my first encounter with Sauternes— Chateau Caillou, alas, not d'Yquem—I might have said that it was sweet, but not syrupy, like perfectly ripe summer fruits that fill your mouth, sort of the wine equivalent of the best foi gras. I might have gone on at length and never been fully satisfied, but not because I failed to capture "it." There is no "it" and thus there is no perfect way to put it. If there is no perfect way to put it, there is no clear sense of what counts as adequate. That's what we have poets for.

But it's precisely at this point that Taves and others are likely to see the importance of EXREL's search for "cognitive mechanisms." For even if it's a mistake to reify the notion of experience, there are clearly events in the organism, particularly the brain, that are relevant for understanding what's going on. The cognitive science approach to the study, unlike vague references to our subjective experiences, provides us with hard evidence. Perhaps the most engaging introduction to this movement is Pascal Boyer's *Religion Explained*, which opens with the claim that "the explanation for religious beliefs and behaviors is to be found in the way all human minds work...because what matters here are properties of minds that are found in all members of our species with normal brains"

(Boyer 2001, 2). For all its aspirations, however, *Religion Explained* doesn't deliver much. The bulk of the book relies on anthropology and the history of religions to deploy a variety of beliefs and rituals for analysis. The analysis depends on the claim that the mind "comprises lots of specialized explanatory devices, more properly called *inference systems*, each of which is adapted to particular kinds of events and automatically suggests explanations for these events" (ibid., 17). These devices are instantiated in the brain and apparently process the raw data delivered through the senses to produce explanations of events. The programs for these devices, if we're to take seriously his endorsement of Pinker, are written in mentalese and have evolved along with the rest of the human organism (ibid., 331).

An important example of how this is supposed to work comes out in Boyer's discussion of infant imitation:

> the fact than an infant can imitate adults' facial gestures (sticking out the tongue, pursing the lips, frowning, etc.) shows that the newborn's brain is equipped with highly specialized capacities. To imitate, you need to match *visual* information from the outside with *motor* control from inside. Infants start doing all this before they have ever seen their own faces in mirrors and before parents react to that behavior. The child does not learn to imitate but uses imitation to learn. [Ibid., 110]

I imagine that the master impressionist Rich Little goes through something like this as he develops a character: Identify the cadence of the voice, shift pitch, exaggerate facial or bodily characteristics, etc. But Mr. Little is already a practiced language-user, who has honed his craft in response to audiences over more than half a century. Babies aren't. What we see is that, at some point, the baby responds to my noises and facial expressions with something that I choose to count as similar noises and facial expressions. The baby doesn't know or attempt anything. It just reacts. To interpret its reaction as if it were that of a mature language-user doesn't explain any more than attributing to it an instinct. The benefit of instinct language is that it doesn't tempt us into the fallacy of Boyer's final sentence, which attributes intention to a being for which we have, at this point, no evidence for intentionality.

That, I think, is the real issue. The mechanisms that most of the cognitivists put forward trade on intentional piracy, stealing from those critters who provide the paradigm of agency—ordinary mature human beings—and slipping it in illegitimately. Paul Churchland states the project boldly:

> The conviction of methodological materialism is that if we set about to understand the physical, chemical, electrical, and developmental behavior

of neurons, and especially of systems of neurons... then we will be on our way toward understanding everything there is to know about natural intelligence. [Churchland 1988, 97]

Churchland envisions this project being realized in the AI dream of building a computer that genuinely thinks. The analogy works, for Churchland, because the "microstructure" of "artificial networks... is similar in many respects to that of the brain, and they have at least some of the same hard-to-simulate functional properties" (ibid., 164). He is willing, at least early on, to gloss over the problem of getting the program into the machine, but this is a problem that can't be ignored forever.

At the beginning of a subsequent volume, Churchland writes that "we are now in a position to explain how our vivid sensory experience arises in the sensory cortex of our brains" (1995, 3). But he immediately equates this with "how the infant brain slowly develops a framework of concepts with which to comprehend the world" (ibid., 4). More piracy. Brains don't develop concepts. Brains are complex, highly articulated masses of soft tissue. The parts have their own architecture and configuration of neurons and synapses that pass electrical charges and release neurotransmitters that connect the brain to the rest of the nervous system. There are no concepts in the brain. More cautious writers than Churchland often avoid even the language of control. Take the following passage from Gerald Edelman:

> The cortex is subdivided into regions that mediate different sensory modalities, such as hearing, touch, and sight. There are other cortical regions dedicated to motor functions, the activity of which ultimately drives our muscles. [Edelman 2004, 17]

Laying out the physical organization of the brain, Edelman recognizes the danger of begging the crucial questions and thus falls back on the language of "mediation" and "dedication," which doesn't imply agency.

But maintaining this level of control is difficult, even for molecular biologists. Take a June 2000 article from *Scientific American*, which begins as follows:

> As anyone familiar with the party game "telephone" knows, when people try to pass a message from one individual to another in a line, they usually garble the words beyond recognition. It might seem surprising, then, that mere molecules inside our cells constantly enact their own version of telephone without distorting the relayed information in the least. [Scott and Pawson 2000, 72]

Scott and Pawson then go on to tell in brief the story of research into cell-signaling, dropping, for the most part, the intentional language of "signaling" for the more appropriate language of chemical reactions:

The typical receptor is a protein, a folded chain of amino acids. It includes at least three domains: an external docking region for a hormone or other messenger, a component that spans the cell's outer membrane, and a "tail" that extends a distance into the cytoplasm. [Ibid., 73]

Here it becomes clear that they're talking about types of chemical interaction, as in their description of platelet-derived growth factor:

This factor is often released after a blood vessel is injured. Its attachment to a unique receptor tyrosine kinase on a smooth muscle cell in the blood vessel wall causes such receptors to cluster and become phosphorylated on tyrosine. [Ibid., 76]

So too with the discussion of electrical impulses, at least until the last sentence, where they write that "for the impulse to be produced, many components of the signaling system must jump into action virtually simultaneously" (ibid., 77). The temptation to overwork the metaphor comes out even more brazenly in their final section where Scott and Pawson write that, "by mixing and matching existing modules, a cell can generate many molecules and combinations of molecules and can build an array of interconnected pathways" (ibid., 78).

It is only at the level of formal instruction that the metaphor comes to be seen as only a metaphor. Alberts et al., for example, are happy to use the language of signaling, but make it clear that this is shorthand for a variety of chemical reactions:

Regardless of the nature of the signal, the *target cell* responds by means of a **receptor**, which specifically binds the signal molecule and then initiates a response in the target cell. The extracellular signal molecules often act at very low concentrations (typically $\leq 10^{-8}$ M), and the receptors that recognize them usually bind them with high affinity (affinity constant $K_a \geq 10^8$ liters/ mole). [Alberts et al. 2008, 881]

Here the picture comes out as clearly as possible. In the course of evolution, when certain molecules come into the proximity of certain other molecules, even at very low concentrations, they lock on to each other extremely tightly, thus initiating a wide variety of other reactions. This, going back to Scott and Pawson, is what ensures the proper sequence of events they describe as "relaying information."

"Proper," in this context, means no more than the generally predictable sequence of reactions that are associated with the success of this particular molecular complex in the struggle for survival. I have tried to be cautious in describing the determinism of the causal chain because the "famous 'laws' or 'rules' of variation," as Richard Lewontin puts it, "are really only expressions of tendencies rather than rigid relationships...

Causal claims are usually *ceteris paribus*, but in biology all other things are almost never equal" (Lewontin 2000, 95). This is the part of Peirce that is too often neglected. Science, in the modern sense, requires regularity, but not determinism. The more we study the details, the more natural phenomena, particularly organic phenomena, approximate to the description of habits, as opposed to digital watches. We know that mature human beings base their actions on beliefs and plan accordingly, so we regularly adopt what Dennett calls "the intentional" as opposed to the "physical" or "design stance" (Dennett 1996, 27ff.). But to attribute agency to anything short of a mature human being is a risky move, and well before things get to the molecular level most of us want to leave the intentional stance behind (ibid., 159ff).

If caution prevails, as it does with Edelman, there will be no agency attributed to physical events per se, thus, "although C [conscious process] accompanies C'[underlying neural activity], it is C' that is causal of other neural events and certain bodily actions. The world is causally closed" (Edelman 2004, 78). Having begun along the path laid out by William James, Edelman arrives at the position of Donald Davidson. In a paper of 1970, Davidson distinguishes mental from physical events. The natural sciences pursue explanations that can be couched in solely physical terms, which describe the component parts in such a way that their interactions can be, for all intents and purposes, fully defined and fully predicted. This requires a "comprehensive closed system guaranteed to yield a standardized, unique description" (Davidson 1970, 223). The hope of early modern science "that all genuine effects in nature were to prove explicable based on ordinary, comprehensible mechanical and material causes" (Shapin 1996, 45), founders, however, on the language of the mental. Human beings are clearly part of the natural world, but as long as we persist in treating them as rational, we will need to use intentional language, the language of beliefs, wants, rejects, and the like. And this language is "anomalous."

What does Davidson mean? Take the common mosquito. While the male typically feeds exclusively on plant nectars, the female has evolved to use blood in order to generate eggs. So while both feed on nectar, the female also needs a blood-bearing host for reproduction. In the process of evolution, the female has developed antennae that respond to the carbon dioxide and aldehydes generated by potential hosts. So in the process of randomly flying around, when the female detects these chemicals at some threshold concentration she acts like a heat-seeking missile and homes in mechanically on the potential host. In principle, all of this could be formally described and the interactions of mosquitoes and other species predicted in the ways familiar to biologists everywhere.

Some human behavior looks like mosquito behavior. There is a local barbeque place I occasionally walk by and the smell of the wood smoke invariably pulls me up short. I breathe deeply and consider going in. But here's where the similarity ends. "We know too much about thought and behaviour," writes Davidson, "to trust exact and universal statements linking them" (1970b, 217). So, as I pass by Extra Billy's and catch a whiff of hickory smoke, I might be tempted, but I might not. I might simply think "I love that smell!" and carry on. Or I might think that I'll stop in for lunch and then change my mind. "Beliefs and desires issue in behaviour," Davidson continues, "only as modified and mediated by further beliefs and desires, attitudes and attendings" (ibid.). As a result, language that involves beliefs, desires, judgments and the like can only marginally approximate the language scientists use for the non-rational parts of the natural world. This is not because one incorporates probabilities and the other doesn't. Any follower of Peirce will require that theory acknowledge the reality of chance within the regularities of physical events; it just took the emergence of quantum physics to convince philosophers of this.

Unlike our theorizing about the rest of the natural world, generalizations about rational individuals and groups have to invoke a language that both has different origins and is subject to unanticipatable change for any member of the group. "We make sense of particular beliefs," as Davidson puts it, "only as they cohere with other beliefs, with preferences, with intentions, hopes, fears, expectations, and the rest . . . the content of a propositional attitude derives from its place in the pattern" (ibid., 221). To make sense of rational behavior requires attributing truth to the bulk of an individual's beliefs and consistency in his actions on those beliefs. Otherwise our subject would be opaque to the point of unintelligibility.

Sometimes, of course, that happens. When James accuses scholars of "medical materialism," he's not denying that some neuropathologies lead to bizarre behavior (James 1902, 13–14).

Almost twenty years earlier Gilles de la Tourette had described what we now know as "Tourette's syndrome" and a century later Oliver Sacks has made a career writing up his experiences with patients. But identifying the sorts of neuropathy Sacks discusses depends on the *failure* of our ordinary ways of explaining behavior in terms of intentions, desires, expectations, and the like. Take this early passage from the title essay of Sacks's book:

> It was while examining his reflexes—a trifle abnormal on the left side—that the first bizarre experience occurred. I had taken off his left shoe and

scratched the sole of his foot with a key—a frivolous-seeming but essential test of a reflex—and then, excusing myself to screw my ophthalmoscope together, left him to put on the shoe himself. To my surprise, a minute later, he had not done this.

"Can I help?" I asked.

"Help what? Help whom?"

"Help you put on your shoe."

"Ach," he said, "I had forgotten the shoe," adding, *sotto voce*, "The shoe? The shoe?" He seemed to be baffled. [Sacks 1985, 9–10]

Sacks initially interprets Dr. P. as a "lovely man," with "no trace of dementia in the ordinary sense" (ibid., 9). Therefore he assumes that, in the context of an office visit, after taking off the shoe he can leave Dr. P. to replace it himself. When the patient not only fails to replace the shoe, but mistakes it for his foot, Sacks wonders, "was he joking? Was he mad? Was he blind? If this was one of his 'strange mistakes', it was the strangest mistake I had ever come across" (ibid., 10).

It is only when a "mistake" is too big to assimilate to the ordinary levels of indifference or distraction that it demands an explanation beyond the common invocation of intentions and desires. And it is only when that "mistake" becomes both regular and likely to interfere with the successful carrying out of everyday activities that we usually feel compelled to look for pathology. James's medical materialist has adopted the attitude that all human behavior needs, ultimately, some sort of neurochemical explanation that eliminates intentions, desires, and the full panoply of the mental. But in reality, he doesn't act on this any more than Sacks does. As James notes, if the medical materialist really believed what he professed, then there would be no grounds for distinguishing which of our beliefs were true, as opposed to false, and which of our actions were reasonable, as opposed to problematic. "It is needless to say," he continues, "that medical materialism draws in point of fact no such sweeping skeptical conclusion. It is sure, just as every simple man is sure, that some states of mind are inwardly superior to others" (James 1902, 14).

This is Davidson's point as well. The language that we use for mental events is *anomalous* when compared to scientific language about the physical world. We interpret the beliefs and desires of others on the basis of their observed behavior, including linguistic behavior, as well as what we know about the ways human communities, including our own, have behaved elsewhere and at other times. This gives us generalizations, rules of thumb, points of comparison for understanding the groups that interest us, but even the best of these will be indexed for a particular time and subject to broad levels of uncertainty for individual members of the population. On the other hand, "physical theory," Davidson argues, "promises a comprehensive closed system guaranteed to yield a standardized, unique description of every physical event couched in a vocabulary amenable to law" (ibid., 223–24). Because human beings are not uniform, when it comes to their mental lives, and subject to unpredictable change, "nomological slack between the mental and the physical is essential as long as we conceive of man as a rational animal" (ibid., 223).

The semantics of natural language and the primacy of the idiolect

The anomalousness of the mental ought to be enough to make us think twice about any account of religion that hopes "to develop models for simulating future courses of transformation in specified religious systems" (EXREL, *Project Overview*). But cognitivists and their partisans are likely to think I've been unfair. After all, they may argue, language itself is a product, perhaps the most important product, of human evolution, and all they are doing is modeling their approach to religion, particularly ritual, on the most successful recent approach to the study of language. This is clearly true of Lawson and McCauley, who emphasize the "analogy with language" and argue for "the promise of the competence approach to theorizing as a means of generating theories for the study of religious ritual systems—looking at the work of Chomsky and Sperber for inspiration" (1990, 170–71).

By the "competence approach" they mean formulating and testing "theories about the cognitive representations that an idealized participant's implicit knowledge about such systems suggests" (1990, 2). Such systems characteristically: 1. "Involve symbolic phenomena;" 2. "are usually not explicitly codified;" 3. "are relatively restricted both in their use and in their transmission;" 4. "typically, are not explicitly taught;" and 5. "require that participants must have some form of *implicit* knowledge" (1990, 2–3). The goal is to make this knowledge explicit. They do so by attempting to specify the building blocks of a language and the rules that must go into the regular production of well-formed instances of linguistic behavior. The idea goes back at least to Chomsky's famous review of Skinner's *Verbal Behavior* (Chomsky 1959).

While Lawson and McCauley don't argue the point, Chomsky's thesis rests on the systematic critique of the theoretical adequacy of the entire vocabulary of behaviorism. Thus:

We are no doubt to interpret the terms "strength" and "probability" in this context as paraphrases of more familiar locutions such as "justified belief" or "warranted assertability"... or that "our belief in what someone tells us is similarly a function of, or identical with, our tendency to act upon the verbal stimuli which he provides" (160). [Chomsky 1959, 35]

These and other functional equivalents result in the original linguistic products losing whatever claim on objectivity they appeared to carry (cf. 36ff.). While "reinforcement" and the rest of the conceptual arsenal Skinner deploys are "important factors" in language acquisition, Chomsky insists that they are inadequate without understanding:

the remarkable capacity of the child to generalize, hypothesize, and 'process information' in a variety of very special and apparently highly complex ways which we cannot yet describe or begin to understand, and which may be largely innate, or may develop through some sort of learning or through maturation of the nervous system. [1959, 43]

These innate processing abilities become the object of Chomsky's subsequent research program. The formal models of deep structure are supposed to represent the processes, presumably instantiated in some sort of neural matrix, that make language acquisition and use possible. Lawson and McCauley's embrace of this program, at least in its broadest outlines, stretches from their early work to their most recent, where they reaffirm that "the forces on which we are concentrating are *psychological* rather than social" (2002, 72–73) and that the explanation of these psychological forces is ultimately to be found in "the possible neural underpinnings for such a system" (2002, 77; see Davis 2007 for details).

But here too Davidson seems to have cut them off at the pass. In a watershed essay of 1986, Davidson concludes that:

there is no such thing as a language, not if a language is anything like what many philosophers and linguists have supposed. There is therefore no such thing to be learned, mastered, or born with. We must give up the idea of a clearly defined shared structure which language-users acquire and then apply to cases. [1986, 107]

A few years later he acknowledged that, "this is the sort of remark for which one can expect to be pilloried" (1994, 109), but he doesn't take it back. Nor should he. The object of Davidson's attack is exemplified by David Lewis, who writes:

What is a language? Something which assigns meanings to certain strings of types of sounds or of marks. It could therefore be a function, a set of ordered pairs of strings and meaning. The entities in the domain of the function are certain finite sequences of types of vocal sounds, or of types of inscribable marks; if σ is in the domain of a language £, let us call σ a *sentence* of £. [Lewis 1975, 163][1]

Language, construed *this* way, is unabashedly formal, "a set-theoretic entity which can be discussed in complete abstraction from human affairs" (ibid., 176). There are all sorts of reasons to study language in this sense, just as there are for studying systems of logic: consistency, simplicity, the ontological commitments necessary to say certain things. The problem, as Davidson sees it, comes when students of these artificial languages attempt to draw substantive conclusions about communication, thought, and action. For if these set-theoretic entities are artificial, what Lewis calls "rational reconstructions" (1975, 188), then it's hard to see what causal role they could play in any but a very narrow slice of human behavior. And this, in turn, makes it hard to see what explanatory role they could serve in our studies of human behavior.

Consider Archie Bunker's "we need a few laughs to break up the monogamy" or Goodman Ace's "we're all cremated equal." Davidson notes that "what is interesting is the fact that in all these cases the hearer has no trouble understanding the speaker in the way the speaker intends." (Davidson 1986, 90) These and other "mistakes," intended or not, threaten the formal account of language because "the intended meaning seems to take over from the standard meaning" (ibid., 91).[2] Languages in Lewis's sense churn out well-formed sentences that are interpretable given the grammar, vocabulary, and universe associated with them. "All that really matters," as John Burgess puts it, "is the *number* of elements in the domain of the model, and the *pattern* of distinguished relations among them" (2009, 10). In natural languages, what Davidson calls "first meaning... will be what should be found by consulting a dictionary based on actual usage" (1986, 91). On most ordinary occasions, the normal "way to distinguish first meaning is through the intentions of the speaker. The intentions with which an act is performed are usually unambiguously ordered by the relation of means to ends" (ibid., 92). So "close the door" would normally register my intention that someone close the door and "John has already closed

---

[1] Davidson cites this article in various places, usually in order to identify Lewis as the sort of philosopher of language against whom he is arguing. The earliest seems to be Davidson 1982. In fairness it should be said that Lewis acknowledges the social practice aspect of language from the very beginning and goes on to argue that both are full partners in the philosophy of language. But that's not the interesting point here.

[2] I put "mistakes" in scare quotes because in a great many cases there is no error at all. Carroll O'Connor, playing the part of Archie Bunker, is clearly not making a mistake, but hewing to the script as he generates malapropism after malapropism. The point is that the audience doesn't know what is coming, but can be relied on to generate the relevant interpretive moves to get the joke in next to no time.

the door" will be true, spoken by a particular individual at a particular time and place, if John has already closed the door.

In characterizing what the speaker and hearer share that allows communication to succeed, the "usual answer" is "a system which makes possible the articulation of logical relations between utterances and explains the ability to interpret novel utterances in an organised way" (ibid., 93). Just the sort of thing, in other words, that Lewis recommends. At the very least, it would seem that any such system conforms to the following "three plausible principles:"

1. *First meaning is systematic* . . . there must be systematic relations between the meanings of utterances.

2. *First meanings are shared.* For speaker and interpreter to communicate successfully and regularly, they must share a method of interpretation of the sort described in (1).

3. *First meanings are governed by learned conventions or regularities.* The systematic knowledge or competence of the speaker or interpreter is learned in advance or occasions of interpretation and is conventional in character. [Ibid.]

Unfortunately, the plausibility of each is undermined by the fact of linguistic innovation, of which malapropisms are but one example. When Archie substitutes "monogamy" for "monotony" he violates the first usage in a way that the theory must flag as unintelligible. But it isn't; "the interpreter adjusts his theory so that it yields the speaker's intended interpretation" (ibid., 99). The same would be true of names, local rules for the use of names, definite descriptions associated with names, in short:

> There is no word or construction that cannot be converted to a new use by an ingenious or ignorant speaker . . . learning to interpret a word that expresses a concept we do not already have is a far deeper and more interesting phenomenon than explaining the ability to use a word new to us for an old concept. But both require a change in one's way of interpreting the speech of another, or in speaking to someone who has the use of the word. [Ibid., 100]

Given these facts it turns out that principle (1) is, at best, woefully incomplete. If (1) is incomplete, then (2) must be false, at least for a substantial number of utterances they may be called upon to interpret. And (3) is simply false. For all we can say, even the most mature language-user is likely to encounter numerous interpretive situations that cannot be specified in advance. "To put it differently," writes Davidson, "the theory we actually use to interpret an utterance is geared to the occasion" (ibid., 101).

Even if we continue to be interested in studying languages as represented by formal systems, the upshot of Davidson's argument is that the "idiolect," the way of talking, writing, and thinking associated with an individual, is "conceptually primary" (Davidson 1994, 109). What does this mean? Consider a view of mind popularized by Steven Pinker, another figure who features prominently in cognitivist studies. "According to Pinker, Fodor, and a number of others," writes Davidson:

> the extraordinary ease with which language develops, added to the apparent existence of linguistic universals, shows that what is innate—that is, genetically programmed—is an internal language, the which they call the language of thought, or mentalese. [Davidson 1997, 132]

On this view, mentalese is hardwired into the brain. When the infant learns the language into which it is born it is translating mental language into a natural language. The details of those natural languages, then, are constrained by the structure of the mental. Since our thoughts are articulated in language, mentalese sets the parameters for what we can think and studying the brain can provide insight into the biological constraints on human thought.

This sounds pretty exciting, but "the arguments for the existence of a language of thought... are feeble" (ibid., 133). Both the "extraordinary ease" and the "linguistic universals" are matters of serious debate, and even together they don't license the move to an innate internal language.[3] Davidson is happy to embrace "the idea of inborn constraints on syntax, for which Chomsky has argued so vigorously," but:

> there is no reason to suppose that ideas, concepts, or meanings are innate if this is taken to mean anything more than that people have come to have languages and thoughts that reflect the needs and interests of human animals. [Ibid., 134]

Ideas, concepts, and meanings are matters of semantics; syntax, even with a comprehensive dictionary, cannot yield semantics (see Davidson 1967). The meanings of words are inseparable from their uses, and uses must be learned. In this, Davidson is simply endorsing Quine's point that "language aptitude is innate; language learning, on the other hand, in which that aptitude is put to work, turns on intersubjectively observable features

---

[3] Consider the young Mozart, famous for his musical precocity. He apparently learned the language of Western music with extraordinary ease, at the very same time that he was learning his native language. According to Grove, Leopold Mozart taught his children not only music, but math, language, and the rest. Wolfgang's earliest compositions were at five and he was playing in public at six. But none of this shows that there are musical universals or that there is a mental language of music that facilitates this precocious learning.

of human behavior and its environing circumstances" (Quine 1968, 306).[4] If we human beings hadn't evolved the way we did, we might never have become language-users. The primate line might have topped out with bonobos. But it didn't. How much hardwiring do we need to postulate in order to explain "the sounds and marks people make, and the habits and expectations that go with them?" (ibid.).

The answer is "not much." If you start with a standard-model baby, the only thing that's really essential is a well-disposed language-using adult. It is natural for babies to babble, by which I mean no more than that, if you watch enough babies, you'll notice that at some point most of them start making noises with their vocal chords, and there seems to be something like an instinct to mimicry. The adult produces sounds and the baby produces sounds. When the product sounds sufficiently like the input to the adult, she laughs and smiles and says "yes!" and repeats. "By the time he is two," write the Maurers, "the baby learns to form rudimentary sentences. He makes innumerable errors, of course ... But, like calling an orange 'ball,' his errors tend to be understandable" (Maurer and Maurer 1988, 203). Like Pavlov's dogs, the baby can be trained to respond differentially, so that "ball" comes to be associated with various inedible round things and "orange" with a particular kind of edible roundish thing. Of course, real languages being messy, he is also being trained to differentiate between "orange," "blue," and the like. But eventually the toddler can be counted on to produce unprompted noises very similar to the ones his teacher is likely to produce under similar circumstances. Davidson picks up the story. "By three years," he writes, "most children glibly generate sentences, and have the basic grammar of their environment right" (1997, 131). In the process, the learner picks up basic beliefs about the way the world is, how he relates to the bits and pieces of it, and how he should interact with the other sentient beings he encounters:

> Involved in our picture there are now not two but three similarity patterns. The child finds tables similar; we find tables similar; and we find the child's responses in the presences of tables similar. It now makes sense for us to call the responses of the child responses to tables. [Davidson 1992, 119]

At this point, only two more components need be added in order to attribute thought to our youngster. "The first," writes Davidson, "is the

---

[4] Goodman puts it less charitably when he writes that, "the emperor needs to be told that his wise men, like his tailors, deceive him; that just as the body covered with the miraculous cloth has nothing on it, the mind packed with innate ideas has nothing in it" (Goodman 1969, 79).

concept of error, that is, the appreciation of the distinction between belief and truth" (1997, 141). The making of mistakes, when they are recognized as such by the agent, sets up the distinction between what he is initially inclined to say and the way things are. When he comes to understand this distinction then he is in a position to understand "truth" and its cognates. "The primitive triangle, constituted by two (and typically more than two) creatures reacting in concert to features of the world and to each other's reactions," Davidson then concludes, "thus provides the framework in which thought and language can evolve" (ibid.). The noises are now systematically related as assertings, requestings, and warnings that are confirmed, rejected, or ignored by the world and the other people in it.

In the process, the adult imparts her norms and standards to the child, who modifies them as he matures. By the time the youngster is ready to strike out on his own, he has an idiolect capacious enough to identify the components of his world, rank them hierarchically for various purposes, and make plans for the future. He and his mother speak the same dialect, even though they may have different purposes, preferences, and desires for the future, because at every stage they have adjusted their ways of communicating to be recognizably similar to each other's. As they move out into the wider world (where they probably were all along), they encounter fellow beings who have developed in pretty much the same way and they treat each other as speaking the same language and sharing the same beliefs, even though it's unlikely that anyone speaks or believes exactly the same things in exactly the same way. This is Davidson's point about the conceptual primacy of the idiolect. While there is no objection in principle to studying languages as abstract entities, in complete isolation from what people actually do, having either a formal syntax or a formal semantics is neither necessary nor sufficient for the development of the idiolect in the child and the sharing of information between language-users that constitutes communication.

Understanding religions without theories

Davidson's arguments render the EXREL project pretty much pointless. For what could it mean to "characterize precisely the main elements of the universal religious repertoire and the extent of its variation?" (EXREL, *Project Overview*). If the idiolect is primary, then the only thing a "universal" component of the "repertoire" could possibly be is something that researchers have claimed to find in all of the instances examined to date. But even this is too strong, since that first objective itself acknowledges "variations." The plurality of idiolects makes it impossible to define a single system that could serve as the generative base for the "ritual forms, cult organizations, and social structures found among the Mountain Ok" (Barth 1987, 1). Even if we could make sense of the idea that "every person's mind is full of representations of cultural objects, which are handled by mental processes and in due course give shape to the person's acts" (ibid., 28), there is no reason to believe that we could write a rule for identifying "the same" object across a population without engaging in the usual intentional judgments of exclusion and inclusion that constitute our ordinary discriminations among categories. In other words, "representations of cultural objects" cashes out as "ways of talking that everybody agrees are about more or less the same things."

At the level of cultural innovation, it is equally hard to see what we might learn from cognitive accounts of ritual. Consider the *bat mitzvah*. Although it may have its precursor in late medieval Italian Jewish culture, in its present form it represents an American reformist attempt to affirm the religious equality of women in a tradition where orthodoxy has traditionally excluded them.[5] Despite its absence from Torah and early rabbinic tradition, the *bar mitzvah* emerged as a celebration of young man's first *aliyah*, the recitation of the blessing at service. So the *bat mitzvah* is something like a second generation ritual innovation. It has become ubiquitous in American Reformed Judaism and has made some inroads among the Orthodox. But when Orthodox do celebrate it, they typically treat the *bat mitzvah* as nothing more than a coming-of-age party.

This is only one example that tests the limits of Lawson and McCauley's approach. Having proposed an approach to ritual that will have the ability to identify "what will count" as a probably acceptable ritual form for a given tradition, they confront the fact that the most famous early Zulu leader mandated a dramatic ritual innovation early in his career. Oliver and Atmore set the stage:

> Cattle, which required a large area of pasture, were essential in the lives of the South African Bantu: they were the outward sign of their wealth and power, and no man could marry without handing over cattle to his bride's family. [2005, 105]

Because of the arrival of the Boers, who were establishing themselves to the south and west, previously the lands of least resistance, the Zulu

---

[5] The *Encyclopedia Judaica* (available online) has an up-to-date account of *bar/bat mitzvah*. Solomon 1996 is a very nice introduction to Judaism, with basic bibliography. On the fluidity of ritual in Judaism the classic source is Schauss 1938.

now had to turn against their Bantu neighbors, particularly the Nguni. Shaka inherited Zulu leadership in 1816 and reorganized the male social order. "Young warriors," continue Oliver and Atwater, "were formed into age regiments [*impi*], and were not allowed to marry until they had completed their military service at the age of thirty, or even later" (ibid.). In his introduction to African religions, Lawson sketches the life cycle of a Zulu headman, from the point at which his mother senses his destiny until the day his heir assumes the post:

> She knew that her first son's birth would be auspicious, because before his birth she saw an ancestor in the form of a snake . . . before he was permitted to drink his mother's milk, he was fed cows' milk or *amasi*, the specially treated curds of milk. The religious significance lay in the fact that Zulu identity is intimately connected with the imagery of cattle. [Lawson 1984, 33–34]

Lawson describes the movement to puberty, marriage, and death, noting Shaka's military organization and remarking that "an important stage in the career of the young Zulu male was induction into one of these regiments," while admitting that "even though this ritual induction into the regiment is fast disappearing today, the concept still survives" (ibid., 36). But what is it that survives?

There is comparatively little information on the Zulu before the time of Shaka, when they were a small group apparently living among the more populace Nguni.[6] It is completely unclear what the Zulu tradition looked like before the time of Shaka. Given the impact of Shaka, the *ukubuthwa* of the Zulu male described by Lawson may well have been complete innovation (see Lawson 1984, 36–38). However it is dealt with now, it is clear that, under Shaka, the induction was not likely to be "little more than a week or two," or even merely "as long as six months depending upon the king's decision," and in any case, the inductee "was now ready for marriage" in only the most formal sense (ibid., 38). If Shaka was free to manipulate traditional forms with minimal constraint, then it is impossible to say what constitutes a "main element of the universal religious repertoire" and what a "variation."

Two points: None of this much matters if you are going back and forth between various texts attempting to argue one interpretation over and against another. You don't need, for example, a theory of ritual warfare

---

[6] The problem of pre-modern Bantu demographics is laid out in Oliver and Mathew 1963, 80ff. Later the Nguni are described as "in origin close relatives of the Zulus. Their leaders formed one of several groups which moved away from Natal in order to avoid forcible incorporation in the empire of the tyrant Shaka" (ibid., 208). More recently, Oliver and Atmore accord the Nguni more importance, eclipsed "with the rise of the Zulu nation just after the end of our period" (Oliver and Atmore 2001, 214–19).

in order to understand, criticize, and argue over the latest account of the crusades. All you need is an adequate grasp of the sources and the previous scholarship. Not only that, but the test for a good piece of scholarship has nothing to do with adopting the formal mode or couching the discussion in terms of diagrams; what counts is the ability to force a reinterpretation, or at least a qualification, of previous findings.

Take a well-known essay by Giles Constable. Popular scholarship on the First Crusade has frequently fostered a world-weary cynicism about the motives of the crusaders. Steven Runciman, long the most frequently read historian of the crusades in English, writes that "western knights responded readily to the appeal of the holy war. Their motives were in part genuinely religious... But there was also a land-hunger to incite them" (Runciman 1951, 92). Constable asks a comparatively simple question; are the printed sources as close as we can get to the motives and intentions of the first crusaders? The answer, he suggests, is no. Looking at medieval archives, Constable notices "the number of references to the crusades especially in French charters of the eleventh and twelfth centuries" (ibid.). These are legal records of judgments, bequests, treaties, and potentially any other transaction that might at some point be contested. A minor knight might offer the earnings of his mill, or something similar, over a specified period of time, in exchange for the liquid capital necessary to mount a pilgrimage. Why go on pilgrimage? "I have already stressed," writes Constable:

> the expressions of religious love, hope, and fear which are found in crusading charters... the burning love and desire of the knight Milo, whom divine fire roused to good works; the desire for salvation for himself and his family of Arnold Seschaves. [Ibid., 147]

Constable hardly denies that some went for venal motives and others in hope of bettering their state in life. He has intended "to muddy the scholarly waters and to blur the distinctions drawn from sources less close to the events," to insist that historians and their audiences have to take seriously the texts closest to the events, which "show how a spirit of sacrifice and devotion, even when it covered secular motives, remained uppermost in the minds of the men, and the women, who made the crusades" (ibid., 153). This is the sort of scholarship that pushes inquiry forward.

Understanding the crusades requires understanding the beliefs and desires, including the religious beliefs and desires, of the individuals involved. This will have to include the full spectrum of evidence—inscriptions, charters, letters, and chronicles—that they have left behind. When we find ourselves stumped it may be necessary to imagine the chastened functional possibilities articulated by Douglas and others. In very rare instances we may need to entertain the possibility of pathology, but pathological explanations typically face a heavy burden of proof. The reconstructed intentions of the agents will always be tipping the scales.

Because mental verbs "express propositional attitudes like believing, intending, desiring, hoping, knowing, perceiving, noticing, remembering, and so on" (Davidson 1970, 210), a purely physical description will not capture the content of any report of a mental event. There is nothing mystical, private, or metaphysical about this; it's simply a function of the ways that we describe human agents. Imagine, for example, that I am at the firing range, relaxing with my vintage BAR. I unload twenty rounds at a target 500 yards away and one round glances off a steel support killing an assassin who had positioned himself to take out a visiting dignitary later in the afternoon. The physical description works pretty straightforwardly: my index finger contracted, squeezing the trigger, which engaged a mechanism that discharged the 0.30 caliber bullet, which exited with a muzzle velocity of 860 meters per second... and so on. But this leaves open what I did. To address *that* question it's necessary to know what I saw, what I believed, and what I intended. The physical account in accord with causal laws can't capture this as long as you are willing to treat me as a rational agent, as opposed to a mechanism. So if I am a recreational shooter, ignorant of the assassin's presence, then perhaps what I did was miss the target, with the bullet ricocheting off the bar, accidentally killing the assassin. If I am a superstar marksman, perhaps I intended to give the appearance of missing the target, but meant to hit the assassin, thereby averting an international incident. The possibilities are vast.

We are rational agents, interpreting the doings of other beings more or less like us, deploying the rough generalizations that we've learned from the cradle. Understanding each other requires using intentional language, and so "we must stand prepared, as the evidence accumulates, to adjust our theory in the light of considerations of overall cogency" (ibid., 223). In doing so, we acknowledge not just the explanatory primacy of history and ethnography, but two other facts about understanding intentional enterprises as well. The first is the connection between the social and the linguistic division of labor.[7] There are no societies in which every member is equally responsible for every aspect

---

[7] I believe that Hilary Putnam introduced this notion in his 1975, though it is clearly implied by Durkheim's discussion of the emergence of logic out of social life in the conclusion of *Elementary Forms*. See Durkheim 1995, 433ff.

of social life. Along with this division of social labor we are likely to find a division of linguistic labor. "We could hardly use such words as 'elm' and 'aluminum,'" writes Hilary Putnam, "if no one possessed a way of recognizing elm trees and aluminum metal; but not everyone to whom the distinction is important has to be able to make the distinction" (Putnam 1975, 227). What's true for metallurgy will typically be true of religion as well and there is no particularly good reason to privilege one group's understanding of that language over another. For some purposes we might want to study one subset of the population—say priests—while for other purposes we might be interested in lay women. There is no a priori reason to look at one part of the population as opposed to another, thus there is no way to predict exactly what the language of our target population will look like.

And this brings me to a final consequence of Davidson's argument. Theologians may do battle over the essence of one religion or another, but there is no reason for students of religion to imitate them. If the idiolect bears conceptual primacy in the study of language, then local practice will hold a similar position in the study of religion. Deciding that Branch Davidians, the Pope in Rome, and some Mennonite congregation in central Kansas are all Christians will rest on the giving and taking of reasons, the same as any other judgment about the world and its inhabitants. This isn't a matter of inadequate historical knowledge or an imprecise, "unscientific" understanding of religion. All the evidence we could possibly have isn't enough to generate more than the rough generalizations that we currently use to imagine what somebody's going to do next.

We don't need a theory of religion to study religion any more than we need a theory of science to study science. Nor do we need a theory of history to study the history of either science or religion. "Various global games," writes Arthur Fine, "including the game of demarcation, have been the style setters in philosophy of science from Mach through Kuhn" (Fine 1996, 10). The same can be said for philosophy of religion. Back in the 1950s, there was a well-established set of questions that constituted philosophy of religion in the analytic vein: the existence of god, religious language, the divine attributes, miracles, etc. It's still a matter of professional responsibility to be able to teach Aquinas's "five ways" and Hume on miracles. But beginning in the 1940s, with John Wisdom's now neglected essay "Gods," a new "disciplinary matrix" was beginning to emerge. There is an interesting story to be told about the trajectory from "Gods" to the debate on falsification to Bryan Wilson's 1970 *Rationality*. This watershed collection of essays brings together Wittgenstein, Popper, and the nature of rationality in the social sciences, particularly anthropology, in ways that set a new agenda for the philosophical study of religion, and particularly what I have been calling the pragmatic turn epitomized by Proudfoot. The upshot of that turn is to recognize that understanding religion and religious practices needs nothing more, theoretically, than the imaginative juxtaposition of the sort of data provided by history and ethnography. Understanding the practices of religion is no different in principle from understanding the practices of the natural sciences.

This chapter uses Davidson to further an argument parallel to Fine's "natural ontological attitude," which insists that "philosophy of science connect with on-going science" (Fine 1996, 11). "The war between Einstein, the realist, and Bohr, the nonrealist," writes Fine, "was not, I believe, just a sideshow in physics, nor an idle intellectual exercise. It was an important endeavor undertaken by Bohr on behalf of the enterprise of physics as a progressive science" (1984a, 124). Bohr, on Fine's reading, worried that Einstein was setting himself up as an impediment to inquiry. Louisa Gilder reconstructs the situation at the Solvey Conference:

> One day, after Einstein had asked for the umpteenth time if Bohr really believed God played dice to determine the future, a smile dawned on Bohr's face. "Einstein," he said, "stop telling God how to run the world." "After the game had continued for a few days," remembered Heisenberg, Ehrenfest looked over at Einstein in bemused semi-exasperation. "Einstein," he said, "I am ashamed of you; you are arguing against the new quantum theory just as your opponents argue about relativity theory." Heisenberg gave Pauli a look that said: *Finally someone's said it.* [Gilder 2008, 113–14]

There seem to be good philosophical reasons for worrying about quantum physics, just as there seemed to be good philosophical reasons for worrying about relativity. But they shouldn't be the physicists' reasons. They, if they're any good, want to get on with the business of science.

Fine's move—a move I identify with Peirce's attitude to inquiry—is to ask what really separates the two camps. The realist of a less philosophical and more common-sense sort, feels answerable to "a more simple and homely sort of argument" (1984a, 126). On the one hand, it would be absurd to doubt "the evidence of my senses, on the whole, with regard to the existence and features of everyday objects," while, on the other, "I have similar confidence in the system of 'check, double-check, check, triple-check' of scientific investigation, as well as the other safeguards built into the institutions of science" (ibid., 126–27). The various nonrealists, who want to identify the entities postulated by a theory with instrument readings, dispositions on the part of the observer, or any construction that eliminates reference to the objects of the theory, want to deny that I'm talking about, referring to, the things that the theory claims are there. But this is no more credible than urging me to deny that Murphy exists and replace him with my dispositions to respond to Murphyesque sense data:

> It seems, then, that I had better be a realist. One can summarize this homely and compelling line as follows: it is possible to accept the evidence of one's senses and to accept *in the same way*, the confirmed results of science only for a realist; hence I should be one (and so should you!). [Ibid., 127]

This is the common-sense realism that I have attributed to Rorty from the beginning of his career to the end. Unfortunately, the realism/anti-realism debate has become such a fraught philosophical battleground that it is just simpler to drop the terms altogether. Both sides want to accept Fine's "homely and compelling line," but both want to add to or qualify it with something that the other side doesn't trust. Hence, Fine writes, we would be better off adopting "a third alternative...the core position itself, *and all by itself.* If I am correct," he continues:

> in thinking that, at heart, the grip of realism only extends to the homely connection of everyday truths with scientific truths, and that good sense dictates our acceptance of the one on the same basis as our acceptance of the other, then the homely line makes the core position, all by itself, a compelling one. [Ibid., 129–30]

My eyes tell me yonder is an African violet, happily flowering by the window. The physicists tell me that molecules are made up of atoms, which are made up of various subatomic particles all the way down to quarks, or whatever the next big accelerator comes up with. There's no reason not to believe both.

Similarly, Dogon parents believe that it is essential to nurse their infants. I can see this plainly in a number of Agnès Pataux's photos (see Pataux 2004). At the same time, at least some Dogon believe that the serpent spirit Lébé visits the house of the Hogon, the village leader, every night and licks him, giving him "the strength to live for one day" (Griaule 1965, 118). There's no reason for the Dogon not to believe both. Or, what's the real point, there is no more reason for the Dogon not to believe both than there is for me not to believe both the ordinary deliveries of my senses and the best available statements of current physical research. That doesn't mean that I have compelling reasons for believing in the relation of the Hogon to Lébé, but then most Dogon don't have much reason to believe in quantum physics.

If we adopt Fine's natural ontological attitude with regard to the physical sciences, we might as well adopt it for the study of religion. Once we do, then disputes between cognitivist and non-cognitivist studies of religion have no traction. Proudfoot's critique of Phillips still holds, but not because it is "non-cognitivist;" it just gets in the way of inquiry. Davidson's critique of Pinker, and my related critique of Boyer et al., still hold, but not because they are "cognitivist;" they just don't tell us anything interesting about the inferential relations that hold between our target population's beliefs, desires, expectations, and the like. When we want to know about gods, ghosts, rituals, and rewards, we should go to the scholars who can tells what, in their best estimations, the people we're interested in said or wrote about those topics and how that information fits into the web and woof of their lives. "Many a dangerous temptation," writes Matthew Henry, "comes to us in gay fine colours that are but skin-deep, and seem to come from above" (Henry 1706, on Genesis 3). Henry was writing about the temptation of Eve and Adam. Academic temptations are not likely to have such shattering consequences, but they mislead us nonetheless.

6

The Base of Design

Relativism and fieldwork in contemporary anthropology

Here's a handful of relativists: Paul Feyerabend, "who famously wrote in *Against Method* that 'science is much closer to myth than a scientific philosophy is prepared to admit';" Thomas Kuhn, who argued "that science proceeds through a succession of 'incommensurable' paradigms;" Wittgenstein, who asked "is it wrong for 'primitives' to consult an oracle and be guided by it;" Richard Rorty, "who sped down the relativist road with scarcely a glance behind;" Clifford Geertz, who "deviously defended relativism by criticizing 'anti-relativism:'" and Mary Douglas, who describes universal norms of justice as "the legitimating principles of the conventions created to maintain a particular set of institutions, to wit, those of Western industrial society" (Lukes 2008, 4–5, 9–10, 24–26). Since these are among the heroes of this book, it looks like I'm in trouble. The trouble, some people are going to say, is of my own making. For all my protestation about Peirce's commitment to truth and Rorty's common-sense realism, neither provides a sure-fire method for deciding between competing claims about the way the world is.

That's true, but so what? Nobody can definitively fix our beliefs, to use Peirce's phrase. Those methods that rely on enforcing consensus are always going to be subject to rebellion. Someone who adopts "the method of tenacity... will find that other men think differently from him, and it will be apt to occur to him, in some saner moment, that their opinions are quite as good as his own" (Peirce 1877, 116). Authority will run up against the limits of its power and the a priori method turns out to be a version of authority (ibid., 117–19). The methods of the natural sciences, as long as their practitioners remain honest, will have to acknowledge that all theories are under-determined, fallible, and subject to revision. So the persistence of disagreement is not a sign of pervasive malice, conceptual or moral.

Confusion about relativism comes out particularly clearly in Steven Lukes's little book. He opens with the worry that "relativism seems to be a threat to intellectual certainties, on the one hand, and to moral seriousness, on the other" (Lukes 2008, 1). Shortly thereafter he characterizes "moral relativists" as "denying the rational basis and universal applicability of moral norms" (ibid., 28). By the end, he shifts back to the first formulation:

> The problem with moral relativism as we have discussed it throughout this book is that it debunks the authority of moral standards, claiming that it derives from social norms or conventions; and that it denies the reality of moral disagreements. [Ibid., 158]

"Bunk," as in Henry Ford's "history is more or less bunk" (*OED*, "bunk"), is a wonderful word with a colorful history. Synonyms might be "drivel," "clap trap," and the ever popular "bullshit." So when Lukes accuses the "relativist" of "debunking" authority he clearly implies that the critic holds that authority and moral standards are nothing but humbug. But that's not true either. The importance of the pragmatist story, from Peirce to Rorty, is to distinguish serious inquiry, conceptual and moral, from specious claims of certainty and universalism. Royce, whom Peirce called "America's greatest pragmatist," (Brent 1993, 293) saw clearly that:

> Since an interpretation of a sign is, in its turn, the expression of the interpreter's mind, it constitutes a new sign, which again calls for interpretation; and so on without end; unless the process is arbitrarily interrupted . . . we live, as selves, by interpreting the events and the meaning of our experience. History consists of such interpretations. [Royce 1982, 391]

There is no such thing as Morality, any more than there is such a thing as Language; there are the ongoing disputes about what we should do and how we should live. When Lukes endorses Ronald Dworkin's suggestion that "ethics includes convictions about which kinds of lives are good or bad for a person to lead, and morality includes principles about how a person should treat other people" (Lukes 2008, 135), he is simply making one more suggestion about how to interpret our normative vocabularies. It is an interpretation meant to elicit further interpretations and it carries no certainty or universal authority.

Sometimes Lukes seems to acknowledge this, as when he admits to "the surviving truth in moral relativism—that there are multiple best ways for human beings to live" (ibid., 159). At other times he pulls back, as when he retails the story of Franca Viola, who refused to marry a rejected suitor after he had kidnapped and raped her. Franca:

> took her rich suitor to court, charging him with rape, and in consequence she and her family "were threatened with vengeance for her violation of the ancient code." She subsequently married another man, who carried a gun on their wedding day for protection. [Ibid., 68]

A few pages later Lukes asks, rhetorically it seems, "do we not want to insist that Franca Viola's rich suitor *raped* her, and do we not want to do so, whether or not he and the local community so described his action?" (ibid., 76; italics in original).

I suppose I do, but probably not for the reasons Lukes is looking for. He seems to be gesturing toward some neutral concept of rape (hence the italics), which we might define as the unjust taking of sexual gratification accompanied by force. But this won't get him what he wants. For just as communities disagree about whether some killings are unjust, hence murders, they also disagree about whether some takings of sexual gratification, even accompanied by force, are unjust and, if so, what to do about them. In this particular case there is no disagreement about what happened. But there are two competing interpretations of what should be done about it: that of the once-dominant local culture and that of the reigning rule of law. That both are available is evident from the story itself. One segment of the community seems to think that the appropriate response to rape is to admit that you are rendered impure and dishonored and accept the rapist as the only available man. The other is to have the rapist charged and take control of your life. At least Franca, her husband to be, and some part of the community, chose the second course.

Disagreements are a fact of life. They can be disagreements about fact or policy, but both sorts are grounded on interpretations of ourselves and the way the world is. Anyone who expects to eliminate disagreement altogether is in the grip of a serious delusion. But disagreements can be explained. Some can be explained in terms of the personalities involved, others by the positions taken by differing communities. Sometimes it takes both a historical and sociological reconstruction of the individual biography and of the group. If relativism of any sort is to be either interesting or worrisome, Lukes and his ilk need to identify a serious thinker who insists that at least some disagreements cannot be given a plausible explanation if we can only reconstruct enough history and ethnography. Otherwise they're in no better position than Fine's "realist," who feels compelled to add "a desk-thumping, foot-stamping shout of 'Really!'" to the findings of my Peircean inquirer (Fine 1984, 129).

Donald Davidson and the limits of relativism

Davidson's argument for the primacy of the idiolect might seem to fit the bill. If there is no language that serves as the norm, against which the idiolects of the many may be judged, then it seems that anything goes. And this brings us, finally, to Davidson's "On the Very Idea of a Conceptual Scheme," the essay by which Rorty's "philosophical views were shaken up, and began to be transformed" (Rorty 1999, 575). Early on, Davidson writes:

> We are encouraged to imagine we understand massive conceptual change or profound contrasts by legitimate examples of a familiar sort. Sometimes an idea, like that of simultaneity as defined in relativity theory, is so important that with its addition a whole department of science takes on a new look. Sometimes revisions in the list of sentences held true in a discipline are so central that we may feel that the terms involved have changed their meanings. [1974, 183]

But in all these cases it turns out that ethnography and history give us exactly what we need to make sense of the changes. Take the case of Feyerabend, often thought of as the most extreme relativist in the philosophy of science. In a long paper from the early 1960s Feyerabend argues that in the transition from medieval to Newtonian physics there is not a simple tinkering with received ideas, but the wholesale overthrow of one theory for another. As a result:

> *the concept of impetus, as fixed by the usage established in the impetus theory, cannot be defined in a reasonable way within Newton's theory.* And this is not further surprising. For this usage involves laws, such as (7), which are inconsistent with the Newtonian physics. [Feyerabend 1962, 57; emphasis original]

Different ways of talking involve different laws or presuppositions about the world, which implies that they are talking about different worlds. This would seem to be as relativist as it gets.

But if we work our way through the rhetoric, it turns out that *Against Method*, the upshot of Feyerabend's early essays, advocates the emphasis on ethnography and history I've attributed to pragmatism. The test of any account of scientific method is the actual practice of inventive scientists. Ian Hacking insists, against Feyerabend's critics, that he "never meant for one minute that anything *except* the scientific method (whatever that is) 'goes'" (Feyerabend 2010, xiii). The methods of real scientists, as opposed to the strictures of philosophers, are what are important in the pursuit of inquiry, and we discover what these are by the judicious exercise of our historical and ethnographic skills. When we do, it turns out that:

the principles of critical rationalism... give an inadequate account of the past development of science and are liable to hinder science in the future. They give an inadequate account of science because science is much more "sloppy" and "irrational" than its methodological image. And, they are liable to hinder it, because the attempt to make science more "rational" and more precise is bound to wipe it out. [Feyerabend 1975, 179]

Philosophically dictated methodology, in other words, risks blocking the road to inquiry. If Galileo succeeded in a major, and fruitful, rethinking of how to describe the cosmos, then he must have been doing something right. And if he violated the "rules," this says more about the limits of rule-making than scientific rationality.

So Feyerabend, the arch-relativist, turns out to be a pragmatist of my Peircean sort. And he says as much in his last book, where he writes, against the "normative" philosophers of science, that "pragmatists and the later Wittgenstein, on the other hand, point to the complexity of scientific or, more generally, epistemic practice and invite us to 'look, not to think'" (Feyerabend 1999, 84).[1] As with Davidson, what begins by shocking turns out to revolve around the familiar old notions of belief, argument, and justification based on the available evidence. And this leaves us with common old disagreement. For something to count as an alternative conceptual scheme, and thus provide something to which our conceptual scheme could be relative, it would have to be inaccessible from where we normally find ourselves, and the best test for this is the failure of translatability.

It's probably important to cut off a potential misunderstanding. First, to produce a translation doesn't require producing a perfect translation; much of the time there's no such thing. Simple declarative sentences may map one to one from language to language, but they needn't. My friends who do exciting languages like Arabic and Chinese never tire of explaining the difficulties of their subjects. The fact that I have four translations of Confucius's *Analects* testifies to the scope of scholarly disagreement. But you don't have to go so far afield to find examples. Ficino's *Platonic Theology* opens as follows:

Plato, philosophorum pater, magnanime Laurenti, cum intellegeret quemadmodum se habet visus ad solis lumen, ita se habere mentes omnes ad deum...

---

[1] Feyerabend can't bring himself to sign up with any group, but while he insists that no group has the full story, it's clear where his sympathies lie. In approaching Feyerabend it's worth noting that subsequent editions of *Against Method* are much revised and reorganized. Hacking's introduction to the 4th edition is quite helpful.

which Michael Allen renders:

> Noble-souled Lorenzo! Plato, the father of philosophers, realizing that our minds bear the same relationship to God as our sight to the light of the Sun... [Ficino 2001, 8–9]

The translator has obviously decided that the parenthetical vocative would sound stilted in English, so he has shifted it to an initial greeting. He has also changed the Latinized Laurentius to Lorenzo; who's ever heard of Laurentius de' Medici? Furthermore, he has turned Ficino's imperfect subjunctive "intelligeret" into the participial phrase "realizing that." This is all perfectly legitimate if the translator's goal is to render intelligible an author writing in a language unknown to potential readers. The standard is whether or not the translation helps or misleads the reader. The jury is a representative body of people familiar with both languages.

A second mistake would be to worry about technical terms. Fifty years ago the only people who had a familiarity with quarks were scholars of James Joyce. Then, so the story goes, Murray Gell-Mann introduced the term for the speculative components of the hadron (itself a recent coinage). Over the next decade a variety of quarks were identified. But part of Davidson's point is that all mature language-users develop the capacity to accommodate new usages. Given time enough and a good teacher, there is no reason to assume that any term is beyond the capacity of at least some users of a language.

If we don't let ourselves get distracted by these sorts of worries, Davidson's strategy will seem obvious. Whatever a conceptual scheme might turn out to be, the best evidence for its structure and content would have to be what its adherents believe. And our best evidence for this has to be what they say and write. So a truly alternative scheme would be one where our access to what they say and write is blocked, and the best evidence for that would have to be failure of translation. Why should we doubt that this is at least possible? "Speech," writes Davidson, "requires a multitude of finely discriminated intentions and beliefs" (1974, 186). Talking to someone, as opposed to merely making noise, requires that I hold certain beliefs and that I intend to communicate them. I also intend that my interlocutor recognize that first intention and thus I must believe a variety of things about her abilities and dispositions. This, Davidson suggests, might be the place at which conceptual schemes gain a foothold. The particular beliefs and intentions I ascribe to my partner in discourse have to be either sentences in her language or close translations of those sentences. A conceptual scheme is a lot like a comprehensive scientific theory and an alternative conceptual scheme would, on this analogy, be another comprehensive scientific theory that uses a different conceptual structure. So in the Ptolemaic account of the heavens, the planets are carried on crystalline spheres whose rotations produce the various motions seen in the night sky (Kuhn 1957, ch. 2). When the details of that system became too cumbersome, astronomy underwent a paradigm change, leading first to the Copernican system and then to the modern "big bang" (Kuhn 1970, 68–69; Weinberg 1993). According to Kuhn and Feyerabend, "we must not describe this change simply as a matter their coming to view old falsehoods as truths...A change has come over the meaning of the sentence because it now belongs to a new language" (Davidson 1974, 188). What it means for the earth to orbit the sun in accord with Newton's laws is wholly different from the heliocentrism of Aristarchus (Kuhn 1957, 42). The basic theoretical vocabulary provides the scheme; when the variables are given actual values, we get the empirical content that describes the world according to this or that theory.

Unfortunately, Davidson argues, it's not possible to make much sense of this dualism, which is no more than "a dogma of empiricism" (Davidson 1974, 189). Whether its advocates want to talk in terms of organizing the world or fitting language to experience, we are still going to have to talk about which sentences are true in which language. But truth, as we've already seen, is best summed up by Aristotle or, in its modern form, by Tarski. So the question becomes "how well we understand the notion of truth, as applied to language, independent of the notion of translation. The answer is, I think, that we do not understand it independently at all" (ibid., 194). Suppose we are interested in analyzing the sort of sentence exemplified by:

The mango grows in Venezuela.

Using quotation marks to distinguish mention from use, the relevant description of this sentence is:

"The mango grows in Venezuela."

Thus, on the familiar Tarskian model:

"The mango grows in Venezuela"

is true if and only if the mango grows in Venezuela. What else, after all, could make such a statement true? Neither intending, nor asserting, nor the fact that "the mango grows in Venezuela," coheres with other sentences I am disposed to utter would make it true if mangoes didn't grow in Venezuela. Now consider the sentence:

El mango se crece en Venezuela.

In order to formulate the theory of truth we give its description:

"El mango se crece en Venezuela."

We then notice that, since we already have an unproblematic translation of the Spanish:

"El mango se crece en Venezuela"

is true if and only if the mango grows in Venezuela. Of course, this does not tell us "why" the mango grows in Venezuela, or "how" we come to be able to translate Spanish into English, and vice versa, but those questions are not directly relevant to the truth of the sentence.

When interpreting an alien language, failure to secure a credible match of my sentences with my subject's will, in most cases, boil down either to confusion on the part of the translator or to simple difference in opinion, value, or belief. The more false statements I attribute to the subject, the more evidence that something is amiss with the translation. For, while we may not know, at the outset, which of our subject population's beliefs are false, we do know that the vast majority of them cannot be. If, in writing up my field notes, I repeatedly come across native claims that lead to:

"El mango se crece en Venezuela" is true if and only if the mango gives birth through Caesarian section

I have evidence either for my inadequacy as a speaker of Spanish or for the existence of a very peculiar belief. If an expanded grasp of the language supports my original then we may indeed have encountered a community with odd beliefs about mangos. Of course, the only thing that could confirm this would be my ability successfully to translate the majority of true sentences in Spanish into true sentences of English. From considerations like this, Davidson concludes that, if it is strongly differentiated from difference in belief, the notion of a conceptual scheme cannot be intelligibly formulated. It is a minimal demand of such schemes that a substantial body of true statements in one be false in the other. Otherwise they wouldn't be *alternative* conceptual schemes.

Not only do we not have alternatives, but we don't even share the same scheme. Schemes require some unschematized reality upon which to impose a structure, a flux of we know not what that each community must come to grips with by imposing some perhaps "untranslatable" or "incommensurable" template. Davidson suggests that we drop the scheme/reality distinction as unilluminating:

> Without the dogma this kind of relativity goes by the board. Of course truth
> of sentences remains relative to language, but that is as objective as can be. In
> giving up the dualism of scheme and world, we do not give up the world, but
> reestablish unmediated touch with the familiar objects whose antics make
> our sentences and opinions true or false. [1974, 198]

"Truth of sentences remains relative to language," for the simple reason
that sentences have to be in some language or another. But we are left
with a basic realism "that is as objective as can be," for what else are we
to use in saying true things about our world but some language or other.
The alternative is either silence or the continued elaboration of philosophical programs that are neither perspicuous nor necessary.

Conceptual schemes *redivivus*

Where Davidson's critics frequently go wrong is in confusing the intellectual or psychological *importance* of a linguistic domain with its place
in supporting the web of language as a whole. The disputes that typically interest us as students of ethics and religion are those that can have
a profound impact on how we live our lives, thus we are inclined to
investigate changes in religious belief, scientific theory, ethical practice,
and the political organization of societies. But interpreting changes and
developments in these areas requires sharing unproblematic beliefs
about hominids, insects, trees, the tensile strength of various metals
and a host of other facts about the world. Even if we allowed, for
example, that creationism were a theory in competition with the cosmology of Stephen Hawking, the level of disagreement is insufficient to
warrant calling them different conceptual schemes. They are different
cosmologies, which involve different beliefs about God, the good life for
human beings, and the ultimate end of the universe, but despite the
obstacles, Hawking and Falwell understand each other. They couldn't
argue about the age of the earth unless they agreed about what it meant
to be a fossil. They agree about the size, manner of reproduction, and
fossil precursors of various species of tree, about the composition of
water, and probably about the wickedness of murder.

A failure to grasp this point underlies the criticisms of Davidson
offered by Nicholas Rescher. According to Rescher, the notion of conceptual schemes is of value in the "disciplinary settings" of descriptive
sociology, intellectual history, history of science and philosophical epistemology, and to reject it "smacks of the unrealism of one who closes
one's mind toward what people are actually saying and doing" (Rescher

131

1980, 324). Rescher's claim here seems to rest on the view not merely that people act on the basis of beliefs, which differ from time to time and place to place, but on the stronger position that those beliefs are determined by conceptual schemes, which are themselves "correlative with and embedded in a substantive position as to how things work in the world" (ibid., 330). Concepts that cannot be formulated within a particular scheme are not simply unknown, they are outside those individuals's "conceptual horizons." As Rescher puts it, "it is not just that Caesar did not *know* what the half-life of californium is, but that he could not have *understood* this fact if someone had told it to him . . . he could not have understood it if the Recording Angel had whispered it into his ear" (ibid., 330–33).

Rescher's claim, however, admits of two distinctly different interpretations. On the one hand, there is the undeniable truth that no first-century Roman was in a position to develop an account of the elements based on their subatomic structure, and thus in no position to provide an account of radioactive decay based on that structure. Since no one could formulate such a theory it also follows that no one was in a position to learn it, a disability that extends to Caesar himself. But Rescher intends something much stronger than this. "Difference between schemes," he insists, is:

> a matter of difference in orientation rather than one of disagreement in *doctrine*. It is less like that between the Christian heresies than like that between Christianity and Buddhism. The denizens of different schemes live in—to at least some extent—different "thought worlds." [Ibid., 333]

The contrast between difference in orientation and disagreement in doctrine rests on the lessons of history, for "the original Copernican revolution made the point that there is nothing *ontologically* privileged about our own position in space." Acknowledging the importance of conceptual schemes signals the further constraint that "there is nothing *cognitively* privileged about our own position in time" (ibid., 335). Changes in our fundamental way of understanding the world create chasms that separate us from the inhabitants of other schemes. We can reconstruct the way things looked to them, just as we can describe the world as given by our own way of approaching it, but beyond that "comparison cannot be made on the basis of comparative *correctness*." There is no neutral framework that we can adopt that would allow us to judge between the way the ancient Romans divided up the world and our own. Davidson's attempt to approach interpretation through truth leaves us with "little alternative but to advance our own scheme automatically into a position of standard of comparison and so run afoul of the strictures of a cognitive Copernicanism" (ibid., 342).

The invocation of Copernicus is telling. Rescher seems to think that without conceptual schemes it will prove impossible to explain the facts of conceptual change. As he puts it:

> One conceptual scheme will envisage assertions that have no even remote equivalents in the other framework. They lie beyond the reach of effective transportation exactly because they involve different factual commitments and presuppositions. Given the change, it is not just that one says things differently but that one says altogether different things. [Ibid., 331]

The examples of caloric and phlogiston are by now too familiar to admit denying the last sentence in Rescher's remarks. The question is whether or not recognizing that different theories refer to different things forces the conclusion that talk in the competing theories lies "beyond the reach of effective transportation." When Caesar died most educated people believed that there were at most five elements, four in the sublunary realm, and an immutable fifth in the heavens. These elements were, in themselves, simple, and the ordinary objects of the workaday world were compounded out of various portions of them. If you knew enough about them you could predict what they would do, how they would hold together, and what was needed to produce an acceptable system of, say, water management. Two thousand years later people think that there are about one hundred elements occurring naturally on earth and that they are not simple but highly complex. Nonetheless, the ordinary objects of the workaday world are compounded out of them, and if you know enough you can predict how they will hold together and what would be needed to produce an acceptable system of mass slaughter. There is nothing mysterious about someone not understanding a theoretical term developed 2,000 years after his death. There would be a serious epistemological puzzle only if Caesar were *necessarily incapable* of learning the term.

Do we have any reason to believe this latter claim? Neither Plutarch nor Suetonius offers much information on Caesar's education. Marrou suggests that the sciences were much neglected in the Roman curriculum, but this was a function of culture, not intelligibility (Marrou 1956, 281–82). Had he desired, Caesar or any other student of means and leisure could acquire a basic grounding in the mathematical arts of arithmetic, geometry, music and astronomy, the sort of learning Newton would have been absorbing at Grantham before going up to Cambridge in 1661, though at that point "probably the most that anyone could have said of him was that he was a bright boy, with a real gift for making models and drawing" (Andrade 1954, 36). From here it is less a chasm than a step to algebra and trigonometry. On this basis Newton wrote the *Optics* and *Principia*, he and Leibniz developed the calculus, and the foundations of modern physics were laid. There is no reason, other than the problem of time travel, to doubt that a bright Roman fourteen-year-old, given the opportunity, could make as much sense of the half-life of californium as the average twentieth-century college student. To believe otherwise is to believe that someone who has learned Euclid cannot learn algebra, or that someone who has learned algebra cannot learn Cartesian geometry, cannot learn the calculus, cannot learn Newtonian physics, and so forth. That no one has lived long enough to learn these things as they were developed is, perhaps, unfortunate but not surprising. It is not grounds for thinking that anyone is incapable of learning them because of the barriers erected by his conceptual scheme. In principle there seems no more of an obstacle to teaching quantum electrodynamics to a second-century Roman, or a contemporary Baktaman tribesman, than there is to teaching it to a high-school freshman. It might take longer, I or my student might not be up to the task, but these are the trials of pedagogy, not the tribulations of epistemology.

Is there any reason to believe that Caesar's ignorance of quantum physics obtains under all conceivable circumstances? Consider the possibility that greater and earlier conceptual trade with India might have led to the development of a Greek algebra, which might have led some fourth-century BC Descartes or Galileo or Newton to achieve what was actually achieved 2,000 years later. And it's only 300 years from Descartes to quantum theory, which, but for his untimely assassination, would have made what we call modern physics easily available to Caesar. A murdered man is clearly "beyond the reach of effective transportation" but not in the way Rescher needs. Granted that it did not turn out this way, what argument has been put forward, or could be put forward, to say that it could not have?

There is, I think, an obvious argument, the one that makes do with beliefs and trade routes, technology and desires, values and vacuum tubes. In the actual doing of cultural and intellectual history, as opposed to generalizing about it, this is the level at which we say understanding has been achieved. I am not saying that intellectual historians agree about which explanation to adopt of a given phenomenon, nor that disagreements will not rest on deeper philosophical differences—Marxists vs. Liberals, falsificationists vs. methodological anarchists—but there is nothing mysterious about these disagreements. When it comes down to the hard work of explanation and understanding, conceptual schemes have nothing to do, they dissolve into beliefs, desires, and the stories we can tell about who discovered what, when, and how it was received.

Don't misunderstand me. I am not claiming that we will inevitably succeed in interpreting any and every language we come upon, much less the people who speak them. There are countless possible obstacles to interpretation, from incompetence to obstinance to extinction. Davíd Carrasco, for example, recounts the story of an early Spanish landing in Mexico. "Attempting to figure out their location," he writes, "the Spaniards shouted, 'What is this place called?' The natives replied, 'Uic athan,' meaning, 'We do not understand your words'" (Carrasco, 1990: 1). The Land of the Turkey and the Deer continues to be known as the Yucatan Peninsula. But what allows for translation is the regular pattern of relations among linguistic phenomena.

Truth, translation, and thick description

Once we've disposed of conceptual schemes, there remains nothing mystical, or mystifying, about translation. The richer our history and ethnography, the more nuanced our translations. The better our translations, the more nuance we can add to our history and ethnography. The best statement of the practice generally is by Clifford Geertz. But to see what Geertz is after in "Thick Description," however, it will be helpful to start a few years earlier. In *Islam Observed*, Geertz attempts to relate Sukarno's conception of the role of the president to "Mataram kingship" and the "theater state." His methodological allegiances are ultimately Weberian, but much modified by a pervasive interpretive pragmatism. Thus he sketches a classical Indonesian style comprising "the Exemplary Center," "Graded Spirituality," and "the Theater State." Politics, religion, and the social order are brought into harmony because "the welfare of the country proceeds from the excellence of its capital, the excellence of the capital from the brilliance of its court, the brilliance of its court from the spirituality of its king" (Geertz 1968, 36). This ideal is recognized and reinforced by texts emphasizing the honor due each member by those below him, thus "the lord should honor the prince, the prince should honor the priest, the priest should honor the god-king," and so on (ibid., 37).

In reality, Geertz insists, these ideals are put under pressure by unpredictable, external forces, such as the arrival, first of Islam, and then of the Dutch. Competing material and spiritual cultures produce various upheavals, but when the charismatic leader emerges, the classical style remained available to be developed for contemporary purposes. Thus Sukarno, who "had only ideology and those men to whom ideology most appeals—the intelligentsia," used his intellectual and political skills to bring together Muslim and secularist in "the recreation of a theater state, the revival, in the face of both the scripturalist and the Marxist brands of purism, of exemplary politics" (ibid., 83–84). Nonetheless, the changes brought about by history rarely make recreating the whole past possible, and despite Sukarno's claim to "grasp the entire gamut between Marxism and theism," and to "know all the trends and understand them," Geertz emphasizes the fact that "things did not work themselves out as harmoniously in the society at large; the world around did not automatically shape itself in the image of its exemplary leader" (ibid., 85). Sukarno was deposed and Indonesia emerged from a period of bloody chaos with a military dictatorship.

It is possible, no doubt, for historians and anthropologists to dispute the details of Geertz's story, but this is beside the point.[2] To the vocabulary drawn from Weber, Parsons, and others he adds historical research, details of political biography, and the occasional insight from Don Marquis or Sigmund Freud, whatever it takes to put together a "perspicuous representation" of the way things developed. But important as the presentation may be, it is not the whole thing. As Davidson puts it, any "linguistic utterance," be it written or verbal, "has an ulterior purpose" (1982, 272). In Geertz's case, the purpose is to make true statements about religion and politics in Indonesia, and about religious development in general. Simply put, this is a matter of "looking for facts" (Geertz 1995, 167). Before and after the appearance of *Islam Observed*, Geertz explored further facets of Indonesian religion and politics (cf. Geertz 1964, 1972, 1977, and 1980). All of these stand together as a body of evidence that may be tested against other interpreters and made subject to qualification or correction. This isn't a defect; it is the nature of honest inquiry.

While admirable in its attempt to broaden the intellectual sources for the anthropological study of religion, the early essay "Religion as a Cultural System" takes "the problem of meaning" to be considerably more uniform than the fieldwork shows it to be (cf. Geertz 1966, 108). In "Thick Description" Geertz writes of theory that "there appears to be little profit in it, because the essential task of theory building here is not

---

[2] Matters of historical dispute lie beyond the purview of this essay. They also have little impact on the methodological issues that are under investigation here. Nonetheless, Geertz was sufficiently sensitive to them to equip his follow up volume, *Negara*, with a scholarly apparatus that takes up half the volume (see Geertz 1980).

to codify abstract regularities, but to make thick description possible" (1973a, 26). Theory for theory's sake is pointless; theories are useful only to the extent that they help organize and arrange details into a perspicuous whole and when they cease to do this they should be, if possible, discarded (ibid., 27, n. 5). More recently, reflecting on his professional career, Geertz has written that "the sequence of settings into which you are projected...does far more to shape the pattern of your work, to discipline it and give it form, than do theoretical arguments" (Geertz 1995, 134). If ethnography begins in field notes, often a shorthand account of the day's research, those notes become the center, around which layers of comment, suggestion, revision, and further comment adhere. Eventually the successful anthropologist achieves thick description. At each step, theoretical formulations move further away from the center, to be replaced by the particular story that seems most pertinent to the occasion. In *Works and Lives* and *After the Fact* Geertz turns to anecdote and thick description of the vagaries of anthropological writing, including his own, to assess the methods and institutional presuppositions that have informed recent anthropology.

This brings me to a further complication. Even if we can happily ignore philosophical arguments for and against relativism, there is a practical relativism generated by the cultural biases identified in historians and anthropologists alike. In particular, I seem to have failed to address the ways that ethnography, and hence Davidson's "radical interpretation," is shaped by power relations, ideology, and the unarticulated presuppositions at work in producing ethnographic texts.[3] This, at least, seems to be the conclusion of recent reflections on ethnography, loosely unified by their concern with the "post-modern" predicament. According to Stephen Tyler, post-modern ethnography has become "a superordinate discourse to which all other discourses are relativized and in which they find their meaning and justification," an enterprise that:

> *describes* no knowledge and *produces* no action. It transcends instead by *evoking*...beyond truth and immune to the judgment of performance. It

---

[3] Several colleagues have suggested that a discussion of Talal Asad's *Genealogies of Religion* would be helpful here, and since I'm not going to discuss Asad in the body of the text let me explain my thinking. Rereading the book after a decade I find it even more confused that I originally thought. Indicating why I think it is confused would require dedicating an entire chapter to Asad, and that would be excessive. But if we begin with Davidson's emphasis on the idiolect, treat the critique of conceptual schemes as a check on any hermeneutic of suspicion, and then apply the critique of Foucault's anthropological followers that comes below, the argument should translate straightforwardly to Asad.

overcomes the separation of the sensible and the conceivable, of form and content, of self and other, of language and the world. [Tyler 1986, 123]

This is strong stuff. If we grasp other peoples through ethnography, and if ethnography transcends truth, then Davidson's arguments about shared beliefs would appear to break down.

What leads Tyler to talk as he does? There are two converging reasons. On the one hand, that paradigm of the search for knowledge, modern Western science, depends, for Tyler, on the possibility of perfect representation. But this is a mere will-o'-the-wisp, a myth based on an oversimplified account of language. Critics, from Nietzsche to Heidegger to Derrida, have exposed as untenable the concept of language as representation, and hence the pretentions of science as perfect representation. We're left with discourse, a fluid interaction of involved participants which need take no predetermined form. The assumption that any particular form of discourse is privileged, and this brings us to the second argument, rests on the imposition of power, which in anthropology has typically meant "the theoretical and commonsense categories of the hegemonic western tradition" (ibid., 129). If we wish to avoid such hegemonic skewing of discourse it is necessary to acknowledge that there is no "meta-narrative" or overarching representation of the way things must be or happen, "neither the scientific illusion of reality nor the religious reality of illusion is congruent with the reality of fantasy in the fantasy reality of the post-modern world" (ibid., 135). Even if there is no definitive form of post-modern ethnography—that would be a contradiction in terms—there is ethnography that struggles to free itself from the pressures of scientific, religious and political hegemonies, becoming genuinely post-modern, a "meditative vehicle" that opens up a new grasp of reality because "we come to it neither as to a map of knowledge or as a guide to action, nor even for entertainment. We come to it as the start of a different kind of journey" (ibid., 140).

Paul Rabinow's contribution to the same collection is less breathless, but no less demanding, in its call to revise our understanding of social facts. Rabinow begins with a generally positive account of Rorty's attack on epistemology "as an accidental, but eventually sterile, turning in Western culture," but chastises him for failing to provide "any discussion of how thought and social practices interconnect" (Rabinow 1986, 234–39). Because social practices are not only discursive, but political and historical as well, we need to be sensitive, as Foucault insists, to possibly unrecognized motives and relations of power that propel our practices, including the practice of ethnography. Specifically, the realism of the ethnographic mainstream "does not escape the general strictures of those critics of 'colonial' representation who, since 1950, have rejected discourses that portray the cultural realities of other peoples without placing their own reality in jeopardy" (ibid., 245). Clifford and Foucault make one with Fredric Jameson and Marilyn Strathern in providing us with the analytic tools for investigating not only the macro-political discourses of the West, but the micro-politics of academic culture, all by way of helping us "move against either economic or philosophical hegemony" and create "centers of resistance" (ibid., 241).

Geertz and his ilk are suspect in their interpretations for failing to place "their own reality in jeopardy," but it's hard to see what that might mean. Davidson's argument implies that we already believe most of what the natives believe, just not the interesting stuff. Tyler and Rabinow are right to suspect that "the deconstruction of otherness," as Geertz writes, "is the price of truth" (Geertz 1984, 63).[4] But that would only be problematic if the "other" were being invoked in ways analogous to "conceptual schemes." If Davidson is right about conceptual schemes, his argument goes through equally well for "otherness;" our access to any other is no more problematic, conceptually, that our access to ourselves.

On my reading, Geertz turns out to be the same sort of common-sense realist as Rorty. What, then, of his "deviously defending relativism?" The essay Lukes refers to, "Anti Anti-Relativism," is hardly a defense. It is, rather, an essay on the politics of interpreting what inquiry turns up:

> The realization that news from elsewhere about ghost marriage, ritual destruction of property, initiatory fellatio, royal immolation, and nonchalant adolescent sex naturally inclines the mind to an "other beasts other mores" view of things has led to arguments, outraged, desperate, and exultant by turns, designed to persuade us either to resist that inclination in the name of reason, or to embrace it on the same grounds. What looks like a debate about the broader implications of anthropological research is really a debate about how to live with them. [Geertz 1984, 45]

So suppose the phone rings and it is the father of a young woman in my comparative ethics course. He is appalled that I have his daughter reading Gilbert Herdt on initiatory fellatio. "What are you doing," he says, trying to hold himself in check, "assigning such disgusting material to my little girl?" How should I respond? I'm inclined simply to recount the facts: Herdt is a well-credentialed anthropologist, whose

---

[4] In addition to Geertz 1984, see 1983, 222–4, for his relations to Rorty, and 1988 for his relations to Rabinow et al.

initial fieldwork was in New Guinea; the people Herdt calls the Sambia live in the isolated highlands and part of their male initiation system involves the oral ingestion of sexual fluids; I assigned Herdt's introduction precisely to generate a discussion of sexuality and sexual ethics; we're also reading Pope Paul VI and Gilbert Meilaender. But this is unlikely to assuage my student's father. He, for whatever reasons, is disturbed that I have brought the facts about a particular community's sexual practices to the attention of his daughter.

But that's just overprotective middle-class squeamishness, the sort of thing an education is supposed to help us get over. "What the relativists, so-called, want us to worry about," writes Geertz, "is provincialism—the danger that our perceptions will be dulled, our intellects constricted, and our sympathies narrowed by the overlearned and overvalued acceptances of our own society" (1984, 46). So-called relativism (which I'll take from now on as a term of art) is the creation of a certain kind of fear-mongerer, who worries that if we allow that people in other times and places can live out their lives acting on what we consider disturbing beliefs, then we won't be able to say no to anything. Geertz cites "Paul Johnson's ferocious book... *Modern Times,*" which:

> accounts for the whole modern disaster—Lenin and Hitler, Amin, Bokassa, Sukarno, Mao, Nasser, and Hammerskjöld, Structuralism, the New Deal, the Holocaust, both world wars, 1968, inflation, Shinto militarism, OPEC, and the independence of India—as outcomes of something called "the relativist heresy." [Ibid., 48–49]

Johnson happens to be a political conservative, but Steven Lukes isn't. *Moral Relativism* builds toward a defense of human rights along the lines of Martha Nussbaum, whose liberal credentials are substantial (see Lukes 2008, 144–51). Lukes seems to lump Rorty, Geertz, et al. together because they have all provided aid and comfort to rights skeptics. But their skepticism, such as it is, has to do with the philosophical theory of rights. "On the account of rationality I am recommending," writes Rorty, non-Westerners are justified in being skeptical of the universalist claims, but "this is not to deny that these societies *should* adopt recent Western ways by, for example, abandoning slavery, practicing religious toleration, educating women... and so on" (Rorty 1997, 54–5). Neither Rorty nor Geertz is interested in denying that slavery is unjust or that freedom for women, gays, and even Republicans is a good thing. So it turns out that so-called relativism is no more than a bogey, something to accuse your rivals of in one political argument or another. There is no cure for politics. Anthropology plays the important role of pointing out the temporal and geographical limits of the "certainties" and "absurdities" that politicians use with abandon. "If we wanted home truths," Geertz concludes, "we should have stayed at home" (1984, 65).

Metaphysics as Midrash

In three giant steps we've seen that the philosophically interesting sense of relativism can't get started because it is impossible to make sense of an inherently untranslatable language, that without scheme-content dualism there's no work for "conceptual schemes" to do that can't be done by reference to disagreement about particular beliefs and practices, and that without a strong sense of "conceptual schemes" the specter of postmodernism deflates into old-fashioned politics as usual. But there is still a worry about fieldwork. What are we to think when it turns out that the claims of fieldwork cannot be repeated and confirmed? When investigators in the natural sciences can't replicate the results of an experiment—think "cold fusion"—the entire research program risks being dumped. If ethnography doesn't measure up, then perhaps the study of human beings really is lacking in rationality. A test case will help.

The Dutch ethnographer W. E. A. van Beek, in a 1991 critique of Marcel Griaule, argues that "the Dogon ethnography produced by Griaule after World War II cannot be taken at face value." First, van Beek's fieldwork uncovers no creation myth, nor anyone who will acknowledge the versions reported by Griaule and Dieterlen. Second, the "'supernatural' world of the Dogon is more diverse and much more vague, ambivalent, and capricious than represented in *DE* or *RP*."[5] The body and number symbolism invoked by Griaule is not acknowledged by informants and the "crucial concept of *nyama*, allegedly 'vital force,' is irrelevant to Dogon religion." Finally, the religious symbolism and feeling Griaule portrays as pervasive simply doesn't appear in the ethnography (van Beek 1991, 148). These anomalies lead van Beek to conclude that there is no systematic Dogon cosmology, that the

---

[5] *DE* and *RP* refer, respectively, to the French titles of *Conversations with Ogotemmêli* and Griaule's posthumous volume, published by Germaine Dieterlen, *The Pale Fox*. Part of what motivates van Beek is the evident difficulty created by the fact that Griaule and Dieterlen 1954 and later *The Pale Fox* seem to be working with a creation myth at odds with the one given in *Conversations with Ogotemmêli*. For our purposes there is no point in distinguishing between *Conversations with Ogotemmêli* and *The Pale Fox*, both of which van Beek treats as, at best, collaborative fabrications by Griaule, Dieterlen, and their informants. His bibliography is very full and an accessible place to begin for anyone interested in the details of the critical dispute or in pursuing Dogon matters further, though Clifford 1983 is a more balanced discussion of the problems with Griaule and his fieldwork, particularly when read in conjunction with Stocking 1983.

mythology available to the ethnographer is a hodgepodge from various sources, and that some Dogon myths derive from Christian, and perhaps Islamic, sources, others inventive play, and others the sort of *bricolage* practiced by his principal informants.

Van Beek identifies "four ethnographic periods" in Dogon anthropology, of which "the first period is characterized by valid description, the second and third by the creation of a culture that creates culture, and the fourth by a return to descriptive validity" (ibid., 157). In the early work, most notably *Masques Dogons*, Griaule documented institutions and practices that persist, and for which current ethnography such as van Beek's gives independent corroboration. But in *Conversations with Ogotemmêli*, *The Pale Fox*, and his and Dieterlen's contribution to Forde's *African Worlds*, he and his co-workers were led astray by their liberal aspirations in favor of Africa and the Dogon. Dogon thought, as a system, is increasingly, in the post-war years, the fabrication of Griaule's quest for an African philosophy the equal of any European system. "The tendency towards the creation of increasingly 'deep knowledge'," writes van Beek, "shows itself much more towards the end of Griaule's life, with a decreasing amount of 'Dogon-ness' marking the texts." Since Griaule's death, as his influence has waned over students of the Dogon, there has been a return to sound ethnographic practice.

Van Beek is aware of a certain irony here, for during the period in which he and Dieterlen elaborated Dogon cosmology, Griaule insisted, in the introduction to ethnography he taught in Paris, on the need to be wary of the motives and ways in which the fieldworker may be deceived by informants. Specifically, "the most dangerous informant is the forgetful, or the liar by omission, who provides apparently coherent and, what is more, candid information, all the while masking the essential principles of the institution" (Griaule 1957, 56). "It is hard to understand," van Beek concludes, "how someone who warned so eloquently against inventive informants remained naive about what was happening between him and his informants" (van Beek 1991, 157). Indeed it is. On van Beek's account Griaule should have held Ogotemelli up as the very kind of informant to avoid; instead, the European bought the blind hunter's fabrications lock, stock, and barrel.

In any field of inquiry, if there is some reason to believe that something less than credible is going on, we reconsider the evidence, attempt both to verify and disconfirm, and look for larger bodies of evidence within which to integrate the problematic case. In this case, we should probably try to imagine how Griaule might have been led to say what he does and why that might be at odds with other things we have discovered. There is no methodological perspective, traditional, philosophical or post-modern, that can make this problem go away; nonetheless, the problem need not paralyze us. Particular gaps in our knowledge do not render everything mere speculation nor belief mere opinion. Whatever Griaule's agenda, he makes claims about the claims that at least some Dogon make, and we may ask whether any or all of those claims are true. The methods we use are those familiar from everyday life and the extent of our success is unpredictable at the outset. If we turn up reasons to believe that Griaule distorted his material, or that he was misled, for whatever reasons, this may constitute evidence against, but it will remain part of the larger body of evidence that includes what we know of Griaule's other work, of the subsequent history of the Dogon, and a great deal more. Couching debate in terms of post-modernism and global politics not only provokes a lot of unnecessary epistemological hand-wringing, it distracts attention from alternate accounts of what is going on between Ogotemmêli and the "European." Consider van Beek's comment on Griaule's "overdifferentiation" as possibly "the product of the inability to take no for an answer and, for that matter, an unwillingness on the part of the informants to disappoint the researcher." Van Beek goes on to remark that "something similar happened to me when I was looking into colour terms," prompting the general reflection that:

> Given their general fascination with objects, there is a Dogon conviction that they should in fact be able to name and classify anything that comes their way, a kind of mild cultural hubris that may lure them into ridiculously detailed descriptions. The other reason is that naming becomes a game; it is fun to try to find ingenious—and sometimes correct—names for new objects. Afterwards they acknowledged to me that it was not at all necessary, but they did have a good time doing it. [1991, 154]

Failure to reflect on the import of this passage suggests an opportunity lost. For it is possible that the various mythic accounts provided by Griaule's informers are incommensurable, that they are only selectively related to the religious and cosmological information shared by the majority of Dogon on the street, and that nonetheless they tell us something extremely important, not only about Dogon belief but about religious belief and its interpretation in general. For what we see in the later work of Griaule and Dieterlen may be the origins of Midrash.

David Weiss Halivni, reflecting on the Mishnah, finds the document odd given "the Jewish predilection for justified law." Scripture places God's law within a narrative structure that moves from creation to Canaan. The Mishnah arranges these laws systematically and provides the decisions of the most notable teachers of Israel. But from early on,

Halivni argues, a need was felt to give an account of the "give and take" by which judgments were reached, for, he suggests, study and the process of justification are at least as important as the decisions reached:

> Theoretical learning was a main mode of worship, worth pursuing even if it does not lead to practical decision making. Any decision, however, that is the result of honest discussion and an attempt to seek out the truth through discussion is acceptable... The task of the Stammaim was to complete what was missing (usually through conjectural restoration) and to integrate the whole into a flowing discourse. [Halivni 1986, 77]

What is being restored is the underlying basis for a commandment, the inner momentum that links the practices enjoined by God to his plan for creation as a whole. Slowly but surely this practice became an institution, and the study of this give and take became the way in which the teachers of classical Judaism were trained from late antiquity to the present: an exegetical tradition made into a formal institution.

Law, written or oral, has a purpose only as part of the life of a community, and it is not in the least surprising that this community understands itself in terms both of the narrative that accounts for its present situation and the precedents set and standards articulated by its acknowledged masters. Halivni talks of a "Jewish predilection for justified law," but there is no reason to think of this predilection as uniquely, or even essentially, associated with one culture. Explanation and justification are continuous enterprises and there is no telling where they are likely to be found or the ways in which they are developed, but understanding a culture, with its beliefs and practices, will have to take into account the relations between narrative, justification, practice and belief, the changes they may undergo, and the new forms of explanation, justification, and argument that those changes may prompt.

Griaule's Dogon sound rather like Rabbinic Jews; van Beek's sound more like Fredrik Barth's Baktaman, who "have no exegetical tradition" (Barth 1975, 226).[6] Barth was tempted, during his field work, to seek "a Baktaman version of the Wise Man of the Dogon," but, while he came to believe that "it would have been relatively easy to make certain Baktaman informants schematize" the concepts and relations at work in their

---

[6] Barth's reflections on "the lack of factual comparative evidence in the anthropological literature on the presence and degree of development of native exegetical tradition and praxis," strike me as extremely important. His "strong suspicion... that the bodies of native explanation that we find in anthropological literature are often created as an artefact of the anthropologist's activity" (1975, 226), points to a middle area between Griaule and van Beek. My point is that once a tradition of exegesis emerges, whether from some internal or external impetus, it *can* take on a life of its own that becomes central to the community. Even if it doesn't, that fact in itself may tell us something important.

daily lives, he concluded "that no such string of associations has ever been constructed by them to date" (ibid., 228). This does not mean that exegesis will never develop among the Baktaman. If the Dogon, or at least some Dogon, were experimenting with exegesis this could have flourished during and because of Griaule, only to fade away. Perhaps, before the arrival of Griaule, there were few, if any, who inclined toward Midrash as a way of clarifying their "diverse, vague, ambivalent and capricious" relations with the "supernatural" world. On the other hand, van Beek himself notes the "cultural hubris" which assumes anything can be classified, understood, and comprehended by a Dogon, suggesting that there is at least something of an informal urge to classification. Leaving aside the problematic question of secret knowledge, and the possibility that knowledgeable Dogon are less disposed to confide in van Beek than, or perhaps because of, Griaule, it would not be in the least surprising if Griaule and his co-workers received differing creation stories *because*, as we saw earlier, those stories lack as much import as those at the foundations of community practice. If any or all of this should turn out to be true, van Beek would have to rethink his division of Dogon anthropology along the following lines: the study of Dogon public social and material culture, 1930s and 1940s; the study of Dogon and Bambara religious thought, 1940s to the 1960s; the study of Dogon public culture, 1982—the date of van Beek's first essay on the Dogon—to the present.

If the Dogon and the Baktaman and the rabbis of classical Judaism differ in the role they give exegesis, we learn this as a result of history, fieldwork, and critical debate. Neither the "relativist," the "cognitivist," nor the "post-modernist" can determine the truth of this, or any other claim, without them. The relativist so-called, who seemed initially to be Davidson's target, is inclined to think there are no constraints on how communities act and speak and give accounts of themselves. Rescher, in his criticism of Davidson, failed to get the point, and thus left Davidson's critique of conceptual schemes untouched. As alternative worlds, literally understood, conceptual schemes are nonsense. The cognitivist, in mortal fear for our moral selves, urges us to put the study of cultures on a "scientific" footing.[7] An unexpected upshot of Davidson's work, however, is its highlighting of "the normative element in interpretation

---

[7] Rorty frequently writes as though nobody really talks like this. Lawson and McCauley have kindly supplied evidence to the contrary. In discussing the post-colonial guilt that motivates Rabinow and his colleagues, they write that: "If epistemic virtues collapse, can moral virtues be far behind? . . . With the collapse of epistemic distinctions, what will happen to the moral awareness that kindled the guilt and precipitated anthropology's crisis of conscience in the first place?" (1993: 206).

introduced by the necessity of appealing to charity in matching the sentences of others to our own" (Davidson 1995, 4). Neither our accounts of language, nor the accounts of cultures which we base on them, can be evaded. Cognitivists will no doubt insist that such a reduction is no intention of theirs, but "unless the meanings of expressions can be tied in lawlike ways to specific neural configurations, there is no hope for a serious account of linguistic phenomena" (Davidson, 1995, 6). Davidson, of course, sees nothing less than serious about beliefs, intentions, and the desires that play a key role in our linguistic behavior. That a complete account of language cannot do away with them tells us something fundamental about what we take humans to be.

Nonetheless, it may happen that we have reached a point "where there is no such thing as a justification and we ought simply to have said: *that's how we do it.*" (Wittgenstein *RFM*, II-74) Our inclination is to think Wittgenstein's response is the last resort, but perhaps we think so only because we have inherited so many forms of explanation and justification. Knowing when there is nothing further to say is not the end of rationality, it is part of being rational. Human beings, however, can go about their business in many and unpredictable ways. This is why rational animals are unavoidably political animals, a burden borne by Marcel Griaule, Richard Rorty, and Paul Rabinow alike. There is no approach to ethnography that will insulate our political selves from our interpretive ones. But political claims are in the same boat as all the rest. We embrace them on the basis of education, experience, and critical debate, all of which remain as public as ever.

7

Explaining Innovation

From the history of art to comparative ethics and religion

When Arthur Danto's *Mysticism and Morality* appeared in 1972 it was greeted by a chorus of abuse. Danto's argument that the "mystical" ideas found in Indian and Chinese thought are rationally untenable because morally incoherent drew such comments as "predictably parochial," "pedestrian" (Staal 1974, 177) and "trapped in nineteenth century scholarship for twentieth century needs," the latter in a review article entitle "Cultural Lobotomy: The Failure of Philosophy" (de Nicolas 1977, 113). It's a contentious book, to say the least. To write that Indian pollution beliefs "probably originated in sanitary precautions, as many prohibitions doubtless do" (Danto 1972, 33), is an embarrassing bit of "medical materialism," while presenting the doctrine of *karma* as encouraging a "metaphysical boredom" that "goes with the sense of the meaninglessness of things" (ibid., 51) suggests that believers are mired in the moral stupor of Homer's lotus-eaters. And at more than one point Danto implies that all religious belief is suspect, as in the backhanded compliment that the "humanity of the Buddha shines through the features of the institutions he generated, even if his thought was to degenerate into a religion like the rest" (ibid., 83). Nonetheless, Danto raises a legitimate worry. "The animating metaethical thesis of *Mysticism and Morality*," he writes, is that the fundamental vocabulary of these traditions is "at odds with beliefs of *ours* about the world, propositions which the logic of belief requires us to hold for true" (ibid., 38). We cannot embrace the view of the world that gives meaning to *karma*, *nirvana*, or *wu wei*, he thinks, without disenfranchising our own moral vocabulary and making us unintelligible to ourselves.

Furthermore, adherents of those traditions are morally and intellectually blameless only insofar as they don't understand the implications of their own beliefs.

For Danto, morality involves the relations among multiple agents competing to secure goods. Unlike economics, however, the goods sought are not only material, but also include fairness, justice and virtue. Failure to attain material goods may put an individual at a disadvantage, but failure of justice or virtue renders the agent defective. A religion, though it may have some structurally similar forms, only qualifies as morality if it can be said to have embedded a moral commitment. Thus when Danto turns to Buddhism's Four Noble Truths and the Eightfold Path he acknowledges that they seek to overcome suffering and the cravings that arise from the illusion of the self, but "selflessness is a metaphysical thesis of Buddhism, not an ethical teaching" (ibid., 75).

The same turns out to be true for the quest for nirvana. The *arhat* of the Theravada tradition effectively abrogates any ethical commitments in turning away from the world, but even the *boddhisattva* ideal of the Mahayana is only a specious moral principle since its selfless compassion cannot provide a rule for discriminating between blameworthy and praiseworthy human interaction. When combined with the Mahayana emphasis on the identity of *nirvana* and *samsara*, the tradition suffers a collapse of the ideal into the actual, the "should be" into the "is," and as a result our day-to-day world becomes "the nirvana world without any alteration" (ibid., 81). At best there is an acceptance of all things as somehow sanctified, but Danto does "not believe it will do as a moral philosophy" since it makes it impossible, for example, to distinguish between torture and love. To realize the identity of *nirvana* and *samsara* is to perceive the emptiness of moral distinctions along with any others, and is no less than antinomianism. The conditions for morality cannot get a foothold.

Danto is not saying that Buddhists are inherently immoral, nor "that Buddhism is lacking in moral rules. It is only that they are not internal to the theory of Buddhism" (ibid., 82). In fact, the persistence of a moral order that cannot be theoretically squared with basic Buddhist teachings points up the moral inadequacy of the tradition. Though he is unaware of it, the Buddhist demonstrates in his day-to-day life that his approach to practical reasoning is at odds with the basic structure of his world view. "Ethics," as Danto puts it, "has to do with how we should treat one another, not merely with how we are to treat ourselves alone" (ibid.). If our religious or philosophical resources are incapable of accounting for our norms of practice they will inevitably require supplementing with a genuinely moral system of imperatives and prohibitions. Morality is not an option. Fairness, justice, and the rest of our basic moral vocabulary are essential to life and part of what it means to be a reasonable agent is acknowledging that there are no circumstances, no enterprises, in which they can be suspended.

It clearly won't do to say, as does one of Danto's reviewers, "that no one in the East... shared in any way his presupposition" (de Nicolas 1977, 102). This fails to address the metaethical argument and leaves us in the untenable interpretive position of explaining how a society can achieve internal stability and maintain its integrity over time, can give, in short, every appearance of moral order without possessing any genuine moral concepts. In a symposium on Danto's book, Proudfoot suggests that the Buddhist emphasis on the monistic may provide the "critical leverage" necessary; "whatever else the world may be like," he writes, the mystical experience assures him that, "I am not alone and am not identified with all that is... I cannot ignore that other existence, because it exerts on me a fascination... a claim that cannot be denied" (Proudfoot 1976, 15–18). Still, Danto seems correct in suspecting that something "would hardly seem a *mystical* experience if it did not alter *everything*: facts, values, attitudes and, most profoundly, the entire categorial structures which define common experience" (Danto 1976, 45). In doing so it may set itself over and against any communally recognizable standards of practical reasonableness. Proudfoot does, however, hint at a better approach when he notes that our own moral world is not "fixed as firmly as Danto seems to suggest" (1976, 25). The irony is that Danto himself was in the best position to see this.

Art worlds and historical narratives

In 1981, shortly before becoming art critic for *The Nation*, Danto mused on his early reaction to Andy Warhol:

> I recall the philosophical intoxication that survived the aesthetic repugnance of his exhibition in 1964, at what was then the Stable Gallery on East 74th Street, where facsimiles of Brillo cartons were piled one upon the other, as though the gallery had been pressed into service as a warehouse for surplus scouring pads... My philosophical responses to the Brillo boxes were delivered in an invited paper to the American Philosophical Association in 1965. Its title was "The Artworld," and I had the morbid satisfaction of not having it understood at all. [Danto 1981, vi–vii]

Danto opens that earlier essay with a contrast between the imitation theory of art and the reality theory of art. "The Imitation Theory of Art (IT) is," he writes, "an exceedingly powerful theory, explaining a great many phenomena connected with the causation and evaluation of art-works" (1964, 572). A fair number of artists, from the Greeks through the Realists, modified and refined it to develop new ways of representing the world, but something like a revolution:

> transpired with the advent of post-impressionist paintings. In terms of the prevailing artistic theory (IT), it was impossible to accept these as art unless inept art: otherwise they could be discounted as hoaxes, self-advertisements, or the visual counterparts of madmen's ravings. To to get them accepted *as* art... required not so much a revolution in taste as a theoretical revision of rather considerable portions. [Ibid., 573]

Despite some acknowledged oversimplifying—Cezanne is but one of the contributors to the real theory—complication only proves his point. Within a comparatively short period of time, "the Post-Impressionists won a victory in ontology" (ibid., 574). Artworks were no longer restricted to imitation, but had become real things to be taken on their own terms. "It is in terms of RT," Danto continues, "that we must understand the artworks around us today. Thus Roy Lichtenstein paints comic-strip paens, though ten or twelve feet high... it is precisely the scale that counts" (ibid.). Jasper Johns makes and paints numerals, Rauschenburg and Old-enburg make beds, Warhol builds Brillo boxes. All of them would have been not just ridiculed, the way Cezanne was in 1865, but totally unintel-ligible to the art world of the late nineteenth century.

But they can be made intelligible. Understanding how certain moves count as creating artworks in one context but not another requires imaginary entry to the relevant art world. The eager appreciator first needs to grasp "the *is of artistic identification* ... it is a necessary condition for something to be an artwork that some part or property of it be designable by the subject of a sentence that employs this special *is*" (ibid., 577). This, in turn, requires learning how to give reasons. So, in an introductory art history course, or through regular museum and gallery visits with an informed friend, I might learn how to identify the relevant features of particular paintings. I might, for example, be intrigued by Mu Qi's "Six Persimmons." As a novice, I might be inclined to connect it to Cezanne's "Still Life with Fruit Dish," but what I have to say becomes more interesting the deeper I go into the art world of Mu Qi himself. I discover than he was a thirteenth century Chan monk, that he is identified with the "spontaneous style," that the painting is perhaps to be associated with the sudden enlightenment central to Chan Bud-dhist thought. Cezanne starts to fade out of the discussion here and it's not quite clear whether "still life" in the western sense is quite what we want. "Acceptance of one identification rather than another," writes

Danto, "is in effect to exchange one *world* for another." (ibid., 578) Cezanne *might* have painted what we know as "Five Apples" so that it was visually indistinguishable from Mu Qi's "Six Persimmons," but they would still be two distinct paintings, from distinct art worlds, to be considered in terms of two very different sets of vocabularies.

Danto's art worlds are not the "conceptual schemes" of relativism. In *Analytical Philosophy of History*, a volume contemporary with "Artworlds," Danto develops the notion of "narrative sentences" in a technical sense. "Their most general characteristic," he writes, "is that they refer to at least two time-separated events though they only *describe* (are only *about*) the earliest event to which they refer" (1964a, 142). Among their important features, narrative sentences "help show why the proper answer to the tedious question 'Is history art or science?' is: 'Neither'" (ibid.). What Danto has in mind are sentences like this:

> The successful Trinity test on 16 July, 1945, showed that the design of Fat Man, subsequently detonated over Nagasaki, was viable.

This is a paradigmatic historical statement of a not very controversial sort. Nonetheless, the historian is committed to articulating the truth, so presumably he is committed to measuring his claims against what actually happened. One way to think of this is in terms of the *"full description* of an event *E,"* by which Danto means, "a set of sentences which, taken together, state absolutely everything that happened in *E"* (ibid., 148). Given the reasonable belief that the past is fixed, Danto suggests that we think of past events as contained in an "Ideal Chronicle (hereafter referred to as I.C.). Once *E* is safely in the Past, its full description is in the I.C. We may now think of the various parts of the I.C. as accounts to which practicing historians endeavour to approximate their own accounts" (ibid., 149). The I.C. is complete, in the sense of "an Ideal Witness," but it won't solve the historian's problems, because "the whole truth concerning an event can only be known after, and sometimes only *long* after the event itself has taken place" (ibid., 151).

In the case of Trinity, the witness simply records what happens in the New Mexican desert, without mention of Fat Man or Nagasaki. It might have been the case that someone, maybe Teller, said "that proves that the design for Fat Man is viable" an instant after the blast, but as part of the chronicle that merely reflects one man's judgment at the time. It's not the equivalent of the historian's judgment. Danto himself illustrates the point with a passage from Yeats's "Leda and the Swan:"

> A shudder in the loins engenders there
> The broken wall, the burning roof and tower
> And Agamemnon dead.

"The *sentence* itself," writes Danto:

> is of a kind which could not appear in the I.C. even if the event happened - in contrast with 'He holds her helpless breast upon his breast' which conceivably could appear there...nobody could witness the act under the description "Zeus engenders the death of Agamemnon". [Ibid.]

Only the historian, as opposed to the chronicler, can use Danto's narrative sentences to weave together an account of events that describes and explains the consequences of earlier acts. As the result of the historian's inquiry and deliberation upon the results of that inquiry, they are both fallible and revisable, but this isn't relativism. It's history writing. We all expect the historian to be aiming for truth, but to imagine that his product is certain, much less infallible, would be irrational in the extreme.

The art critic sees particular works or exhibitions "as requiring explanations" (Danto 1994a, 14). This is a crucial step because it registers the equivalent of Peirce's genuine doubt. The critic is confronted by something that challenges the status quo. Think of it this way. If I'm walking along the beach at San Gregorio, the expanse of sand isn't going to make me pause and take notice. But if I wander up and around the little head north of the state beach, I might look up and catch my breath at the sight of a beautiful naked woman. That's different! But then I realize I've wandered up to the nude beach, which is on private property. Danto's critic does the same thing, "inferring to the best explanation of why they have the form they do have. The explanations are historical and causal" (ibid.). Danto illustrates, in an earlier essay:

> The "real" Brillo box was designed by an artist, Steve Harvey, who was a second-generation Abstract Expressionist more or less forced to take up commercial art...Where Warhol's is cool, it is hot, even urgent, in proclaiming the newness of the product it contains, the speed with which it shines aluminum, and the fact that its twenty-four packages are GIANT SIZE...my hunch is that Harvey was influenced, in his motif, by certain themes in hardedge abstraction. [1993, 385]

Two visually indistinguishable artifacts but two different art worlds, thus dramatically contrasting interpretations. "For all that they resemble one another," writes Danto, "they belong to different histories, and though Steve Harvey's work would be unthinkable without a certain kind of abstraction...Warhol's was itself in no way dependent upon those kinds of abstraction" (ibid., 386).

Danto's art worlds are, loosely, institutional, not in the sense of conferring art status on particular works, but in the sense of embodying a shared history, style, and set of theoretical commitments:

What in the end makes the difference between a Brillo box and a work of art consisting of a Brillo Box, is a certain theory of art ... without the theory, one is unlikely to see it as art, and in order to see it as part of the artworld, one must have mastered a good deal of artistic theory as well as a considerable amount of the history of recent New York painting. [1964, 581]

First and foremost, the theory that helps the critic, and thus his audience, understand is the one with which the artist is working. To inhabit an art world is to be one of "a loose affiliation of individuals who know enough by way of theory and history that they are able to practice what the art historian Michael Baxandall terms 'inferential art criticism'" (Danto 1990, 42). A look at Baxandall will, I believe, prove instructive.

Baxandall's first book, *Giotto and the Orators*, addresses "two related problems, one of them general, the other more local." The general question turns on the relation of "the grammar and rhetoric of a language" to "our manner of describing and, then, of attending to pictures and some other visual experiences." The more focused question turns on Alberti's development of "the concept of pictorial 'composition'... as a special case of the general problem" (Baxandall 1971, vii).

Central to Baxandall's analysis is understanding who the Italian humanists thought they were:

"Humanist" is not a word the early Italian humanists themselves knew; neither is "humanism". It seems that the term *humanista* grew out of late fifteenth-century university slang, where it was used of a professional teacher of the *studia humanitatis* ... When the early humanists wanted a term to describe themselves as a class—for instance, as one section in a classified collection of biographies—the word they generally used was *orator*, or occasionally *rhetoricus*. [Ibid., 1]

The figures we call humanists called themselves orators, and by this they intended to signal their training in the classical rhetorical tradition, or what was available of it. For the early humanists this meant the rigorous embrace of Cicero. "The early humanists' Ciceronianism," as Baxandall puts it, "was an epic affair" (ibid., 7). Writers trained in the oratorical manuals displayed a connoisseur's awareness of the distinction, for instance between *facies* and *vultus* (ibid., 10). They developed their vocabularies in sentences designed to display the sorts of period appropriate to the topic:

In some of the more punctilious statements of classical theory the first section of the periodic sentences (*protasis*) is seen as inducing suspense and the second section (*apodosis*) as resolving it: if A, then B; though A, yet B; as A, so too B; and so on. [Ibid., 20]

Literary composition based on the models of the ancients gave rise, on Baxandall's telling, to a rhetoric of comparison which, in turned paved the way for humanist reflection on painting as the pinnacle of the arts (ibid., 51ff).

When *Giotto and the Orators* appeared, Baxandall was preparing the lectures that became *Painting and Experience in Fifteenth Century Italy*. The first page launches into the complex interplay of areas necessary to understanding individual pieces of art:

> On one side there was a painter who made the picture, or at least supervised its making. On the other side there was somebody else who asked him to make it, provided funds for him to make it and, after he had made it, reckoned on using it in some way or another. [Baxandall 1972, 1]

He has moved us from the rarified atmosphere of the humanists into the marketplace inhabited by the client and the craftsman. "Both parties," he makes clear, "worked within institutions and conventions—commercial, religious, perceptual, in the widest sense social—that were different from ours and influenced the forms of what they together made" (ibid.). Since major works were "done to order," with the client specifying size, subject, and the quality of the materials, each work is likely to have an individual history in which unexpected problems may shape the final product and its impact on the viewer.

Baxandall's first example, a triptych painted by Filippo Lippi in 1457, was negotiated a generation after Alberti's *De pictura*. Since the painting was intended as a kingly gift from a powerful Medici, Filippo was attentive to his client. "To keep you informed," he writes, "I send a drawing of how the triptych is made of wood, and with its height and breadth. Out of friendship to you I do not want to take more than the labour costs of 100 florins for this: I ask no more" (ibid., 4). This is a world where such modern dualisms as public/private or art/craft get in the way of understanding. "One paid for a picture," writes Baxandall, "under these same two headings, matter and skill, material and labour, as Giovanni d'Agnolo de'Bardi paid Botticelli for an altarpiece to go in the family chapel" (ibid., 16).

Having sketched the "conditions for trade," Baxandall shifts to "the period eye," by which he means "how Quattrocento people, painters and public, attended to visual experience in distinctively Quattrocento ways, and how the quality of this attention became a part of their pictorial style" (ibid., 27). Ulrich Middeldorf worries that, "we have only the scantiest and vaguest utterances on works of art from the period; we are forced to rely on ingenious reconstructions and guesswork"(Middeldorf 1975, 284). Another commentator notes

"Gombrich's suspicious reaction" (Langdale 1999, 33 n. 21).[1] Such suspicions seem odd coming to *Painting and Experience* down the road we have travelled. Baxandall seems like nothing so much as the art historical analogue to the anthropologist, attempting to reconstruct the components of their subjects' worlds, in order to make sense of their beliefs, products, and actions.

Not only that, but Baxandall appears to be following out the methodological strictures announced by Gombrich himself, at precisely the point Baxandall chose to work with him. In a lecture of 1957, Gombrich identified "the physiognomic fallacy" with the "tendency to see the past in terms of its typical style" (Gombrich 1957, 108). The proper historian of art investigates "the causes and roots of styles" (ibid., 110). The "physiognomist" blocks this by attributing some mythic causal efficacy to the "spirit of the age." Gombrich cites, by way of example, the popular nineteenth-century view that "the only possible explanation of naturalism was sensuality," revealed to an oppressed and benighted medieval world by "a colourful Renaissance teeming with supermen who said 'yea' to life" (ibid., 115).

Painting and Experience reads like an introduction to the interpretation of art in the manner of Gombrich and his predecessor, Aby Warburg. Baxandall's closing discussion of Cristoforo Landino, which Middeldorf calls "a highly specialized enterprise, which signally fails to throw any light on the style of Renaissance painting" (Middeldorf 1975, 285), illustrates the radical nature of Baxandall's enterprise. He opens the chapter remarking "that the Quattrocento man invoked by this last chapter is just a church-going business man, with a taste for dancing" (Baxandall 1972, 109). They are Landino's audience, the sort of well-to-do civic leaders who commissioned Quattrocento paintings. Landino both lectured at the university and served as secretary to the Signoria. "In short," writes Baxandall, "his profession was the exact use of language. Two other things equipped him to say things about the painters: he was a friend of Leon Battista Alberti (1404–72), and he was the translator of Pliny's *Natural History* (A.D. 77)" (ibid., 114). As a friend of Alberti, Landino, who died in 1498, is as close as we're likely to come to the tradition of thinking about painting that closed *Giotto and the Orators*. As the translator of Pliny, he was turning one of the most important sources for classical reflection on painting into contemporary Italian. Landino, then, is an important figure in determining and transmitting a language of artistic judgment to the sorts of people most likely

---

[1] The interview in question exists as an appendix to Langdale's 1995 UCLA dissertation and I have not found a version in print.

to commission works of art, at least in the first third of the sixteenth century.

Specialists in the art and history of Renaissance Italy may debate how much weight to give Landino, and thus Baxandall's use of him, but the development from the puzzles of chapter I, through the components of looking in chapter II, to the criticism of Landino, exemplifies "that outward spiralling movement," that Gombrich recommends, "the attempt to draw in new evidence from ever-widening circles, which may offer new vistas onto the particular" (Gombrich 1957, 117). In discussing Masaccio, Baxandall notes that Landino's description of him as "a very good imitator of nature" and devoted "to imitation of the truth" were "the easiest cliché of praise one could use and they set up an unspecified realism as a uniform standard of quality." Nonetheless, "the fact that Masaccio is the one Quattrocento painter Landino credits with this virtue suggests that it had a meaning for him" (1972, 119). Leonardo, in the next generation, shares Landino's judgment and this allows Baxandall to bring in yet more evidence; one judgment may be idiosyncratic, while two suggest (if only suggest) a shared judgment over time. Incorporating Leonardo also allows Baxandall to expand on the "unspecified realism" of Landino. The imitator of nature works independently, without relying on "pattern-books and formulas," basing his work on "the appearance of actual objects ... studying and representing these appearances particularly through their perspective and their relief" (ibid., 121). Baxandall contrasts Landino on Masaccio with his discussion of Filippo Lippi to bring out, not simply how these artists look different to us, but how they appeared to a sophisticated period eye and what he said about their differences.

From comparative styles to comparative ethics

I still haven't met the challenge put forth by Danto. For all I have done so far is to illustrate, by way of Baxandall, the sorts of considerations necessary for a rational agent to undertake creative action that responds to the demands of his particular role in society. But Baxandall also helps us explain how the producer and the consumer can come to share a period eye, despite their differences in training, knowledge, and social location. When Danto writes that "one reason moral propositions might lie outside the logical reach of factual ones is that they consist in *rules*" (Danto 1972, 9), he commits to a particular view of ethics. These sorts of rules, he implies, require a distinctive human psychology.

But when he insist that moral rules "are not internal to the theory of Buddhism" (ibid., 82), he commits Gombrich's "physiognomic fallacy."

Danto cites a reasonably broad set of Buddhists classics, from the *Questions of Milinda* to the *Lotus Sutra*, but he does so in order to trace one set of technical questions dealing with selflessness, "a metaphysical thesis" (ibid., 75). This simply isolates one set of questions interesting to the elite theorists of Buddhism and identifies it with the "theory of Buddhism." To put it back in Baxandall's terms, this is no more plausible than identifying European, or even Renaissance, art with the critical interests of Florentine orators in the fifteenth century. And much the same goes for Danto's readings of the rest of South and East Asian thought. A more plausible strategy would be to follow Baxandall's lead and attempt to discern whether and to what extent the musings of the theorists influenced the products of the workshop, keeping in mind, of course, that when it comes to the moral world pretty much everybody is a journeyman.

If this is enough to dispel the worries generated by Danto's critique of "oriental thought," it still doesn't give me a substantive example of comparison at work. For this, we need to return to Baxandall. Not long after the appearance of *Painting and Experience*, he was appointed to the Slade Professorship at Oxford for 1974. The lectures he gave under that aegis appeared in 1980 as *The Limewood Sculptors of Renaissance Germany*. If *Painting and Experience* is a "primer in the social history of pictorial style," *Limewood Sculptors* shows what can be done investigating in depth a particular style in its historical locale. "Most of the sculpture discussed in this book," he begins, "was produced within three generations, between 1475 and 1525, a turning point for Germany" (1980, 1). Not only the time, but the place is closely circumscribed, "the southern half of modern Germany, shading over at its periphery into Alsace, northern Switzerland and Austria" (ibid., 3). Material and artistic possibility are indistinguishable in Baxandall's story. While:

> many sculptors worked also in stone—sandstone, limestone, marble—and a few in bronze... What distinguishes the region is not just that sculptors used limewood in preference to other woods, but that limewood was a central medium in the sense that it was used for a central genre of the culture, the retable altarpiece. [Ibid., 27]

The pieces were big, complex, public, and expensive. In the fifty years that define Baxandall's study, these pieces were being created not by church workshops, nor by the regular employees of the wealthy, but by "the masters of independent workshops in the cities and operated in a framework much like that of other craftsmen" (ibid., 95). Because there were a limited number of true masters, the dynamic between craftsman and client was complex. A Fugger of Augsburg could contract with a master such as Michael Erhart, but "conspicuous talent had its price and its own power," and when Erhart refused to deliver, the richest of the rich could be pressured to meet a higher price; "even a Fugger must bend a little" (ibid., 106).

When Baxandall reaches "the period eye," we have learned about the heft and cellular structure of the wood, the personalities of the tools, and the ways in which artistic practices were shaped by the practices of the Mastersingers. Baxandall connects the flourishes of the Mastersong to the attention to line in contemporary treatises on penmanship and fencing. When it comes to interpreting the individual figures, Baxandall warns his reader against using the treatises on physiognomy to over-interpret the sculptures. "The stage-directions of miracle plays," he writes, "offer a good corrective to over-interpretation" (ibid., 158). These plays, attended by the multitude, would have been familiar in ways that technical treatises would not. Familiar tones, gestures, and poses could be appropriated by an individual sculptor for his own interests and stylistic flourishes.

When juxtaposed to *Painting and Experience*, *Limewood Sculptors* shows us one aspect of the comparative process in action. The artists of fifteenth-century Italy, with Florence in the ascendant, developed their vocabulary and applied it to producing the sorts of works demanded by that market. Those of southern Germany did the same and it's now possible to see how different were the social, economic, and intellectual forces behind them. Not only that, but at the end of the period the two will be flowing together into yet another style. "In 1500," writes Baxandall, "Dürer, with his Italianate intellectual interests and energy, was a nonesuch in Germany, and it would be fraudulent to present his books as the verbal account of the Florid sculptors' values" (ibid., 144). Dürer, particularly Dürer the printmaker, will be important for a different generation.

Baxandall himself almost immediately undertook spelling out the implications of his approach in what became *Patterns of Intention*. To "conditions of trade" and "the period eye," *Patterns of Intention* adds three new terms, "charge," "brief," and "*troc*." The charge of a bridge builder is "span!" but to say that a bridge is the way it is because it is a bridge doesn't tell you anything. It doesn't, for example account for why the Bay Bridge doesn't look like the Golden Gate. Discussing the Forth Bridge, Baxandall lists 24 "cause-suggesting features of the narrative," and then writes:

What I shall call the Brief consists of local conditions in the special case. Specific items are:

7. [A mile-long crossing but] a rocky islet in mid-stream
8. The silted bottom of the Forth
9. The demand for shiproom
14. The strength of side winds

These surely are objective circumstances, in the sense of having a real presence apart from Baker's mind. However, what is less stable is their weighting, their relative mass in the thinking that made the design. [1985, 25–30]

The Forth Bridge is an artifact of a specific time and place. It has the look it has because of choices made by its designer, Benjamin Baker. But those choices are themselves objects of study beyond the simple charge to build a bridge. The demand for shiproom is a constraint put on the designer by an external authority, the Admiralty. This means that height and space between supports must be taken into account. The little island at the approximate mid-point commends itself as one anchor point, while the silted bottom adds a further constraint to the remaining supports. The side winds are a particular issue because, at the very beginning of the project, the Tay Bridge, designed by the original head of the Forth project, "blew over in an easterly gale, taking a passenger train with it. Bouch was discredited and work on his Forth Bridge ceased" (ibid., 17).

What, if anything, changes when we approach a portrait? First, "a painter's Charge is indeed more elusive than a bridge-builder's... Visual interest is secondary and, even though not excluded, incidental" (ibid., 43). If Baker's charge was "span!" Picasso's was "paint!" But this "is featureless. Character begins with the Brief" (ibid., 44). Baxandall suggests three components, namely the need to represent three dimensional things "and yet also positively acknowledge the two-dimensional plane of the canvas;" decide on "the relative importance of form and of colour;" and settle on the moment to be captured, the painting's "fictive instantaneousness" (ibid., 44–45). This brings Baxandall to *troc*, not the earlier conditions of trade, but the market in which cultural goods are bartered:

a *form* of relation in which two classes of people, both within the same culture, are free to make choices in the course of an exchange, any choice affecting the universe of the exchange and so the other participants. [Ibid., 48]

This doesn't mean that *troc* is unrelated the conditions of trade, for "while the basic relation of *troc* is simple and fluid, in any particular case it is partly encased in actual market institutions that are less so" (ibid., 49). Without being overly systematic, *troc* is an exchange for trading cultural goods, existing somewhere between the actual market and the period eye.

The early twentieth-century painter is charged with producing works of "intentional visual interest." At this particular moment in time painters generally, and Picasso certainly, were free to formulate their own briefs, based on the particular goods and values they embraced. Baxandall finds it "important to assert that both *troc* and market offer the painter choice and that the painter acts reciprocally back on his culture" (ibid., 73). As the culture, which is really made up of lots of little knots of individuals situated in smaller or larger institutions, negotiates its responses to the various candidates for cultural consumption this recreates both *troc* and market. The art world, as Baxandall recommends studying it, is no different in kind—as far as action, intention, and objectivity go—from the ethical world as Fingarette conceives it. When we attempt to explain what people believe and why they act the way they do, we act as observers, not as participants, but it doesn't matter. "The account of intention," Baxandall insists, "is not a narrative of what went on in the painter's mind but an analytical construct about his ends and means, as we infer them from the relation of the object to the identifiable circumstances" (ibid., 109). Since we always start in *medias res*, and since we can never, for complex acts and events, be sure we have all the evidence we need for the best possible explanation, our interpretations, hence our comparisons, will always be subject to revision.

"The participant," writes Baxandall, "understands and knows his culture with an immediacy and spontaneity the observer does not share . . . His culture, for him, is like the language he has learned, informally, since infancy" (ibid.). Remembering Davidson, we might say that the participant has his own cultural idiolect, making it easy to interpret the idiolects of his near neighbors. The further he wanders from home, and the more his idiolect has been shaped by cantankerous and combative institutions, the shakier interpretation can become. Thus the more self-critical we must become. Baxandall thinks this is all to the good. Explanations and judgments should be up for grabs because "there is an obligation to demonstrate the need to invoke this or that bit of circumstance. The explanation must pay its way" (Baxandall 1985, 119). To make sure that explanations pay up, Baxandall recommends holding them to "three self-critical moods of a commonsense sort . . . (historical) *legitimacy*, (pictorial and expositive) *order*, and (critical) *necessity* or fertility" (ibid., 120). The first calls for avoiding anachronism without ruling out "individuality or inadvertence or defiance" (ibid.). Here, as always, the quality of the evidence will prove crucial. Picasso's defiance and individuality, for example, are a critical commonplace, but it is nigh on impossible to determine the intentions of most carvers of medieval gargoyles, beyond the charge to move rainwater away from the foundation of the buildings.

As for order, Baxandall intends "articulation, system, integrality, ensemble...an intentional unity and cogency" (ibid.). It is obvious that a self-critical stance here will build on legitimacy, because it's hard to imagine the purpose of attributing to an actor an intention that could not have been formulated in any available vocabulary. Julius Caesar, for example, might have used tactics that could later be modeled game-theoretically; he could not have used game-theory. On the other hand, Piero della Francesca might have consulted a herbalist to discover the healing properties of plants, but "there are various reasons for not reading the plants in the foreground of the *Baptism of Christ* in a symbolic sense of healing" (ibid., 133). Baxandall cites the fact that they appear in other paintings where healing is irrelevant. "The finally decisive thing," is balancing "the relation between picture surface and picture space" (ibid.). This is closely related to Alberti's notion of composition, and Baxandall has already noted that "there are only two important mid-Quattrocento painters one could describe as more than occasionally Albertian: Piero della Francesca and Mantegna" (Baxandall 1971, 133). Thus he is on firm ground when he writes of the problem of *commensurazione* that Piero confronts that, "it was a problem for him, and another man might not have felt it" (ibid.). Given that the plants in the foreground solve a problem that was known to be important to this particular artist tilts the probabilities toward this explanation over others.

And this brings me to necessity. Baxandall's inferential criticism insists that:

> One does not adduce explanatory matter of an inferential kind unless it contributes to experience of the picture as an object of visual perception... there are many fifteenth century circumstances that one could adduce as *consistent* with Piero's *Baptism of Christ* which one does not adduce because they are not necessary to the purpose: which is inferential criticism. It is a pragmatic mood, a demand for a sort of actuality. [Ibid., 121]

As a practicing scientist, Peirce was extremely sensitive to the ability of a theory to explain concrete events in the world. Why else, after all, undertake the complicated scouting necessary to find the ideal place to observe a solar eclipse? "The newly observed effects of the sun's corona and protuberances required new explanatory theories" (Brent 1993, 80). As a historian of philosophy and science, Peirce knows just how many consistent theories can be put forward as explanations of anything. To say, as James often seemed to say, that one was as good as another, as long as it worked (whatever that might mean), was to give up inquiry for self-indulgence.

Baxandall closes *Patterns* by tying his approach "to the scientist's peculiar sense of publication... the experiment must be repeatable and open to testing by other people. If it is not repeatable by other people, the results are not accepted" (1985, 136). Art historical inquiry, like inquiry in general, should avoid the scholasticism of cloaking its findings in a specialized jargon accessible only to the licensed few. "Inferential criticism reduces that apparatus to the heuristic convenience it is, and restores the authority of common visual experience of the pictorial order." In so doing, "inferential criticism is not only rational but sociable" (ibid., 137). If the study of religion and ethics can become both rational and sociable, we will have achieved progress.

War and charity: an exercise in comparative religion and ethics

If an experiment in criticism has to pay up, so should a methodological recommendation. A test case is in order. A few years ago Richard Miller took me and others to task for rejecting the analysis of James Childress, "who proposes to reconstruct the logic of just-war criteria and, in the process, uncover a point of contact between just-war doctrine and its moral alternative, pacifism" (Miller 2002, 174). Childress himself suggests that the fundamental concept is "maleficence," which can either be derived from Rawls's original position or from the Christian "norm of *agape*" (Childress 1978, 69). In earlier writing, Miller suggests that non-religious versions might be based on "the general belief, widely embraced in Western culture, that persons deserve respect, perhaps even care in times of need," while theists maintain "that life is sacred, that God alone is sovereign over life and death" (Miller 1991, 16). Wherever it comes from, for Childress and Miller this duty generates a presumption against harm. Since war inevitably involves harm to others, there is a prima facie duty to reject it as a form of maleficence. If that duty were absolute, then pacifism would be the only moral stance, but when we recognize the broad spectrum of evil that can be inflicted on innocent people, it is possible reasonably to believe that the prima facie duty not to harm can be overridden by the prospect of an even greater evil. Thus war is always an evil, but it can be justified as being the lesser evil. If Thomas Aquinas can be enlisted into the ranks of nonmaleficence theorists then perhaps Childress's critics can be portrayed as the moral outliers.

Miller's first move is to distinguish "rational" from "historical reconstruction:"

> A historical reconstruction, according to Rorty, seeks to give an account of a historical thinker "in his own terms," ignoring whether that thinker's views would survive critical scrutiny today. A rational reconstruction, in contrast, is written "in light of some recent work in philosophy which can reasonably be said to be 'about the same questions' as the great dead thinker was discussing." [Miller 2002, 178]

From here, Miller starts out modestly. His rational reconstruction of Aquinas at this stage is intended to show only "that the language and logic of prima facie duties is compatible with his reasoning" (ibid.). But, after an excursus on the structure of the scholastic *quaestio*, Miller writes that:

> If Aquinas were not intent on instructing readers about the values associated with nonviolence, he would have structured his article on war differently. That is to say, if justice were the font of Aquinas's approach, then he would have had to arrange his *quaestio* so that the virtue of justice provided the horizon within which his inquiry proceeded. [Ibid., 183]

He capitalizes on the fact that Thomas's discussion of war falls under the aegis of charity, which "points to the good of nonviolence, for which Christians should be disposed and prepared" (ibid., 185). This leads to the claim that "a presumption against war informs the manner in which Thomas first answers his question" (ibid., 186).

At this point, however, Miller backs off a bit, writing that "Aquinas's strategy for dealing with it coheres with the pattern of reasoning associated with prima facie duties and the language of a presumption against harm" (ibid., 187). This points to the limits of rational reconstruction, which works at the level of compatibility and coherence. He continues this in the next paragraph, writing that "the language and logic of presumptions and prima facie duties faithfully capture the trade-offs to which Aquinas refers" (ibid.). But Miller soon obscures this. Having discussed the principle of double effect, as found in the question on homicide, he writes that for Aquinas "the soldier does not, strictly speaking, take the sword" (ibid., 199). It is, as Miller reads it, the commander in chief who employs the soldier as a mere instrument. As such, responsibility seems to jump over the individual soldier and lodge in the higher authority, whose, "goals must never include intentional harm against another community...The effect of this point is to restore the presumption against harm that is apparently compromised when Thomas grants soldiers the right intentionally to injure an opponent" (ibid.). This, in turn, licenses the claim that "intentionally killing other soldiers in war is analogous to intentionally disarming an assailant in individual self-defense," which "does not compromise the presumption against harm since such killing is an instrumental rather than a final cause" (ibid., 200). This, finally, allows for Miller's conclusion "that social critics (like the U.S. Catholic bishops) who use patterns of reasoning associated with prima facie duties may claim Thomas's patrimony" (ibid., 203–4).

As Baxandall writes, "things seem over-elaborate." If the point is to claim that Childress develops a position already present in Aquinas, then this sort of "rational reconstruction" is pointless. Miller neglects the dilemma with which Rorty begins:

> either we anachronistically impose enough of our problems and vocabulary on the dead to make them conversational partners, or we confine our interpretive activity to making their falsehoods look less silly by placing them in the context of the benighted times in which they were written. [Rorty 1984, 247]

Rorty dissolves the strategy by suggesting that "we should do both of these things, but do them separately" (ibid.). But if the argument is between two *competing* ways of talking about a subject, then reconstructing one author in a vocabulary he does not use, explicating his thought with concepts that cannot be documented in his works, to defend a position he nowhere entertains, violates the self-critical moods of legitimacy, order, and necessity.

Miller can respond that I have unfairly ignored his own historical analysis. In particular, I have neglected his use of the seminal work of M.-D. Chenu, who observes that "the *quaestio* was a complicated genre, presenting in compressed form 'all the work that was required to raise, discuss, and solve a problem under dispute'" (Miller 2002, 179). In the prooemium to *ST* 2a2ae, 34, Thomas announces that the next set of questions must consider "the vices opposed to charity...in the third instance discord and schism, which are opposed to peace." When it comes to question 40, on war, Thomas divides the discussion into four articles: "first, whether any war is licit; second, whether it is licit for clerics to wage war; third, whether ambushes may be licit; and fourth, whether it may be licit to wage war on feast days." Miller, following Chenu, writes that once a question has been posed, "various opinions (the objections) are brought into play with the aim of pushing inquiry to its limits... Objections represent strong reasons that furnish a presumptive answer to the opening question" (Miller 2002, 179). The objections are followed by the *sed contra*, the response of the master, and then:

> a series of replies that attempt to clarify how the initial objections are to be understood. The idea is not for the replies to destroy the objections but, as Chenu writes, to introduce a set of distinctions that mark "off upon what share of truth [the objection] is founded... There is an effort to embody the truth that the opposing position contains within a wider framework which, far from casting it aside, underwrites its truthfulness." [Ibid., 180]

This last gives Miller an opening, for he can then invoke Bryan Hehir, the principle author of the bishops' letter on peace, to the end that "the question suggests a presumption against war. By starting with the idea that war might be sinful, Aquinas seems to establish a burden of proof in favor of nonviolence and against war" (ibid., 180). Miller admits that, taken by itself, this is a stretch, but then suggests that the objections, "from the Bible, an idea from moral theory, and church law all suggest nonviolent values that ought to dispel the initial uncertainty; they present an affirmative answer to the question" (ibid., 182). Since Bible, moral common sense, and church law are all, ultimately, authoritative, and since Chenu has written that the objection "underwrites its truthfulness," Miller concludes that "the objections are stacked in favor of an affirmative reply to the opening query, which suggests a presumption against war" (ibid., 183).

Having established a presumption against war, Miller now moves to fend off objections:

> If Aquinas were not intent on instructing readers about the values associated with nonviolence, he would have structured his article on war differently. That is to say, if justice were the font of Aquinas's approach, then he would have had to arrange his *quaestio* so that the virtue of justice provided the horizon within which his inquiry proceeded. [Ibid.]

Specifically, he could have invoked biblical passages, moral authorities, and church law to alert "readers to the idea that war can be good and just" (ibid.). Then, in his replies, he could have underwritten the truthfulness of that perspective for his readers. But he doesn't. "The value of nonviolence, not the virtue of justice, generates the intellectual clearing within which he develops his inquiry" (ibid.). This reading, backed by Chenu, reveals a commitment to nonviolence as a primary value of the Thomist tradition. Thus Miller seems to have vindicated the interpretation of Childress over and against obstreperous Aristotelians such as myself. This would seem to justify his rejection of James Johnson's "assertion that 'the presumption against war belongs to pacifism alone'" (ibid., 204).

What's to be said about all this? First, while it is always wise to begin a reading of Thomas with Chenu, Miller doesn't take that precept far enough. Students of Thomas's ethics need to immerse themselves in Chenu's studies of twelfth-century theology. Thomas was born at the end of a century of social and intellectual turmoil. Thinkers had begun to abandon the preoccupations of the cloister to pursue a new set of questions, turning on the "desacralizing of nature—and of the outlook men brought to nature," which "produced an unmistakable crisis both in the recourse to symbolist interpretation which a certain way of looking at nature invited, and in the limitations now placed upon the preternatural" (Chenu 1968, 14). It's William of Conches, not T. H. Huxley, who writes that "when modern divines," hear about the latest account of nature, "they hoot at it right away because they don't find it like this in the Bible . . . modern divines don't want us to inquire into anything that isn't in the scriptures, only to believe simply like a peasant" (ibid., 12).

The new intellectual interests of the twelfth century go hand in hand with a shift away from "monastic evangelism" to the poverty of the "genuine apostolic life." For the older tradition, "the apostles had been monks, and thus monks were the authentic successors to the apostles" (ibid., 206). The quest for the apostolic life may have begun in the cloister, but it quickly took hold among the urban clergy, spreading rapidly to the laity, who "were among the most effective promoters of the *vita apostolica*, the ideals and needs of which were far from being exhausted by the reform of the regular canons" (ibid., 219). Conservatives, notes Chenu, looked on all of this with great suspicion; those on the cutting edge saw the equality of all Christians. Chenu cites Gerhoh of Reichersberg, a particularly distinguished reforming canon:

> Whether rich or poor, noble or serf, merchant or peasant, all who are committed to the Christian faith reject everything inimical to this name and embrace everything conformable to it. Every order and absolutely every profession, in the catholic faith and according to apostolic teaching, has a rule adapted to its character; and under this rule it is possible by striving properly to achieve the crown of glory. [Ibid., 222]

Such a claim would have been outlandish in the previous two centuries and was positively offensive to the lords of the countryside (see Duby 1980, particularly ch. 24). The tools with which to defend the claims of equality, however, were being forged in the newly energized centers of theology.

By the middle of the twelfth century, "the schools became organized and their regulations established, the *licentia docendi* (license to teach) became the prerequisite for this now official title of master. The *licentia* certified one not only as a teacher, but as a theologian" (Chenu 1968, 276). Once again, the conflict between the conservatives and the innovators was open and loud. "At the heart of this difference," writes Chenu, "as shown by the origins of the *quaestio*, there was, in the service of an *intellectus fidei*, the search for causes and reasons. And this is the point upon which Rupert's faith gagged; to look for reasons was to lack respect for God who spoke" (ibid., 303). The outlandish innovation of the masters, from the perspective of Rupert, abbot of Deutz, was to put the pursuit of truth, as found in reasons and causes, before any deference to the old forms. The questions of the schools are the symbol of this defiance.

Placing the *quaestio* in this context suggests a rather different emphasis from Miller's. Inquiry hits a bump in the road, "a proposition carrying doubt" (Chenu 1964, 94). In order to continue it's necessary, in Peirce's phrase, to fix belief in a manner that makes it possible to move on. "The pro and con," writes Chenu, "are brought into play, not with the intention of finding an immediate answer, but in order that, under the action of *dubitatio*, research be pushed to the limit" (ibid.). Whatever the practice in the schools generally, Thomas was engaged in this sort of teaching early on. "Under the Dominican constitutions," writes Simon Tugwell:

> the students held their own sessions with their student master to discuss "difficulties and questions,"... so it was probably in Cologne that Albert first discovered that Thomas instinctively took on the role of the Master rather than that of the student in such a situation. [Tugwell 1988, 210]

By general disposition, even before he began lecturing at Paris in 1251, Thomas was practicing with his brethren the arts of "disputation" and "determination" that prepared bachelors for their "inception."[2]

---

[2] On this see Rashdall 1936, vol. I, 450–62. There is also some nice first hand material in the first three essays collected in Haskins 1929. For example, a student manual of Martino de Fano, professor of law in north-central Italy about the time Thomas began lecturing, describes "the right sort of master" as "one who teaches the necessary things and answers questions readily and satisfactorily, suffering contradiction willingly and giving for his assertions sound reasons based on holy writ." He recommends that the student "search out the reasons for the case, answering objections and seeking parallels...Do not waste time in saying these over by rote, but seek the meaning of the laws" (Haskins 1929, 75). While hard to reconstruct in detail, it is clear that teaching in the school of the master was not *simply* a matter of copying lectures. It was training in disputation and the poor master was likely to find his classroom deserted.

We're moving closer to understanding what Thomas was up to, but we're not quite there yet. What we're after is the equivalent of "Piero's peculiar pictorial idiom," and this means situating Thomas not in the generic atmosphere but in his order. Shortly after Thomas began teaching at Paris, Humbert of Romans became Master of the Order of Preachers and remained in this position for almost a decade, during which time Thomas became regent master at Paris and, in 1261, Conventual Lector at Orvieto, where he was charged with "regular teaching of those who were called the *fratres communes*, which is to say all those who had not been able to study in the *studia generalia* or even the *provincialia*—which was the case for nine out of ten friars" (Torrell 1996, 118–19). This teaching was directed to two ends: preaching and confession. What, according to Humbert, did a preacher need to know? First, there is "knowledge of the holy scriptures, because all preaching ought to be taken from them." Next, there is "knowledge of creatures... Those who know how to read this book well draw from it many things which are very serviceable for helping people grow." Third, "there is knowledge of historical stories. There are many stories told not only among believers but also among unbelievers, which can sometimes be very useful and edifying in a sermon" (Tugwell 1982, 216–17). Humbert finishes this off with knowledge of church law, the mysteries of the church, experience, discretion, and "finally there is knowledge of the Holy Spirit. This was the kind of knowledge which the first apostles had" (ibid., 218).

What were the tools available for imparting all this knowledge? Thomas, who was in the process of completing his *Summa contra Gentiles*, was aware of a number of well-known summaries and mirrors recently produced by his Dominican brothers (see Torrell 1996, 119). Leonard Boyle suggests that it was frustration with the available teaching tools which led Thomas to begin "a *Summa theologiae* at Rome soon after his move there from Orvieto in 1265. Perhaps, indeed, this is precisely why he moved" (Boyle 2002, 4). When Thomas writes that his intention is to provide the basics of Christian doctrine "in a manner appropriate to the instruction of beginners" (*ST*, pro.),[3] he should be

---

[3] I have taken as my text of Thomas that provided in the Corpus Thomisticum, accessible at <http://www.corpusthomisticum.org/>. In translating Thomas's *Summa Theologiae* I have consulted the older translation of the Brothers of the English Dominican Province, which is available in many forms, the handiest is the electronic version of the second, revised edition of 1920 available at <http://www.newadvent.org>. I have also consulted the relevant volumes of the Blackfriars edition, listed individually in the bibliography. When citing secondary works I have, of course, left whatever version the author provided.

taken seriously. And he is not in the least bit shy about why this needs to be done:

> Newcomers to this teaching are greatly hindered by various writings on the subject, partly because of the swarm of pointless questions, articles, and arguments, partly because essential information is given according to the requirements of textual commentary or the occasions of academic debate, not to sound educational method, partly because repetitiousness has bred boredom and muddle in their thinking. [Ibid]

The studium at Santa Sabina, the headquarters of the Dominicans in Rome, writes Boyle, "has the look of what I call a *'studium personale,'* a *studium* set up for or by a given master. The Anagni enactment of 1265 speaks of the students as 'studying with' Thomas, and makes no mention of any assistants or *Sublectores"* (Boyle 2002, 4). After spending the first year lecturing on book one of the Lombard's *Sentences*, "Thomas dropped the *Sentences* altogether and set out on a road of his own." Before being returned to Paris in 1268, "he had completed the *Prima secundae* and had compiled the massive *Secunda secundae"* (ibid., 6).

Consider the implications of Thomas's pedagogy for reading the *Summa Theologiae*. Thomas is completely in charge of a "young and presumably untried bunch of students" (ibid., 4). They have no experience with, nor expectations of, the components of Thomas's teaching. He may or may not have expressed his disdain for the currently available textbooks, but he leaves little doubt of his intention to stave off the "boredom and muddle" of repetition, not to mention the "swarm of pointless questions, articles, and arguments." His goal throughout is "to be concise and clear—brevitur ac delucide prosequi—so far as the matter allows" (*ST*, pro.). We're given every reason to believe that he intends the organization of the *Summa* to be as transparent as possible, with each component building on what comes before. When it comes to the second part of the second part, treating the topics closest to the pastoral concerns of preachers, this clarity is crucial.

Fortunately, Thomas is clear about his procedure and its relation to the first part of the second part: "After consideration of the virtues and vices generally, and other matter pertaining to morals, it is necessary to consider specifics, since talk about morals generally is not very helpful, actions are always about particulars" (*ST* IIaIIae, pro.). Of the ways of proceeding, "to resolve problems about virtues, gifts, vices, and precepts one after another would lead to much repetition" (ibid.). We know that this wouldn't be a good thing, therefore it is not surprising that "everything about morals be reduced to a consideration of the virtues, and that all the virtues be reduced to seven" (ibid.). The theological virtues of faith, hope, and charity define Christian life, and therefore come first. The cardinal virtues are then to be treated in their traditional order "as well as all the virtues and vices that pertain to them in any way. Thus no aspect of morals will be left out" (ibid.).

Good pedagogy, for Thomas, is best served by reducing the specifics of moral analysis to the relevant virtue. There is no talk here of duties, absolute or prima facie. If they come up, they'll be discussed explicitly and in conjunction with the appropriate virtue. Precepts, as Thomas uses the term, are the particular rules or demands of some law—Thomas speaks of *praeceptum caeremoniale, praeceptum ecclesiae, praeceptum tyrannicum* and a host of others—and are in themselves to be discussed in terms of the virtue they serve. There is no talk of presumptions of any sort, as best as I can tell; Thomas uses *praesumptio* only in the sense of audacity, be it virtuous or vicious. There is no talk whatsoever of "stacking the order of the objections" so as to affirm any duty, obligation, or presumption in Miller's sense. There is, then, only one further question to ask: why charity?

Miller suggests that if Thomas were interested in the positive duty to undertake a just war he would have discussed it under the aegis of justice, not charity (Miller 2002, 183). But this is to neglect the substance of Christian charity. Charity as a virtue is a gift of God, making it possible for individuals to enjoy friendship with God. This extends to our neighbors and even to our enemies, for "charity, which above all is friendship, reaches out to sinners whom we love for God's sake" (*ST* IIaIIae, 23, 1 ad 2 & 3). Charity is the principle virtue governing our relations with our neighbors. Those qualities and inclinations of human experience that pertain to it are joy, peace, mercy, kindness, almsgiving, and fraternal correction, each of which receives its own question. Those inclinations that work against charity originate in hatred. "Hatred of the neighbor," writes Thomas, "is the ultimate end of the progress of sin" (*ST* IIaIIae, 34, 6). When combined with indifference to virtue (35), it becomes active as envy and "the good of another conceived as an injury to the self, insofar as his own glory or excellence" (*ST* IIaIIae, 36, 1). Left unchecked, this leads to discord (37), which sets the stage for contention (38), schism (39), and war.

Had Miller followed the order of Thomas's exposition it would have been clear why war is best treated under the virtue of charity. He would also have noticed something odd about 40, 1. The preceding questions on acedia, envy, discord, contention, and schism begin the same way, with minor variations: is this a sin? But 40, 1, begins, "Primo, utrum aliquod bellum sit licitum." May some war be legitimate? This doesn't begin with any presumption against war, only the experience and discretion that come with growing up in thirteenth-century Italy. Thomas's family was deeply embroiled in the wars of the peninsula. Thomas's father was a knight on the side of Frederick II when hostilities broke out against the Pope. Thomas was probably two (see Tugwell 1988, 201–2). Over the course of his life Thomas remained closely involved with his family's affairs. "He remained feudally tied," writes Torrell, "to his milieu and his time, and his language constantly reminds us of that, as when he borrows the vocabulary and metaphors of chivalry and the military profession—something often overlooked" (Torrell 1996, 12). Anyone, even a Dominican brother, would have been personally familiar with destruction and death in war.

Nonetheless, Thomas follows the tradition of Augustine in finding that, when necessary for the protection of the community, war is not only legitimate, but a matter of virtue, imposed upon the authorities by their own sense of charity. War is an expression of the love of neighbor, including the enemy. The discussion of war is housed, so to speak, under charity because that is the primary motivating virtue for the Christian who sees his neighbors menaced by a threat. Note the way that Thomas uses this as a matter of course in discussing nonbelievers:

> They can be restrained by force so that they do not impede the faith, or blaspheme, or prosyletize or, indeed, persecute the faithful. And this is why Christ's faithful frequently engage nonbelievers in war, not so that they can force them to believe. [*ST* IIaIIae, 10, 8]

War is the charitable response to assaults on the faith. Since, by Thomas's lights, such an assault also constitutes a sin on the part of the nonbeliever, it is also an act of charity with regard to him as well. Fraternal correction is one of the benefits of charity. In this case correction is perhaps a by-product of the primary act of aiding the neighbor, but it is a good nonetheless. It is true that "military activities are distressing in the extreme; they greatly impede the soul from contemplating and praising God" (*ST* IIaIIae, 40, 2). Nonetheless, when undertaken by the right people, for the right reasons, in the right way, "to wage a just war is meritorious" (ibid., ad 4).

One last point should suffice. In his quest for clarity, Thomas plainly locates war where he does because its proper intention derives from charity. Justice and propriety constrain the movement of charity toward war. This is obvious in the traditional just-war criteria of question 40, article 1. It continues in play in article 2, where human and divine law, respectively, forbid merchants and clerics "to fight in war, not because it is a sin, but because it is inappropriate to their persons" (ibid., 2 ad 3). In article 3, ambushes are perfectly legitimate, but lying and breaking promises are not: "this is always illicit and nobody should deceive the enemy in such a manner" (ibid., 3). In the modern law of war it's called perfidy (Roberts and Guelff 2000, 442).

The "comparative method"

My point, in discussing Miller, has been to illustrate what Baxandall's self-critical moods look like when trained on the interpretation of Thomas's moral thought. There is no way to *prove* Miller's, or any other reading, wrong. A clever reader can always account for why the plain meaning should be rejected. This was Miller's strategy with prima facie duties. But if we hold ourselves accountable to legitimacy, order, and necessity it is possible to get a fairly sophisticated ordering of interpretations. This is the "comparative method" in religion and ethics. It's a fine-grained comparison of competing interpretations based on the back and forth between close reading and history. It is not the grand comparative enterprise associated with, for example, van der Leeuw's *Religion in Essence and Manifestation*. The English title, perhaps more than the German *Phänomenolgie der Religion*, offers up something I don't believe we can get, or that we need. Van der Leeuw announces in his preface that, "In accordance with the views of Jaspers, I have tried to avoid, above all else, any imperiously dominating theory, and in the Volume there will be found neither evolutionary, nor so-called anti-evolutionary, nor indeed any other theories" (1938, 10). But in his Epilegomena, van der Leeuw talks freely of "homo religiosus" and of "religion" as "always directed towards salvation, never towards life itself as it is given; and in this respect all religion, with no exception, is the religion of deliverance" (ibid., 682). This is either vapid or false; probably it's both. From Hume and Schleiermacher to the present, the tradition of grand comparison has been devoted to one or another agenda, be it laughing believers out of town, exalting Protestant Christianity as the pinnacle of human experience, or latching onto the sacred as the existential center which deracinated modern man longs to recover.

But the cautious comparative endeavor I'm advocating is a much more powerful tool of inquiry. If we are interested in the ways that individuals and groups act, then the place to begin is with what they say, because this is the initial entry into the beliefs that motivate their actions. The reason for beginning with Peirce and closing the circle with Baxandall is to emphasize that understanding isn't about theory in the abstract, or even about the best available explanation; the object of inquiry is truth. We want to know why these people said and did what they said and did. Seeking truth doesn't mean denying the limits of inquiry, however. Another reason for taking the path from Peirce to Baxandall is to emphasize the difficulty of assembling and understanding the available evidence. If truth is saying of what is that it is, then justification is about the quality of the evidence and the circumspection of the inquiry. The Ptolemaic system could technically deal with the individual perturbations that kept presenting themselves, but for cutting-edge investigators it became more and more incapable of allaying their doubts. "Those who have devised eccentric systems," wrote Copernicus, "though they appear to have well-nigh established the seeming motions by calculations agreeable to their assumptions, have yet made many admissions which seem to violate the first principle of uniformity in motion" (Kuhn 1957, 138–39). Baxandall's worries about even his own preliminary interpretation of Piero speak to the same need to fix belief, not just with a satisfying theory, but with a true account.

Peirce's concern for truth as the object of inquiry doesn't merely separate his pragmatism from the standard reading of James and Dewey, it motivates my deployment of Davidson against contemporary temptations of theory in the study of religion: cognitive studies and postmodernist power studies. Only a fool would deny the importance of a healthy and functioning brain to the ability of humans to act on their beliefs, but most of the time you don't need to know anything about Tom's brain to understand why he prefers roast beef to scungilli. Similarly, there are occasions where an analysis based in Foucault will be illuminating. Part of the appeal of such postmodern analyses can be traced to Edward Said's brilliant unmasking of "orientalism" as a component of mainstream American culture. Academic critics of Said typically missed the point, but for a stereotypically alienated Princeton graduate student to read his account of the P-rade was pure illumination.[4] Said uses a combination of history and ethnography to illustrate the way a particular group could be transformed into a symbol that identified insiders from outsiders, good guys from bad guys, and enlisted both nature and society on the side of the insiders.

---

[4] For those who have never experienced it, the P-rade is central to the festivities of the annual Princeton reunions. The younger reunion classes have distinctive costumes; at some point the older classes graduate to more decorous orange blazers. It is an event that calls out for Durkheimian analysis. Said writes that, "the costume for Princeton's tenth-reunion class in 1967 had been planned before the June War." He describes the generically Arab garb and continues, "after the war, when it had become clear that the Arab motif was an embarrassment, a change in the reunion plans was decreed. Wearing the costume as had been originally planned, the class was now to walk in procession, hands above heads in a gesture of abject defeat" (Said 1978, 285).

My critique of Miller was intended to illustrate the ways in which Baxandall's conditions of production, period eye, and *troc* could be translated into the study of moral theology. At the same time it was intended to advance an argument in favor of Baxandall's self-critical demand for legitimacy, order, and necessity. Doubt is the natural product of competing interpretations, which are themselves the precondition for comparative ethics, as opposed to parallel doxographies. If we want to know what people said and did in matters moral, we need to compare interpretations with an eye to eliminating some and using others as the starting points for further inquiry. Those who hope to find moral or policy guidance in comparative ethics and religion are likely to feel disappointed. Ethics, as Fingarette noted, is as cognitive as can be, but it is also regulative, "the norm and the declaration of it being justified by the process and goal of inquiry" (1951, 635). This is a different form of inquiry than comparative ethics in my sense. But that doesn't mean that a commitment to pragmatic inquiry can have no impact on our normative judgments.

8

From Comparisons to Cases

Pragmatism and the politics of virtue

This book has been about how to study ethics and religion comparatively, not what we should believe or how, as believers, we should act. My pragmatists, as students of ethics and religion, treat their subjects as, for the most part, rational agents, acting on what they take to be justified, true beliefs in order to achieve goods, solve problems, and avoid difficulties. I say "for the most part" because any population is likely to have its share of deluded or self-deceived individuals, some even pathological, who will not be able to explain their actions to themselves or to others. This will skew their beliefs about what counts as a good, a problem, or a probable difficulty. Since coming to any judgment, or drawing any conclusion, involves normative acts, there is not likely to be any hard-and-fast line to be drawn between the moral and the nonmoral. Members of the community will have to argue that out for themselves and inquirers will need to register the nature and outcomes of those arguments.

There is nothing inherent in a pragmatist stance to inquiry that dictates one belief over and against another. But there are likely to be certain habits of investigation that prompt questions of justification, about themselves and their subjects. Gilbert Harman, for instance, describes "the naive view" of morality as involving "one or more basic moral demands that everyone accepts, or has reasons to accept, as demands on everyone on which all moral reasons to do things depend" (Harman 1978, 39). Harman, in a move that will sound familiar to the pragmatist, immediately asks "who?" and "why?" We've already had occasion, actually several occasions, to notice that people have believed incompatible beliefs at different times and places without falling into irrationality. So who should we include within the "everyone?"

Robert George, following John Finnis and Germain Grisez, seems to think we should include all human beings who have acknowledged basic human goods and the standing imperative to refrain from any action that would undermine or subvert such goods. Rather than enumerating George's goods, it will be helpful to watch him in action:

> Marriage, considered not as a mere legal convention, but, rather, as a two-in-one-flesh communion of persons that is consummated and actualized by sexual acts of the reproductive type, is an intrinsic (or, in our parlance, "basic") human good. [George 1999, 139]

Putting aside, for the moment, the language of "communion," take a look at what happens when this basic human good is coupled with a second, "the basic human good of integrity" (ibid.). For me to use anyone as a means to my own gratification is an attack on his or her integrity, even if that other person willingly, perhaps eagerly, seeks to engage in the activity. Since any attack on a basic human good is immoral, this rules out prostitution, homosexual acts, masturbation, oral sex of any sort, in fact, any sexual acts other than those of the "reproductive type" within the friendly confines of the "one-flesh communion" of marriage.

The language of communion, it turns out, is central to distinguishing marriage proper from the fictive marriages of mutual utility.[1] But my pragmatist wants to know how, exactly, this language comes to be so central to marriage as a concept. A dip into the fieldwork, historical and anthropological, doesn't suggest that the notion is widespread (see Burguier et al. 1996). If pressed, George is ready to fall back on the fact that "intrinsic value cannot, strictly speaking, be demonstrated ... it must be grasped in non-inferential acts of understanding." This, in turn, involves both "imaginative reflection on data provided by inclination and experience, as well as knowledge of empirical patterns." In the end, it turns out that "longstanding features of our legal and religious traditions testify to the intrinsic value of marriage as a two-in-one-flesh communion" (George 1999, 143). George seems unconcerned that American matrimonial law is one of the few places where the language of communion looks even plausible, not least because it retains substantial vestiges of the clerical language of medieval marriage. Even Justice Douglas, in Griswold, writes of marriage as "a coming together for better or worse, hopefully enduring, and intimate to the degree of being sacred" (Shapiro 1995, 29).[2]

---

[1] George develops this argument on pp. 140–44. For more details see Davis 2001.

[2] For the medieval origins of the theology of marriage, see Brooke 1989. Brundage 1987 provides an exhaustive survey of sex and marriage law from antiquity into the sixteenth century. His appendix 3, "Survivals of Medieval Law," illustrates the persistence of medieval mores. He cites, for example, a 1974 case in which the defendant argued that "the sodomy

Nothing prohibits the pragmatist from embracing Catholicism and even George's position, which Julie Rubio traces to "the words of St. John Chrysostom, who wrote that with their children, husband and wife constitute a three-in-one flesh unity" (Rubio 2010, 29). But as a student of ethics and religion, the pragmatist must be skeptical of the claim that this language, grounded in the history of Christian theology, represents "an important insight into the nature of marriage" (George 1999, 144). In particular, the pragmatist is likely to doubt the claim that "one either understands that spousal genital intercourse has a special significance... or something blocks that understanding and one does not perceive correctly" (ibid.). This sounds a bit too much like fixing belief through the method of authority or its fellow traveller, the *a priori*.

I don't want to leave the appearance, however, that only conservatives kick against the pricks of pragmatist inquiry. In an article from 1999, Harman writes that:

> It seems that ordinary attributions of character traits to people are often deeply misguided and it may even be the case that there is no such thing as character, no ordinary character traits of the sort people think there are, none of the usual moral virtues and vices. [Harman 1999, 165]

The argument for this conclusion rests on identifying the "fundamental attribution error" (ibid., 166). Also called the "correspondence bias," this refers to the tendency, when observing behavior, to conclude that "the person who performed the behavior was predisposed to do so" (Gilbert and Malone 1995, 21). John Doris, in a recent volume cited by Harman, calls it "overattribution" (Doris 2002, 93).[3]

Imagine the following situation. At the very same time in the very same supermarket, separated by half a dozen check-out lines, Jack and Bernie each give the cashier a ten-dollar bill for a five-dollar sandwich. The cashier, having put the bill in the till, counts out fifteen dollars.

---

statute enacted Judeo-Christian religious taboos into public law and hence that it breached the constitutional separation of Church and State" (1987, 613). Brundage goes on to write that, while the appeals court rejected the argument, the California legislature "has now eliminated references to the 'crime against nature' and decriminalized oral and anal sex acts between consenting adults" (ibid.). For marriage law within the modern Catholic church, see not only John Noonan 1972, but his 1965 as well. For a recent account of Catholic thought on marriage, from a perspective substantially different than George's, see Rubio 2010.

[3] Candace Upton has sketched three phases in the development of the "situationist debate," from the early 1990s to the present (Upton 2009). This essay appears in a volume dedicated to the ins and outs of the debate. My sense is that the purported evidence against character is directed at a caricature of virtue held by no one, and that the evidence of Milgram etc. can adequately be handled by the good, old-fashioned, Aristotelian notion of *akrasia*, probably along the lines suggested by Davidson 1970.

Both men say, "excuse me ma'am, but I believe you've given me too much" and then return the extra ten dollars. As they depart, the cashier says to the next person in line, "My it's refreshing to encounter such a decent, honest fellow!"

The cashier's judgment, as uplifting as it is, isn't licensed by the evidence. Put simply, for all we know Jack is an unrepentant utilitarian who initially calculated that that the good he could do with the extra ten was substantially greater than the tiny loss suffered by the supermarket, but he returned the money out of fear that someone else might have noticed the error and that he would be exposed and ridiculed. Bernie, for all we know, is the individual of character, for whom the very idea of keeping the excess is unthinkable. Or maybe they're both cads, or neither. The point is that in an isolated case such as this we don't have enough familiarity with the actors to justify attributing much of anything.

If that were the only point Harman and Doris were making, it wouldn't warrant much discussion; but they seem to be claiming more. What does Harman mean when he archly suggests that "it may even be the case that there is no such thing as character... none of the usual moral virtues and vices?" (1999, 165). He might mean that there are no such things as habits, of which virtues and vices are subspecies, but this seems implausible. Our ability to carry on ordinary conversation depends on acquiring an array of habits that dispose us to respond to bits of verbal behavior in others with a range of behavior on our part. Even if I don't immediately respond to "How's it going?" with "Not bad; how's by you?" the available options are limited. If I break into Donald O'Connor's "make 'em laugh" routine from *Singin' in the Rain*, I had better be ready to offer an explanation. Conversation is made possible by forming habits of response.

This is true of more than talking, of course. Almost any regular daily activity relies on habits, whether it be driving, shaving, or zipping up your pants. Perhaps Harman is relying on the requirement that "character traits" be "*broad-based* dispositions that help to explain what they are dispositions to do" (1999, 167). But it's not clear exactly what this means. He cites young Herbert, who refuses to ride roller-coasters, but is otherwise not particularly cowardly. It would be odd to call Herbert a coward; the inclination is to say he has a quirk about roller-coasters. Plausible attributions of virtue and vice are based on a fairly wide range of experience with the agent in question, so if Herbert avoided not only roller-coasters but bicycles and motorcycles as well, began to get visibly nervous every time the car went over forty, and flattened himself against the subway station wall until the car had come to a complete standstill, we might reasonably say that he was cowardly. If, on the other hand, he failed to jump onto the tracks to save the escaped puppy from the oncoming A train, that probably wouldn't be a strike against him. What if he failed to rescue his own toddler? That would be a tougher call.

The point is not to force a decision about Herbert, but to insist that attributing virtue and vice is always a statement of probabilities trailing a big *ceteris paribus* clause. So, to say that Herb is an honest man registers the belief that, all things being equal, he can be counted on not just to say he would return the extra ten dollars, but to do it. To say that Muriel is a jealous woman indicates that, all things being equal, she is likely to disparage those people who have something she values. Virtues and vices are not mechanisms, churning out identical results over and over. Thus it's hard to see the point of Harman's recourse to the experiments of Milgram and others. In the case of Milgram's shock experiment, the forty test subjects are led to believe that they are merely part of the apparatus, that the actual subject is the individual receiving the shock, and that the experiment has been designed and sanctioned by Yale University. "Typical subjects," writes Milgram, "were postal clerks, high-school teachers, salesmen, engineers, and laborers" (Milgram 1963, 372). Milgram acknowledges that these and other factors contribute to the observed responses. In particular, he notes a conflict in many of his subjects, which he attributes to "the opposition of two deeply ingrained behavior dispositions: first, the disposition not to harm other people, and second, the tendency to obey those whom we perceive to be legitimate authorities" (ibid., 378). Milgram, in fact, sees his experiment as confirming the existence of two sorts of habit, at least one of which would seem to count as a virtue. So it's odd to find Harman and others taking this as evidence for the non-existence of character traits. In any case, there is not much of a case here against the cautious and well-founded use of character language, when appropriate, to explain individual actions and make judgments.

Comparative ethics and the study of abortion

Fortunately, I'm not committed to resolving these points of contemporary moral theory here. My obligation in this final chapter is only to show that comparative religion and ethics, in the pragmatic style I'm recommending, can make a substantive contribution to understanding a contentious moral debate. In the previous chapter, I illustrated the method by comparing competing interpretations of Thomas Aquinas, but there is no reason to confine ourselves exclusively to historical figures. Contemporary issues are fair game as well. But, as with Aquinas, those issues will still have to be located in their historical and ethnographic settings. A recent essay by Anthony Kenny seems headed toward realizing the pragmatist's desiderata, announcing at the very beginning "a survey of some of the ancient answers to this problem within Greek philosophy, in rabbinic texts and among Christian thinkers," as well as "the Warnock Committee that offered a *terminus ante quem* for the origin of individual human life, namely the 14th day" (Kenny 2008, 167). For Kenny, determining the beginning of the individual is important because "any argument that is used to justify abortion, or IVF, or stem-cell research must undergo the following test: would the same argument justify infanticide? If so, then it must be rejected" (ibid., 168).

In the course of his opening survey Kenny provides much useful material, including an account of Aquinas's condemnation of masturbation, a view "natural in the context of a biological belief that only the male gamete provides the active element in conception." In that context "masturbation is then the same kind of thing, on a minor scale, as the exposure of an infant" (ibid.). Kenny concludes "that there is no such thing as *the* Christian consensus on the timing of the origin of the human individual" (ibid., 169). There were many positions and down to the present the question has tended toward confusion. "Life" and "human life" are generic notions, and homicide, which is the issue at hand, is never generic.

It's worth pausing for a minute to be very clear about what's at stake here. At various points Rawls, for example, uses abortion to illustrate the consequences of adopting his approach to political reasoning. In what seems to have been the last published instance, he writes:

> when hotly disputed questions, such as that of abortion, arise which may lead to a stand-off between different political conceptions, citizens must vote on the question according to their complete ordering of political values . . . Some may, of course, reject a legitimate decision, as Roman Catholics may reject a decision to grant a right to abortion. They may present an argument in public reason for denying it and fail to win a majority. But they need not themselves exercise the right to abortion. [Rawls 1997, 606]

Here Rawls, who acknowledges his own commitment to abortion rights in the first trimester, seems unwilling to acknowledge the sort of point Kenny is making. But this point is crucial, and not only for religious conservatives. It is important to get clear on the beginning of an individual's life because, once an individual becomes a member of the community, a very high burden of proof must be met before you can kill him or her. Abortion is not a public policy decision of the same sort as raising taxes or seizing property under eminent domain and however you come down on the issue it's as irresponsible in a citizen to ignore it as it is to ignore the death penalty or targeting civilians in war.

But this doesn't mean that Kenny endorses the official Catholic teaching on abortion, which maintains that "from the time that the ovum is fertilized, a life is begun which is neither that of the father nor the mother," and thus condemns direct abortion "since it is the deliberate killing of an innocent human being" (John Paul II 1995, secs. 60–62). Kenny develops a familiar argument that, even after conception, it is not the case that there is an individual human being. At fertilization the resultant embryo has a specific "blueprint," but "in the case of human beings the possibility of two individuals answering to the same specification is not just a logical possibility: it is a possibility that is realized in the case of identical twins" (Kenny 2008, 172). The temptation to see this as a piece of philosophical legerdemain should be resisted. We should want our policies to do right by fetuses, but they should also do right by women and by all those who might benefit from IVF and embryonic stem-cell research (see ibid., 173). If there is no individual there is no homicide and Kenny is on firm ground in maintaining that before the fourteenth day after fertilization there is no individual. Of course, as he notes, the argument cuts both ways. If, after day fourteen, there is at least one individual, "then late abortion is indeed homicide—and abortion becomes 'late' at an earlier date than was ever dreamt of by Aquinas" (ibid., 174).

Up to this point we have followed Kenny, but we can add something that was advertised but not forthcoming, a discussion of rabbinic texts. Rabbinic teaching on abortion begins with a passage from the *Mishnah*:

> If a woman was in hard travail, the child must be cut up while it is in the womb and brought out member by member, since the life of the mother has priority over the life of the child; but if the greater part of it was already born, it may not be touched, since the claim of one life cannot override the claim of another life. [Danby 1933, Oholoth 7:6]

The text is compressed, but the lesson taken by the rabbis has been unambiguous. The fetus is not *nefesh adam*, not a human being. Once it is born, it is a human being though, writes David Feldman, "we may not be sure that the newborn babe has completed its term and is a *bar kayyama*, fully viable, until thirty days after birth . . . If he dies before his thirtieth day, no funeral or shivah rites are applicable" (Feldman 1986, 384). Fred Rosner notes that, while abortion is required if a pregnancy endangers the mother, it is permissable "if the mother becomes pregnant while nursing a child," for example, "and the pregnancy changes her milk so that the suckling's life is endangered." Under such circumstances, "considerable Rabbinic opinion would permit abortion" (Rosner 1968, 265).

Feldman's *Birth Control, Contraception, and Abortion in Jewish Law* remains the standard text on these matters, but even rabbis who consider the benefits of making "Jewish abortion laws as unconditional as Noahide abortion law seems to be," cite other sections of the *Mishnah* to the end that "inasmuch as a Jewish mother can be saved from a threatening fetus, *it is possible that this is also the case with a non-Jewish mother as well,*" on the principle that "where a fetus threatens the mother's life, it is considered part of her body and may be amputated as one would amputate a gangrenous limb" (Novak 1974, 271). Neither Feldman nor Novak consider abortion acceptable for population control or to maintain economic security—though were people to adopt such strategies they might be despicable, but they would not be guilty of murder.[4] As Feldman puts it, "the difference between fetal life and human life is not determined by the biologist or the physician . . . It's the determination of the culture or the religion that declares not when life begins but when life begins to be human" (Feldman 1986, 384).

Before returning to Kenny, let's add another voice to the mix. William LaFleur's *Liquid Life: Abortion and Buddhism in Japan* self-consciously sets out to bring together ethnography, history, and ethics to explain a cemetery in Kamakura, where he picked up a pamphlet that reads, in part:

> The Kannon is a Buddhist deity whose special task is to help raise healthy children. Many people come and set up small statues, representing their children, so that he can watch over them. More recently, parents have set up statues for miscarried, aborted, or dead-born babies, for the Kannon to protect. These are called Mizuko-jizo and in the Hase-dera there are about 50,000 such Jizos. Mothers and fathers often visit the Mizuko-jizo to pray for the souls of the children they have lost. [LaFleur 1992, 4]

That parents would set up shrines at which to pray for their aborted children might seem "counterintuitive." Richard Gardner relates the response of R. J. Zwi Werblowsky, who:

> is clearly opposed to the practice of *mizuko kuyo* in all of its forms and identifies some of the factors enabling the rise of this "new religion" as the greed of the "gynecologist mafia" and some Buddhist institutions, and the total lack of any theory of social practice within Buddhism. [Gardner 1998, 114]

---

[4] In a more recent discussion, Elliot Dorf warns that "abortion should not be used flippantly as a retroactive form of birth control" but reaffirms the view that "abortion is normally forbidden not as murder but as self-injury" (Dorf 2003, 117).

Werblowsky's essay, published shortly before the appearance of *Liquid Life*, is even more intemperate than Gardner suggests, discussing in outraged detail professional failures of previous scholars, the financial demands of the temples—"Let us not discuss prices and fees at this stage" (Werblowsky 1991, 309)—and the debate against birth control pills that renders abortion "the only legal method of birth control... The pill is dispensed only against specific medical prescription; otherwise doctors prefer abortion to contraception" (ibid., 310). But to cover all of the topics that Werblowsky engages would take us much too far afield.

The most interesting aspect of Werblowsky's article for our purposes comes out in the following remark:

> At the risk of repeating ourselves, let us recall that the attitude of Japanese Buddhists to *mizuko kuyo* is an equivocal affair. There is no doubt that any form of taking life (and life begins at the moment of conception) is a grave matter and generates the worst possible karma. But Buddhism has no theory or practice of concerted social action. Hence a violently anti-abortionist pamphlet like that by Bhikkhu Nyanasobhano (1989) can state the correct Buddhist view, but falls short of advocating an anti-abortionist crusade. [Ibid., 330]

Here's an approach to religion and ethics that might have come from the Danto of *Mysticism and Morality*. The "correct" Buddhist view is that of the classical texts, as interpreted by a contemporary monk. Taking life is not a matter of interpersonal duties or virtues, but a problem because of its karma. Because it lacks the resources for generating a systematic ethics in the western sense, Buddhism also lacks the resources for generating a "theory or practice of concerted social action."

Contrast this with LaFleur's approach. Having noted the puzzle created by the cemetery, LaFleur goes on to explain that Hase-dera is in no way unique. The Purple Cloud Temple, "began its existence as a memorial park to provide rites almost exclusively for deliberately aborted fetuses" (ibid., 5). LaFleur describes the rows of child-sized statues with inexpensive jewelry and bibs. Among the visitors, "one finds there a surprisingly large number of children... there is even a small playground in the middle of the cemetery where children can be seen enjoying themselves" (ibid., 9). How, he asks, is the institutionalization of abortion to be squared with the first precept of Buddhism, "I will not willingly take the life of a living thing?" (ibid., 11).

One of the first things LaFleur does is point out that non-Japanese Buddhists are often perplexed and that not all Japanese are comfortable with the practice either. But even given these conflicts, those who do memorialize their aborted progeny do not try to minimalize or deny what they have done; "many Japanese Buddhists," LaFleur points out, "committed by their religion to refrain from taking life, will nonetheless have an abortion and in doing so refer to the aborted fetus as a child, one that clearly has been alive" (ibid.). In part. abortion comes to be understood in terms of the cycle of birth and death, relating the profane world of adults to the sacred world of spirits and buddhas. Birth and death are passages from one world into another and abortions simply retard the passage from the sacred to the profane world, perhaps because it just wasn't their time (see LaFleur 1992, 31–37).

The middle sections of the book are given over to tracing the development of religious, social, and demographic issues as they interact in early modern and modern Japan, culminating in the Eugenic Protection Law of 1948 and the emergence of abortion as the principal form of contraception for Japanese women (LaFleur 1992, 136). This sets the background for *mizuko kuyo*. "To explore kuyo," writes LaFleur:

> it is first of all important to see that on one level it is shared throughout the Buddhist world in Asia. The root concept comes from the Sanskrit term *pujana*, which refers to those acts of ritual and worship through which Buddhists express their respect for the Buddha, the Teaching, and the Community. [Ibid., 143]

In many of these cultures rites have been extended to the dead and in Japan they have been extended to inanimate objects. "I have been present at temple services," he continues, "where men and women who practice the Japanese tea ceremony bring forward the small bamboo tea whisks which are presented to the altar...and then ritually burned—a kind of Buddhist 'cremation' of a tea whisk" (ibid., 145).

In the case of animals, which also receive *kuyo*, many Japanese combine well-wishes with regret; "these rituals are not just matters of thanks. There is also an element of apology in them" (ibid., 146). This makes the *mizuko kuyo* easier to interpret. Just as Buddhists throughout Asia offer rites to the dead, so too do the Japanese, though they have extended it to non-human animals and even inanimate objects. The aborted fetus entered into the lives of its parents, for which they are thankful, but for whatever reasons it has been felt necessary to terminate the pregnancy and let that spirit wait for a more propitious occasion to return to this world. LaFleur illustrates the resources provided in post-war Japan for dealing in local Buddhist terms with whatever stresses and traumas might be provoked by the emergence of abortion as contraception. "In Japanese," he write, "the differentiation between words of apology and words of thanks is often not sharp...But, as has been argued here before, conceptual imprecision often makes for ease of performance. Apology can overlap with gratitude" (ibid., 147). In lieu of more detailed ethnography, it is enough to acknowledge that these particular people, in these particular circumstances, find themselves in a position to employ practices grounded in Buddhist tradition to address a new situation.

It's not hard to imagine Werblowsky and similar scholars responding, "this isn't Buddhism." He states emphatically that "Christianity does not countenance abortion (just as Buddhism does not)" (1991, 327). But neither Japanese Buddhists nor, for that matter, Christians of any sort, are under obligation to accept these pronouncements. Religions develop and, according to LaFleur, while "the notion that religion is somehow inimical to modernization" may be a common one in the West, it is "openly and emphatically rejected by a lot of Japanese" (1992, 157). Central to my argument is the idea that ethics and religion can be studied the way that other scholars study the art world. The critic, if he hopes to say something both interesting and true, had better have a self-critical grasp of the relevant histories and debates.

A pragmatist perspective on the ethics of abortion

When Danto turns from reading Baxandall to writing about the contemporary art world, he takes the relevant historical understandings with him, but he also takes his knowledge of the contemporary situation and his judgments moral, political, and aesthetic. In discussing the Whitney Biennial 2000, Danto opens with the story of a friend taking an Asian child for a school visit in New York. "The visitors," he writes:

> were shown a chapel, no longer greatly used for devotional purposes but deemed a sight worth seeing. The child was shaken by a picture of Jesus, bleeding and nailed to the cross. "What have they done to that poor man?" she asked, in pained incredulity. [Danto 2007, 19]

This leads Danto to remark on a sign at the Whitney admissions desk: "Sections of the exhibition present artwork or other material that may not be appropriate for some viewers, including children" (ibid.). He uses the child's response to illustrate not only the disparate impact of images common to one culture, but also the dubious political authority of "the forces of artistic repression in our society" (ibid., 20). An image of a man nailed to a couple of posts, his almost nude body wounded and bleeding would be taken by most of the world as inhumanly brutal; Christians see it as an object of devotion. Danto contrasts this to Hans Haacke's "widely deplored installation, *Sanitation*, in which declarations by various politicians, hostile to contemporary art, are lettered on the wall" (ibid.). Because the lettering was done in Fraktur, an angled, broken typeface designed in the early sixteenth century and widely used in German-speaking countries into the twentieth century, Haake was accused of calling Mayor Giuliani, along with Jesse Helms, Pat Robertson, and Pat Buchanan, Nazis. Not altogether unreasonable, since the installation also included garbage cans with speakers playing marching sounds. On the floor Haacke framed a passage from the first amendment. The obvious interpretation is that, while right-wing politicians attempt to suppress freedom of speech by denouncing art they don't approve of as garbage, they themselves are the heirs of the totalitarian regimes America was founded to oppose and the real garbage is coming from them. Nonetheless, Haacke was accused, among other things, of "trivializing the Holocaust," a notion that makes no sense when the installation is interpreted in the light of Baxandall's "inferential criticism." The art alert at the admissions desk, writes Danto, "can be interpreted only as a gesture of deference to the politicians Haacke has quoted" (ibid.). It is a sign that Haacke, and we ourselves, are right to be worried about right-wing assaults on our freedoms.

As a piece of art, Danto doesn't seem much interested in *Sanitation*. He is much more taken by Paul Pfeiffer's *Fragment of a Crucifixion (After Francis Bacon)*:

> At first glance it shows a black athlete standing alone on a stadium floor, distantly surrounded by crowds of spectators . . . The film is a very short loop: The athlete endlessly advances, retreats, advances retreats, advances, retreats. One could let it go at that, until one notices the title. [Ibid., 24]

The connection to Bacon, made explicit in the title, points the viewer toward the tortured visual world of that artist. According to Danto, Pfeiffer "has modified this through digitalization, transforming it into something enough like a painting by Bacon to convert the shout into a scream" (ibid.). Lost in the deafening noise of a distant crowd, the situation "becomes something resembling the lonely space of a Roman arena in which someone has suffered or is undergoing suffering for the entertainment of the prurient crowd" (ibid.). From the chapel crucifixion that horrified a child, dodging the repressive threats of a thuggish political atmosphere, a little masterpiece appears and this Danto offers as something, in his judgment, that observers of the art world should embrace.

There is no reason that the moralist shouldn't approach the problems that interest him in the same way. My pragmatic comparativist has assembled several approaches to the brief "think about abortion as a topic of moral concern." What do they tell him? A certain strand of Christian thinking holds that the fetus is a fully vested member of the human community, whom it would be murderously wicked to attack. Most Jews and some Japanese Buddhists maintain than the fetus is not a full-fledged member of the human community. Its life should not be taken lightly, but to cut it up, piece by piece, and remove it from a woman's body is not murder. Being conceived and being born are both requirements for living a full, and fully choice-worthy, human life, but the different groups disagree about the necessity of birth.

This is a disagreement, at one level, about the facts. One group believes that fetuses are entitled to full recognition, while the other, for various reasons, doesn't. Both groups agree that much of the physical makeup of the individual depends on the particular sequences of base-pairs in the DNA. But nobody believes that's the whole story about individual persons. Once we get beyond the doctrinaire posturing of both sides, everyone will agree that who you become is also dependent on the social and cultural position of your parents, the particular time and place where you happen to be born, and the many choices made for you and by you in the course of the maturation process. Most people on both sides are going to reject infanticide, so Kenny's worry is not in play. Those who opt for birth, however, are likely to reject Kenny's view that "we must deploy concepts that are fundamental to our thinking over a wide range of disciplines, such as those of actuality and potentiality, identity and individuation: and these are the subject matter of metaphysics" (Kenny 2008, 170). If we take seriously the lessons of Douglas and Davidson, we should begin with the particular idiolect and the attitudes and expectations associated with the community within which that language was learned. Since all discourse, including moral discourse, begins in *medias res* the rabbis did not need to seek out a metaphysician to chair their deliberations. They accepted the received wisdom communicated by tradition and built their own deliberations on those foundations. Later generations did the same.

Pre-birth advocates may be tempted to say that that's fine for Jews, but the discourse of contemporary America is framed by another set of attitudes and expectations. Many will turn to John Noonan's "An Almost Absolute Value in History," with its conclusion that:

> when life must be taken to save life, reason alone cannot say that a mother must prefer a child's life to her own. With this exception, now of great rarity, abortion violates the rational humanist tenet of the equality of human lives. [Noonan 1970, 58]

187

Noonan argues that in the Christian tradition, the pagan toleration of abortion and infanticide was rejected in favor of "the commands of the Old Testament to love God with all your heart (Deut. 6:5) and to love your neighbor as yourself (Lev. 19:18)" (ibid., 7). The love commandments that became the New Law were developed to condemn "the offense of abortion," which "was seen as an offense against God because it attacked what He had made. It was associated with the sinful use of drugs to prevent birth and with the slaying of the child" (ibid., 10). The Fathers of the Church affirmed this position and it was perpetuated into the early modern period by theologians and church councils. The casuists of the modern period discussed therapeutic abortion, specifically to preserve the life of the mother, culminating in the work of Alfonso de' Liguori, who:

> held that Sanchez's opinion permitting the intentional killing of the unformed fetus was a probable opinion. But the "more common opinion" held that as it was never licit to expel the seed, even in rape, "so much less is it lawful to expel the fetus which is closer to human life." The more common opinion was "safer" and therefore to be followed. [Ibid., 31]

While the alternative was "probable," meaning held by a recognized authority, thus making it theologically reasonable to "question the absolute prohibition," Noonan notes that "an opposite tendency, to reinforce the prohibition, may be discerned in the legislative activity of the papacy" (ibid., 32). This tendency has persisted into the present.

But what does this show? At most, it shows an arch of analysis within the Catholic magisterial tradition. How and to what extent that tradition should be allowed to shape the discussion remains up in the air. As Ian Shapiro writes:

> That government should regulate or limit women's access to abortion in order to protect the fetus is a relatively recent idea in American law and politics. Historically its emergence seems to have been linked to the increase in abortions sought by white, Protestant, married middle- and upper-class women (as opposed to poor women of other races) in the mid-to-late nineteenth century, and the threat to the existing social order that these developments implied. [Shapiro 1995, 4]

Justice Blackmun had already reached the same opinion, noting that "it has been argued occasionally that these laws were the product of a Victorian social concern to discourage illicit sexual conduct," only to remark that "no court or commentator has taken the argument seriously" (ibid., 57). If law is a sort of barometer for social attitudes, the American situation has never been systematically settled.

This comes out nicely in James Gustafson's "A Protestant Ethical Approach." Rather than adopting the Catholic argument, Gustafson imagines a pregnant woman "in her early twenties. She is a lapsed Catholic, with no significant religious affiliation at the present time... Her pregnancy occurred when she was raped by her former husband and three other men" (Gustafson 1970, 107). Gustafson identifies medical, legal, financial, spiritual, and emotional factors as relevant to the moralist's judgment, in addition to three moral factors: the sanctity of life; rape as "a morally evil deed;" and the relation of ethics to the law (ibid., 112). In coming to a decision, the moralist is not "a systems analyst," but rather an advisor acting out of "respect and concern for the person" (ibid.). Weighing all the salient aspects of the case, Gustafson concludes that, "(a) if I were in the woman's human predicament I believe I could morally justify an abortion, and thus: (b) I would affirm its moral propriety in this instance" (ibid., 117).

It's difficult to know what to make of this. Gustafson clearly believes that there is something important about the rape. This is a common view and many recommendations cite it as an exemption to a proposed ban on abortion, but if the issue is about status in the moral community, it is not clear why. We don't think it is fair to punish children for the crimes of their parents. Pre-birth advocates would seem to be committed to protecting the fetus from any attack and so there is little traction for this exemption to move forward. Nor does there seem to be much room for the pre-birth advocates to use maternal health to generate an exception. We don't kill innocent people to save others. Maimonides toyed with the notion that the fetus in a pathological pregnancy was, de facto, a "pursuer" and thus could legitimately be defended against, but rabbinic opinion on this is divided (see Rosner 1968, 261–62; Feldman 1986, 387–88). In any case, if the rabbis believed that the fetus was a human individual before birth, it is pretty clear that they would have to condemn abortion.

Gustafson, whom I have used as an exemplar of the mainstream Protestant stance prior to Roe v. Wade, also reflects the general history of American law, which prior to the last century had regulated abortion in the name of women's health. Informed by history and ethnography, the pragmatist recognizes the diversity of positions here as indicative of communal lack of clarity about the issue. Prior to Roe v. Wade most people who had anything to say on the subject behaved like birth advocates, regardless of what they actually said. Something of the flavor of the period before Roe v. Wade comes out in the Buzz Kulik film *To Find a Man*, released in 1972. While it was nominated for the Golden Palm at Cannes, the movie has apparently vanished. The original advertising put it forward as a story about a boy who gets a girl "out of trouble" and in the process matures as a moral agent. It centers on Rosalind, who has discovered she is pregnant, and Andy, a long-time friend. When Rosalind is unable to abort the pregnancy on her own, Andy undertakes the search for a doctor willing to perform the abortion. Eventually they find a willing doctor who is, nonetheless, disdainful of Andy, who he assumes is the father. During the procedure, which takes place in his office, Rosalind blurts out the identity of the actual father, the doctor realizes that Andy has been acting out of concern for Rosalind, and Andy realizes the complexity of love and sex in the adult world he is about to enter.[5] When my friends and I saw the movie in the summer of 1972 it seemed fairly accurate in its version of teenage reality and attitudes. Granted, we were a middle- and upper middle-class bunch, who had come of political age in the Bay Area of the civil rights movement, the free-speech movement, Vietnam and the summer of love, but the idea that a girl *wouldn't* abort a problematic pregnancy would have seemed absurd. When I got back to college in the fall a classmate returned with a newborn and, as I remember, what seemed unreasonable to many of us was that she hadn't aborted the pregnancy.

Adolescent anecdotes are not arguments, but they do register division and difference in the American population. A Gallup poll of May 2010 splits down the middle between "pro-life" and "pro-choice," but the Gallup people themselves admit that "it is not entirely clear why Americans have grown more likely to embrace the pro-life label when defining their own views on the issue, especially because there has not been an attendant increase in opposition to abortion on moral grounds" (<http://www.gallup.com/poll/128036>).[6] For the pragmatist's purposes, the "why" may not be all that important, since the point of this exercise has been to determine whether or not the American community speaks a decidedly pre-birth language about the status of the fetus

---

[5] I think I remember the movie pretty well, but I haven't been able to track it down. The advertising poster is available at the Internet Movie Database. The title is not listed on Amazon.com and the Wikipedia entry on it is a stub. I'll leave it to the initiative of readers to see if my account hits the mark.

[6] Reading polls is a notoriously slippery business, shifting with changes in political climate, the wording of the questions, and how the polls are conducted. Polls by the Pew Center, CBS, and others seem generally agreed about the basic split in the population. While the Gallup organization typically phrases the question in terms of "pro-life" or "pro-choice," other polls frame their questions in terms of availability. A CBS News poll of August 20–24, 2010, gives 36% maintaining general availability of abortion, 39% available under stricter limits, and 23% that abortion should not be permitted. The Gallup poll for June 6, 2010 has 47% identifying themselves as "pro-life." If both polls were representative of the country as a whole, this would mean that 24% of the "pro-life" population favored making abortion available under certain conditions.

in the moral community. The answer seems to be that it doesn't. Of course, if the community were strongly committed to formulating its statutes in a way that is consistent with the magisterial teachings of the church, the strategy would be to reformulate the law and educate the citizenry to be good Catholics.

That would, of course, require a dramatic revision of the Constitution, but it wouldn't, in itself, be irrational. Imagine, though, the response of an observant Jew, who discovers shortly after his wife goes into labor that she is in deadly peril. It is not simply a matter of individual desire, but of religious law, that he secure an immediate abortion. The observant Jewish doctor takes it as part of his duty, as a matter of Torah, to cut up the fetus and remove it, bit by bit. Should he, in the United States as it is, be prohibited from exercising his medical skills according to his conscience? Advocates of drawing the line at birth, to which group our doctor and his patients belong, clearly think not. The same with at least some Buddhists and a fair number of the unaffiliated. If, aware of comparative differences in the population, we are uncomfortable with banning abortion for Jews and Buddhists, why should we prohibit it to nonbelievers, even if we could? And if we privilege the life of the woman in some situations, why not in all? If rape, pathology, or mental health licenses the killing of a fetus, what are the reasons for restricting it in others?

This doesn't mean that doctors should be forced to perform abortions if they disapprove; it merely notes the fact that a notable percentage of the population doesn't find the claims of the pre-birth advocates persuasive. But the pragmatist has a bit more to contribute to the debate. Returning to Peirce's ways of fixing belief, he's inclined to remind his compatriots of the limits of authority or the a priori in pursuing the truth. Kenny and others seem to think that once the prospect of twinning has passed there is an individual person, but the rabbis point out that, in this case, science doesn't settle the matter. In this sort of debate, the community does. But the difficulty of achieving consensus shouldn't tempt us back into relativist worries. What Gilbert Harman calls moral relativism is really no more than the pragmatic approach to settling norms that we saw in Fingarette (see Harman 2000, part I). If we begin with the moral realism of Aristotle, as opposed either to the *a priori* theorizing of Kant or the emotivist authority of Mill, we can ask each other what kind of people we think we should become and how individual policies either contribute to or detract from our aspirations. If rationality is found in our approaches to problem-solving, nothing could be more reasonable than this.

The contingency of reasonableness

Early on in his *Ecclesiastical History*, Bede tells the story of St. Alban:

> When infidel rulers were issuing violent edicts against the Christians, Alban, though still a heathen at the time, gave hospitality to a certain cleric who was fleeing from his persecutors . . . Instructed little by little by his teaching about salvation, Alban forsook the darkness of idolatry and became a wholehearted Christian. [Bede *EH*, 1:7]

In a sequence familiar to readers of saints' lives, the evil ruler hears about this affront, Alban offers himself as a martyr, and outrages the authorities with his steadfast devotion:

> As he was being led to his execution, he came to a rapid river whose stream ran between the town wall and the arena where he was to suffer. He saw there a great crowd of people . . . St. Alban, whose ardent desire it was to achieve his martyrdom as soon as possible, came to the torrent and raised his eyes towards heaven. Thereupon the river-bed dried up at that very spot and he saw the waters give way and provide a path for him to walk in. [Ibid.]

The executioner, recognizing the power of Alban's God, refuses to do his duty. After another miracle by the river, Alban is beheaded, but "the one who laid his unholy hands on that holy neck was not permitted to rejoice over his death; for the head of the blessed martyr and the executioner's eyes fell to the ground together" (ibid.). The soldier who would not strike is also beheaded, but Bede assures his reader that, "though he was not washed in the waters of baptism, yet he was cleansed by the washing of his own blood and made worthy to enter the kingdom of heaven" (ibid.).

This is a standard sort of story, with familiar components. The parting of the waters clearly owes much to Exodus 14, but that makes it more, not less, credible. Parting a local river is nothing for a God who can part the sea. The detail of the executioner's eyes is excellent. Unlike his comrade, who had seen the error of his ways, this soldier is blind and deserves to lose his eyes for striking down the saint. I have no idea at all how much, or how literally, Bede's readers believed any of this, but I imagine that most of them believed that it could happen and not a few that it did. And they were perfectly reasonable in doing so. Rationality is about solving everyday problems as they present themselves. Language is the great evolutionary innovation that enables human beings to judge the likelihood of events, assess the evidence for one possible outcome over and against another, and to project those possibilities into the future so that members of the community can exchange reasons for choosing one path over another. Languages, as abstract objects, are generalizations over closely related idiolects, which individuals use to triangulate, in Davidson's sense, between another speaker and the world they share.

If, with Davidson, we think understanding begins with the idiolect, in language as spoken and understood, then the best evidence for particular interpretations will be history and ethnography drawn, as available, from the communities we are studying. Of course, sometimes we just won't have enough evidence and so we will need to formulate hypotheses based on evidence drawn from other parts of the world and test them to see what they can tell us. This is the procedure Mary Douglas adopted with the abominations of Leviticus, and the first three chapters of *Purity and Danger* remain a powerful instrument for weaning beginners off medical materialism. Writing in the mid-1960s, Douglas notes that "pharmacologists are still hard at work on Leviticus XI." She cites one researcher who:

> made muscle extracts from swine, dog, hare... He tested extracts from animals which counted as clean in Leviticus and found them less toxic, but still he reckoned his research proved nothing either way about the medical value of the Mosaic laws. [Douglas 1966, 32]

Not surprising. If God spoke to Moses, then why not take him at his word. If God didn't speak, then there would have been no way for them to identify the causes of any physical pathologies that took, say, forty-eight hours or more to present. Even then, the world being full of potentially malevolent wills, it would be just as likely that you were the victim of witchcraft. In a world teeming with witches, it's reasonable to worry about invisible attacks.

Truly fallacious functional explanations need to be rejected, though these are a little harder to find than sometimes imagined. Attempts at explanation that discount or ignore what the subjects say equally need to be disposed of. Douglas uses the experience of fieldwork, hers and others', to puncture other armchair myths about primitive religion. "The feelings of an Azande man," for example, "on finding that he has been betwitched, are not terror, but hearty indignation as one of us might feel on finding himself the victim of embezzlement" (ibid., 1). "The anthropologists who," having witnessed a rain ritual, "asked if the Bushmen reckoned the rite had produced the rain, were laughed out of court" (ibid., 59). Meyer Schapiro's critique of Freud on Leonardo illustrates the ways that history can deflate the pretentions of grand theory (see Schapiro 1956). Davidson's account of language makes it possible to expose the illegitimate moves of post-modernist idiologues, on the one hand, and neuroscientific popularizers, on the other.

This doesn't mean that we will be done, henceforth, with the temptations of theory. People will always be puzzled about something and will, thus, cast about for an explanation. Part of the power of cognitive science and post-modernist approaches to the study of religion is their simplicity. Learn a basic vocabulary and three or four rhetorical moves and you can do with them what our predecessors did with Marx and Freud. But the real work of argument takes place at the level of detail, which means there are always going to be new interpretive battles to fight. I have tried to illustrate how those take place in my critique of Richard Miller. I suppose it's true that in some possible world Thomas Aquinas does ethics in the manner of James Childress but, in the world for which he actually wrote, Thomas provided an account of the virtues and vices that could be of use to his brothers charged with preaching and the care of souls.

There are a few more things to say about Bede and St. Alban, though. Sometimes the miracles do the trick, as with the instant conversion of the first soldier. But just as often it's the message, not the magic. Alban is won over by the persuasive power of his unnamed guest. And through it all, there is the power of virtue and piety. On the brink of conversion, King Edwin hesitates to accept baptism, sitting "alone for hours at a time, earnestly debating within himself what he ought to do and what religion he should follow" (*EH*, 2:12). Paulinus, who has been instructing him, convinces Edwin to make good on his promise, the king decides to "confer about this with his loyal chief men and his counsellors so that, if they agreed with him, they might be consecrated together" (ibid., 2:13). Coifi, his chief priest, makes the following confession:

> I frankly admit that, for my part, I have found that the religion which we have hitherto held has no virtue nor profit in it. None of your followers has devoted himself more earnestly than I have to the worship of our gods, but nevertheless there are many who receive greater benefits...If the gods had any power they would have helped me more readily, seeing that I have always served them with greater zeal. [Ibid.]

Before Coifi can act, an unnamed member of the entourage offers the simile of the sparrow in the winter storm, flitting through the bright hall, concluding that, "so this life of man appears but for a moment; what follows or indeed what went before, we know not at all. If this new doctrine brings us more certain information, it seems right that we should accept it" (ibid.). Coifi affirms the reasonableness of this and they proceed to the destruction of the idols.

Religion is about both the truth and the good life. We test it against what we consider reasonable expectations to see if it works. But working is not just about being rewarded. Before profaning the idols, Coifi notes that "the more diligently I sought the truth in our cult, the less I found it. Now I confess openly that the truth shines out clearly in this teaching" (ibid.). Right reason demands a change of path. Many years ago Alasdair MacIntyre complained that in the Middle Ages difficulties with Christian teaching were "taken to be tolerable (and treated as apparent and not real) because the concepts were part of a set of concepts which were indispensable to the forms of description used in social and intellectual life," but that in the modern world the connection between Christian belief and social action has been erased. The result is, for MacIntyre, clear:

> The kind of negative theology which refuses to identify any object with the divine (God is not this, not that) has its final fruit in the kind of atheism which Simone Weil and Tillich both see as a recognition of the fact that God cannot be identified with any particular existing object . . . understanding Christianity is incompatible with believing in it, not because Christianity is vulnerable to sceptical objections, but because its peculiar invulnerability belongs to it as a form of belief which has lost the social context which once made it comprehensible. [MacIntyre 1964, 76]

At the level of professional philosophy, the last half century has witnessed numerous attempts to escape MacIntyre's dilemma, the most successful being the anti-foundational epistemology of Nicholas Wolterstorff (see Wolterstorff 1983). But the community at large is not responsible for being up on the latest journal articles. Debate there is best conducted in ways that accept statements of belief at face value.

At the level of public debate, accusations of irrationality are not only, for the most part, unfair; they're unhelpful. I tried, albeit briefly, to illustrate a pragmatic strategy in the third section of this chapter. An inquiry into the varieties of religious approaches to abortion results in the spectrum of positions along what I've called the pre-birth to birth axis of argument. Humans have to be conceived, so the period from conception to birth is clearly essential to my life. But in ordinary parlance, babies have to be born. A notable sector of the community believes that you're not a recognized member of the moral community until birth. However you draw the line there will be a gray area, so it's not surprising that the country is split down the middle and a sizable majority is simple confused.

By calling people confused I seem to be violating my own injunction against incendiary language. So rather than invite sectarian battle it is probably more helpful to illustrate the point by discussing a piece of legislation that can only be described as confused. In Harris v. McRae, Justice Stewart opens the opinion of the court as follows:

> Since September 1976, Congress has prohibited—either by an amendment to the annual appropriations bill for the Department of Health, Education, and Welfare... or by a joint resolution—the use of any federal funds to reimburse the cost of abortions under the Medicaid program except under certain specified circumstances. [Shapiro ed. 1995, 130]

Justice Stewart goes on to note that, for the fiscal year 1980, the version reads:

> None of the funds provided by this joint resolution shall be used to perform abortions except where the life of the mother would be endangered if the fetus were carried to term; or except for such medical procedures necessary for the victims of rape or incest when such rape or incest has been reported promptly to a law enforcement agency or public health service. [Ibid.]

For the last thirty-plus years one or another version of this language has made it into law. The popularly stated justification for the restrictions is the unwillingness of some taxpayers to have their taxes used to support abortions. In finding the Hyde Amendment constitutional, the court notes that it:

> places no governmental obstacle in the path of a woman who chooses to terminate her pregnancy, but rather, by means of unequal subsidization of abortion and other medical services, encourages alternative activity deemed in the public interest. [Ibid., 132]

In allowing reimbursement for abortions where the mother's life is in danger, Hyde seems to join with the birth advocates. In the case of rape and incest, it goes beyond what would be countenanced by more conservative rabbis, who would resist abortion when the mother's life is not in jeopardy. But then it withdraws the exemption if the rape or incest has not been "reported promptly." Why? If the fetus can be killed to save the life of the mother, then it clearly does not have the full status of a member of the community. Allowing the exception for rape and incest would seem to reaffirm this, since it is not a matter of life against life. In those cases it would seem that the injury has been inflicted by a wicked third party and the law is reflecting the unfairness of burdening the woman with the consequences of someone else's crime. If the fetus lacks status, then why should it matter when she reports it? Because some magistrate thinks so? Does he get to decide what counts as "prompt?" That doesn't seem fair.

Suppose the legislator suggests that failure to report suggests that she doesn't experience herself as wounded or aggrieved. That, of course, doesn't follow. Rape and incest are just as likely to paralyze the victim with uncertainty and fear as motivate her to go public. We'd like to think that in twenty-first-century America we are enlightened enough to separate the victim from the crime, but that hardly means reporting it will be easy. If the advocate of the Hyde Amendment falls back on the claim that decisions to take a life can't be "casual," he sets himself up for a dilemma. If by "life" he intends to suggest that the fetus is a fully recognized member of the community, then he would appear to be a pre-birth advocate and shouldn't allow any exceptions at all. If he remains in the birth advocate's camp, then the fetus is obviously not a member of the community and it's not clear, beyond a concern for the quality of the physician and the clinic, why the state has any concern here at all.

Legislators are elected, at least in the American system, to represent their constituents on matters of general concern to the common good. My pragmatist, looking at the variety of positions on abortion, as well as the genuine confusion reflected in the law, is inclined to doubt that there is a whole lot of consensus about the relation of fetuses to the common good. It makes no sense as a matter of inquiry to say that abortion is a murder when done by a conservative Catholic but not when it's done by an orthodox Jew. All this could mean is that conservative Catholics believe that the fetus is a member of the community at conception and draw the conclusion that to kill it would be murder, while the orthodox Jew doesn't. But we know this already. Repeating it doesn't represent progress of any sort. Looked at in the context of American politics after Roe v. Wade, the pragmatic inquirer of a secular Aristotelian bent is likely to conclude, with the dissenters in Harris v. McRae, "that the Hyde Amendment is nothing less than an attempt by Congress to circumvent the dictates of the Constitution and achieve indirectly what *Roe v. Wade* said it could not do directly" (ibid., 135).

I think there are good reasons for seeing this as the point where the inquirer is likely to become an advocate, one way or another. I don't believe that advocates have anything to apologize for, unless their advocacy is based on the ways of fixing belief that block the road of inquiry. I've been happy to write, in other places and at other times, pieces that clearly advocate particular views about war, humanitarian intervention, and pornography. On abortion, I advocate drawing the line at birth and I'm inclined to think that it is hard to defend the pre-birth position without introducing theological and metaphysical positions that there are not compelling reasons to embrace. But that's not what this book is about. My intent has been to advocate a pragmatic approach to inquiry generally and to the study of religion and ethics in particular. Because both are complex human phenomena, they call for the approaches that have proven successful in similar enterprises. And if we can use Peirce's account of inquiry to avoid blind alleys and dead ends, so much the better.

Bibliography

Abbreviations

CP   Peirce, Charles Sanders. *Collected Papers of Charles Sanders Peirce.* Ed. C. Hartshorne, P. Weiss, and A. Burks. 8 vols. Cambridge, MA: Harvard University Press, 1931–1958.

EH   Bede. *Ecclesiastical History of the English People.* Ed. and trans. B. Colgrave and R. A. B. Mynors. 1969; repr. 2001. Oxford: Oxford University Press.

Inf   Dante Alighieri. *Inferno.* Trans. A. Mandelbaum. New York: Bantam Books, 1982.

Meta   Aristotle. *Metaphysics.* Trans. W. D. Ross in Jonathan Barnes, ed. *The Complete Works of Aristotle.* 2 Vols. Princeton: Princeton University Press, 1984.

PI   Wittgenstein, Ludwig. *Philosophical Investigations.* Ed. G. E. M. Anscombe and R. Rhees, trans. G. E. M. Anscombe. 3rd ed. Oxford: Basil Blackwell, 1958.

RFM   Wittgenstein, Ludwig. *Remarks on the Foundations of Mathematics.* Ed. G. H. von Wright, R. Rhees, and G. E. M. Anscombe. Trans. G. E. M. Anscombe. 2nd ed. Oxford: Basil Blackwell, 1978.

ST   Thomas Aquinas, *Summa Theologiae,* Textum Leoninum Romae, in the Corpus Thomisticum, <http://www.corpusthomisticum.org>

Books and Journals

Abiodun, Rowland, Henry Drewel, and John Pemberton, eds. 1994. *The Yoruba Artist: New Theoretical Perspectives on African Arts.* Washington, DC: Smithsonian Press.

Alberts, Bruce, Alexander Johnson, Julian Lewis, Martin Raff, Keith Roberts, and Peter Walters. 2008. *Molecular Biology of the Cell.* Reference edition. 5th ed. New York: Garland Science.

Andrade, E. N. da C. 1954. *Sir Isaac Newton.* London: Collins.

Aquinas, Thomas. 1964. *Summa Theologiae*. Vol. 1: *Christian Theology*. Ed. T. Gilby. London: Eyre and Spittiswoode.

——. 1966. *Summa Theologiae*. Vol. 42: *Courage*. Ed. A. Ross and P. Walsh. London: Eyre and Spottiswoode.

——. 1972. *Summa Theologiae*. Vol. 35: *Consequences of Charity*. Ed. T. Heath. London: Eyre and Spottiswoode.

——. 1974. *Summa Theologiae*. Vol. 31: *Faith*. Ed. T. O'Brien. London: Eyre and Spottiswoode.

——. 1975. *Summa Theologiae*. Vol. 34: *Charity*. Ed. R. Batten. London: Eyre and Spottiswoode.

Aristotle. 1984. *The Complete Works of Aristotle: The Revised Oxford Translation*. Ed. Jonathan Barnes. 2 vols. Princeton: Princeton University Press.

——. 2002. *Nicomachean Ethics*. Trans., intro. and comm. S. Broadie and C. Rowe. Oxford: Oxford University Press.

Arnold, John. 2000. *History: A Very Short Introduction*. Oxford: Oxford University Press.

Auxier, Randall E. and Lewis Edwin Hahn, eds. 2010. *The Philosophy of Richard Rorty*. Chicago: Open Court.

Ayer, A. J. 1946. *Language, Truth and Logic*. 2nd ed. London: Victor Gollancz.

Ayer, A. J., ed. 1959. *Logical Positivism* Glencoe. IL: Free Press.

Baker, Lynne Rudder. 1987. *Saving Belief: A Critique of Physicalism*. Princeton: Princeton University Press.

Baker, P. M. S. 1996. *Wittgenstein's Place in Twentieth-Century Analytic Philosophy*. Oxford: Blackwell Books.

Balmer, Randall. 1993. *Mine Eyes Have Seeen the Glory: A Journey into the Evangelical Subculture in America*. Rev. ed. Oxford: Oxford University Press.

Barnard, G. William. 1992. "Explaining the Unexplainable: Wayne Proudfoot's *Religious Experience*". *Journal of the American Academy of Religion* 60/2, pp. 231–56.

——. 1993. "Explaining the Unexplainable: Rejoinder." *Journal of the American Academy of Religion* 61(4): 803–12.

Barth, Fredrik. 1975. *Ritual and Knowledge among the Baktaman of New Guinea*. New Haven: Yale University Press.

——. 1987. *Cosmologies in the Making: A Generative Approach to Cultural Variation in Inner New Guinea*. Cambridge: Cambridge University Press.

Barth, Karl. 1991. *Karl Barth: Theologian of Freedom*. Trans. C. Green. Minneapolis, MN: Fortress Press.

Baxandall, Michael. 1971. *Giotto and the Orators: Humanist Observers of Painting in Italy and the Discovery of Pictorial Composition, 1350–1450*. Oxford: Oxford University Press.

——. 1972. *Painting and Experience in Fifteenth Century Italy*. Oxford: Oxford University Press.

——. 1980. *The Limewood Sculptors of Renaissance Germany*. New Haven: Yale University Press.

——. 1985. *Patterns of Intention: On the Historical Explanation of Pictures*. New Haven: Yale University Press.

——. 2003. *Words for Pictures*. New Haven: Yale University Press.

Becker, Lawrence C. and Charlotte B. Becker, eds. 2003. *A History of Western Ethics.* 2nd ed. London: Routledge.

Beek, Walter E. A. van. 1991. "Dogon Restudied: A Field Evaluation of the Work of Marcel Griaule." *Current Anthropology* 13(2): 139–67.

Berkeley, George. 1950. *Alciphron, or the Minute Philosopher: Works of George Berkeley, Bishop of Cloyne.* Vol. 3. Ed. T. E. Jessop. London: Thomas Nelson and Sons.

Berlin, Isaiah. 1999. *The Roots of Romanticism.* Ed. H. Hardy. Princeton: Princeton University Press.

Bernard of Clairvaux. 1987. *Selected Writings.* Tr. G. R. Evans. Mahwah, NJ: Paulist Press.

Biardeau, Madeleine. 1989. *Hindusm: The Anthropology of a Civilization.* Trans. Nice. Oxford: Oxford University Press.

Blake, Ralph M. Curt J. Ducasse, and Edward Madden, eds. 1960. *Theories of Scientific Method: The Renaissance through the Nineteenth Century.* Seattle: University of Washington Press.

Bockover, Mary I., ed. 1991. *Rules, Rituals, and Responsibility: Essays Dedicated to Herbert Fingarette.* La Salle, IL: Open Court.

Bosland, P. W. and E. J. Votava. 2000. *Peppers: Vegetable and Spice Capsicums.* Wallingford, UK: CABI Publishing.

Bowler, Peter J. 1993. *The Norton History of the Environmental Sciences.* New York: W. W. Norton.

Boyer, Pascal. 2001. *Religion Explained: The Evolutionary Origins of Religious Thought.* New York: Basic Books.

Boyle, Leonard E. 2002. "The Setting of the *Summa Theologiae* of St. Thomas: Revisited." In Pope, ed. 2002, pp. 1–16.

Bradley, Francis Herbert. 1914. *Essays on Truth and Reality.* Oxford: Oxford University Press.

Brandom, Robert. 2000. *Articulating Reasons: An Introduction to Inferentialism.* Cambridge, MA: Harvard University Press.

——. 2008. *Between Saying and Doing: Towards an Analytic Pragmatism.* Oxford: Oxford University Press.

Brandom, Robert, ed. 2000. *Rorty and His Critics.* Oxford: Blackwell.

Brent, Joseph. 1993. *Charles Sanders Peirce: A Life.* Bloomington, IN Indiana University Press.

Brooke, Christopher. 1989. *The Medieval Idea of Marriage.* Oxford: Oxford University Press.

Brundage, James A. 1987. *Law, Sex, and Christian Society in Medieval Europe.* Chicago: University of Chicago Press.

Bull, Marcus. 1993. "The Roots of Lay Enthusiasm for the First Crusade." Repr. in Madden 2002, pp. 173–93.

Burgess, John P. 2009. *Philosophical Logic.* Princeton: Princeton University Press.

Burguier, Andre, Christiane Klapisch-Zuber, Martine Segalen, and Francois Zonabend, eds. 1996. *A History of the Family.* Trans. Tennison, Morris, and Wilson. 2 vols. Cambridge, MA: Harvard University Press.

Burridge, K. O. L. 1969. *New Heaven, New Earth: A Study of Millenarian Activities.* New York: Schocken Books.

——. 1995. *Mambu: A Melanesian Millennium.* Rev. ed. Princeton: Princeton University Press.

Butterfield, Herbert. 1949. *The Origins of Modern Science, 1300–1800.* London: G. Bell and Sons.

Butts, Robert E. and John W. Davis, eds. 1970. *The Methodological Heritage of Newton.* Oxford: Blackwell.

Carrasco, David. 1990. *Religions of Mesoamerica.* San Francisco: Harper and Row.

Carrier, David. 1998. "Danto and His Critics: Art History, Historiography, and *After the End of Art.*" *History and Theory* 37(4): 1–16.

Cartwright, Nancy. 1989. *Nature's Capacities and their Measurement.* Oxford: Oxford University Press.

Chadwick, Owen. 1975. *The Secularization of the European Mind in the 19th Century.* Cambridge: Cambridge University Press.

Chenu, Marie-Dominique. 1964. *Toward Understanding St. Thomas.* Trans. A. Landry and D. Hughes. Chicago: Henry Regnery Co.

——. 1968. *Nature, Man, and Society in the Twelfth Century: Essays on New Theological Perspectives in the Latin West.* Ed. and trans. J. Taylor and L. Little. Chicago: University of Chicago Press.

——. 1969. *La Théologie comme science au XIIIe siècle.* 3rd ed. Paris: Librairie Philosophique J. Vrin.

——. 2002. *Aquinas and His Role in Theology.* Trans. Paul Philibert. Collegeville, MN: Liturgical Press.

Childress, James F. 1978. "Just-War Criteria." Repr. in Childress 1982, pp. 63–94.

——. 1982. *Moral Responsibility in Conflicts: Essays on Nonviolence, War, and Conscience.* Baton Rouge, LA: Louisiana State University Press.

Chipp, Herschel B., ed. 1968. *Theories of Modern Art: A Source Book by Artists and Critics.* Berkeley: Univesity of California Press.

Chomsky, Noam. 1959. "Verbal behavior." *Language,* 25: 26–58.

——. 1963. "Perception and Language." In *Boston Studies in the Philosophy of Science.* Ed. E. Wartofsky. Dordrecht: D. Reidel Publishing, pp. 199–205.

——. 1980. *Rules and Representations.* New York: Columbia University Press.

Churchland, Paul. 1981. "Eliminative Materialism and Propositional Attitudes." *Journal of Philosophy* 78(2): 67–90.

——. 1988. *Matter and Consciousness.* Rev. ed. Cambridge, MA: MIT Press.

——. 1995. *The Engine of Reason, the Seat of the Soul: A Philosophical Journey into the Brain.* Cambridge, MA: MIT Press.

——. 1998. "Conceptual Similarity and Sensory/Neural Diversity: The Fodor/Lepore Challenge Answered." *Journal of Philosophy* 95(1): 5–32.

Clark, Kenneth. 1956. *The Nude: A Study in Ideal Form.* Princeton: Princeton University Press.

Clebsch, William A. 1973. *American Religious Thought: A History.* Chicago: University of Chicago Press.

Clifford, James. 1983. "Power and Dialogue in Ethnography: Marcel Griaule's Initiation." In Stocking, ed. 1983, 121–56.

Clifford, James and George E. Marcus, eds. 1986. *Writing Culture: The Poetics and Politics of Ethnography*. Berkeley: University of California Press.

Cohen, I. Bernard. 1985. *The Birth of a New Physics*. Rev. ed. New York: W. W. Norton.

Cohen, Morris Raphael. 1916. "Charles S. Peirce and a Tentative Bibliography of his Published Writings." *Journal of Philosophy, Psychology and Scientific Method* 13(26): 726–37.

——. 1949. *A Dreamer's Journey: The Autobiography of Morris Raphael Cohen*. New York: Free Press.

——. 1954. *American Thought: A Sketch*. Ed. Felix Cohen. New York: Free Press.

Cohen, Morris Raphael and Ernest Nagel. 1934. *Introduction to Logic and Scientific Method*. New York: Harcourt, Brace and Co.

Cohn, Norman. 1970. *The Pursuit of the Millennium: Revolutionary Millenarians and Mystical Anarchists of the Middle Ages*. Oxford: Oxford University Press.

Constable, Giles. 1985. "Medieval Charters as a Source for the History of the Crusades." Repr. in Madden 2002, pp. 130–53.

Corson, Trevor. 2007. *The Zen of Fish: The Story of Sushi, from Samurai to Supermarket*. New York: Harper Collins.

Cortes, Hernan. 1986. *Letters from Mexico*. Trans. and ed. Anthony Pagden. Intro. J. H. Elliott. New Haven: Yale University Press.

Creel, H. G. 1960. *Confucius and the Chinese Way*. New York: Harper Torchbooks.

Danby, Herbert. 1933. *The Mishnah, Translated from the Hebrew with Introduction and Brief Explanatory Notes*. Oxford: Oxford University Press.

Danto, Arthur C. 1964. "The Artworld." *Journal of Philosophy* 61(19): 571–84.

——. 1964a. *Analytical Philosophy of History*. Cambridge: Cambridge University Press.

——. 1972. *Mysticism and Morality: Oriental Thought and Moral Philosophy*. New York: Harper and Row.

——. 1973. "Artworks and Real Things." *Theoria* 39: 1–17.

——. 1976. "Ethical Theory and Mystical Experience: A Response to Professors Proudfoot and Wainwright." *Journal of Religious Ethics* 4(1): 37–46.

——. 1981. *The Transfiguration of the Commonplace*. Cambridge, MA: Harvard University Press.

——. 1990. "The Art World Revisited: Comedies of Similarity." Repr. in Danto 1992, pp. 33–54.

——. 1992. *Beyond the Brillo Box: The Visual Arts in Post-Historical Perspective*. New York: Farrar, Straus, Giroux.

——. 1993. "Aesthetics and Art Criticism." Repr. in Danto 1994, pp. 378–87.

——. 1994. *Embodied Meanings: Critical Essays and Aesthetic Meditations*. New York: Farrar, Straus, Giroux.

——. 1994a. "Philosophy and the Criticism of Art: A Personal Narrative." In Danto 1994, pp. 3–14.

——. 1997. *After the End of Art: Contemporary Art and the Pale of History.* Princeton: Princeton University Press.

——. 2007. *Unnatural Wonders: Essays from the Gap between Art and Life.* New York: Columbia University Press.

Darwin, Charles. 2001. *Darwin: A Norton Critical Edition.* Ed. P. Appleman. 3rd ed. New York: W. W. Norton.

——. 2008. *On the Origin of Species.* Ed. G. Beer. Revised. Oxford: Oxford University Press.

Davidson, Donald. 1963. "Actions, Reasons, and Causes." Repr. in Davidson 1980, pp. 3–19.

——. 1965. "Theories of Meaning and Learnable Languages." Repr. in Davidson 1984, pp. 3–15.

——. 1967. "Truth and Meaning." Repr. in Davidson 1984, pp. 17–36

——. 1967a. "The Logical Form of Action Sentences." Repr. with comments in Davidson 1980, pp. 105–48.

——. 1970. "How is Weakness of the Will Possible?" Repr. in Davidson 1980, pp. 21–42.

——. 1970a. "Semantics for Natural Languages." Repr. in Davidson 1984, pp. 55–64.

——. 1970b. "Mental Events." Repr. in Davidson 1980, pp. 207–25.

——. 1973. "Radical Interpretation." Repr. in Davidson 1984, pp. 125–39.

——. 1974. "On the Very Idea of a Conceptual Scheme." Repr. in Davidson 1984, pp. 183–98.

——. 1980. *Essays on Actions and Events.* Oxford: Oxford University Press.

——. 1982. "Communication and Convention." Repr. in Davidson 1984, pp. 165–80.

——. 1984. *Inquiries into Truth and Interpretation.* Oxford: Oxford University Press.

——. 1986. "A Nice Derangement of Epitaphs." Repr. in Davidson 2005, pp. 89–107.

——. 1987. "A Coherence Theory of Truth and Knowledge." Repr. with "Afterthoughts, 1987." In Davidson 2001, pp. 137–57.

——. 1992. "The Second Person." Repr. in Davidson 2001, pp. 107–21.

——. 1994. "The Social Aspect of Language." Repr. in Davidson 2005, pp. 109–25.

——. 1995. "Could There Be a Science of Rationality?" Repr. in Davidson 2004, pp. 117–34.

——. 1996. "The Folly of Attempting to Define Truth." Repr. in Davidson 2005, pp. 19–37.

——. 1997. "Seeing through Language." Repr. in Davidson 2005, pp. 126–41.

——. 1999. "Intellectual Autobiography." In Hahn, ed. 1999, pp. 3–70.

——. 2001. *Subjective, Intersubjective, Objective.* Oxford: Oxford University Press.

——. 2004. *Problems of Rationality.* Oxford: Oxford University Press.

——. 2005. *Truth, Language, and History.* Oxford: Oxford University Press.

Davidson, Donald and Jaako Hintikka, eds. 1969. *Words and Objections: Essays on the Work of W. V. Quine.* Dordrecht: D. Reidel Publishing.

Davis, G. Scott. 1991. "Irony and Argument in *Dialogues* XII." *Religious Studies* 27: 239–57.

———. 1992. *Warcraft and the Fragility of Virtue: An Essay in Aristotelian Ethics.* Moscow, ID: University of Idaho Press.

———. 2001. "Doing What Comes Naturally: Recent Work in the New Natural Law Theory." *Religion* 31: 63–94.

———. 2004. "Wittgenstein and the Recovery of Virtue." In Stout and MacSwain, eds. 2004, pp. 175–96.

———. 2004a. "Nancy Frankenberry, ed. *Religion and Radical Interpretation.*" *Journal of the American Academy of Religion* 72(3): 780–3.

———. 2005. "Introduction" to G. E. Moore, *Principia Ethica: Barnes and Noble Library of Essential Reading.* New York: Barnes and Noble.

———. 2006. "Ethics." In Segal, ed. 2006, pp. 239–54.

———. 2007. "Donald Davidson, Anomalous Monism, and the Study of Religion." *Method and Theory in the Study of Religion* 19(3–4): 200–31.

———. 2007a. "Comment on David Little." *Journal of Religious Ethics* 35(1): 165–70.

———. 2008. "Method and Metaphysics." In Phillips and Ruhr, eds. 2008, pp. 87–115.

———. 2008a. "Two Neglected Classics of Comparative Ethics." *Journal of Religious Ethics*, 36(3): 375–403.

D'Azevedo, Warren, ed. 1973. *The Traditional Artist in African Societies.* Bloomington, IN: Indiana University Press.

Dennett, Daniel. 1996. *Kinds of Minds: Toward an Understanding of Consciousness.* New York: Basic Books.

———. 2000. "The Case for Rorts." In Brandom, ed. 2000, pp. 91–101.

Deutsch, Eliot, ed. 1991. *Culture and Modernity: East-West Philosophical Perspectives.* Honolulu: University of Hawaii Press.

Dickstein, Morris, ed. 1998. *The Revival of Pragmatism: New Essays on Social Though, Law, and Culture.* Durham, NC: Duke University Press.

Dilman, Ilham. 1996. "Wisdom." *Philosophy* 71(278): 577–90.

Donagan, Alan. 2003. "Twentieth-Century Anglo-American Ethics." In Becker and Becker, eds. 2003, pp. 139–51.

Dorf, Elliot. 2003. *Love Your Neighbor and Yourself: A Jewish Approach to Modern Personal Ethics.* Philadelphia: Jewish Publication Society.

Dorf, Elliott and Louis Newman, eds. 1995. *Contemporary Jewish Ethics and Morality: A Reader.* Oxford: Oxford University Press.

Doris, John. 2002. *Lack of Character: Personality and Moral Behavior.* Cambridge: Cambridge University Press.

Douglas, Mary. 1966. *Purity and Danger: An Analysis of Concepts of Pollution and Taboo.* London: Routledge.

———. 1968. "Pollution". Repr. in Douglas 1999, pp. 106–15

———. 1970 "Self-evidence." Repr. in Douglas 1999, pp. 252–83

———. 1985. "Credibility." Repr. in Douglas 1992, pp. 235–54.

———. 1986. *How Institutions Think.* Syracuse, NY: Syracuse University Press.

———. 1989. "The Background of the Grid Dimension: A Comment." *Sociological Analysis* 50(2): 171–6.

———. 1992. *Risk and Blame: Essays in Cultural Theory.* London: Routledge.

———. 1993. "Rightness of Categories." Repr. in Douglas 1999, pp. 284–309.

——. 1996. *Natural Symbols: Explorations in Cosmology*. Rev. ed. London: Routledge.

——. 1999. *Implicit Meanings: Selected Essays in Anthropology*. 2nd ed. London: Routledge.

——. 1999a. *Leviticus as Literature*. Oxford: Oxford University Press.

——. 2001. *In the Wilderness: The Doctrine of Defilement in the Book of Numbers*. Paperback ed. Oxford: Oxford University Press.

Douglas, Mary and Steven Ney. 1998. *Missing Persons: A Critique of the Social Sciences*. Berkeley: University of California Press.

Dreier, James. 2006. *Contemporary Debates in Moral Theory*. Oxford: Blackwell.

Dubois, Jean Antoine. 1906. *Hindu Manners, Customs and Ceremonies*. Trans. H. Beauchamp. 3rd ed. Oxford: Oxford University Press.

Duby, Georges. 1980. *The Three Orders: Feudal Society Imagined*. Trans. A. Goldhammer. Chicago: University of Chicago Press.

Dummett, Michael A. E. 1975. "What is a Theory of Meaning?" In Guttenplan, ed. 1975, pp. 97–138.

——. 1976. "What is a Theory of Meaning? (II)" In Evans and McDowell, eds. 1976, pp. 67–137.

——. 1977. "Can Analytical Philosophy be Systematic, and Ought it to Be?" Repr. in Dummett 1978, pp. 437–58.

——. 1978. *Truth and Other Enigmas*. Cambridge, MA: Harvard University Press.

——. 1993. *Origins of Analytic Philosophy*. Cambridge, MA: Harvard University Press.

Dumont, Louis. 1970. *Homo Hierarchicus: The Caste System and Its Implications*. Trans. M. Sainsbury. Chicago: University of Chicago Press.

Dunlop, Fuschia. 2005. "Culture Shock." *Gourmet: The Magazine of Good Living* 65(8): 62–5.

Durkheim, Emile. 1960. "Pragmatism and Sociology." Trans. C. Blend in Wolff 1960, pp. 386–436.

——. 1975. *Durkheim on Religion: A Selection of Readings with Bibliographies and Introductory Remarks*. Ed. W. Pickering. London: Routledge and Kegal Paul.

——. 1983. *Pragmatism and Sociology*. Ed. J. Allcock, trans. J. Whitehouse. Cambridge: Cambridge University Press.

——. 1995. *The Elementary Forms of Religious Life*. Trans. K. Fields. New York: The Free Press.

——. 2001. *The Elementary Forms of Religious Life*. Ed. M. Cladis, trans. C. Cosman. Oxford: Oxford University Press.

Edelman, Gerald M. 2004. *Wider Than the Sky: The Phenomenal Gift of Consciousness*. New Haven: Yale University Press.

Edelstein, Ludwig. 1967. *Ancient Medicine: Selected Papers of Ludwig Edelstein*. Ed. O. Temkin and L. Temkin. Baltimore: Johns Hopkins University Press.

Einstein, Albert and Leopold Infeld. 1938. *The Evolution of Physics: From Early Concepts to Relativity and Quanta*. New York: Simon and Shcuster.

Eisele, Carolyn. 1979. *Studies in the Scientific and Mathematical Philosophy of Charles S. Peirce*. Ed. R. M. Martin. The Hague: Mouton.

Eliade, Mircea. 1959. *The Sacred and the Profane: The Nature of Religion*. Trans. W. Trask. New York: Harcourt, Brace, Jovanovich.

Ellwood, Robert S. 1979. *Alternative Altars: Unconventional and Eastern Spirituality in America*. Chicago: University of Chicago Press.

Evans, Gareth and John McDowell, eds. 1976. *Truth and Meaning: Essays in Semantics*. Oxford: Oxford University Press.

Evans-Pritchard, E. E. 1956. *Nuer Religion*. Oxford: Oxford University Press.

——. 1965. *Theories of Primitive Religion*. Oxford: Oxford University Press.

Feigl, Herbert and Grover Maxwell, eds. 1962. *Scientific Explanation, Space and Time*. Minneapolis: University of Minnesota.

Feigl, Herbert and Wilfred Sellars, eds. 1949. *Readings in Philosophical Analysis*. New York: Appleton-Century-Crofts.

Feldman, David M. 1986. "This Matter of Abortion." Repr. in Dorf and Newman 1995, pp. 382–91.

Festinger, Leon, Henry W. Riecken, and Stanley Schachter. 1956. *When Prophecy Fails: A Social and Psychological Study of a Modern Group that Predicted the Destruction of the World*. New York: Harper and Row.

Feuer, Lewis. 1936. "Collected Papers of Charles Sanders Peirce (1839–1914), Volume VI: Scientific Metaphysics." *Isis* 26(1): 203–8.

Feyerabend, Paul. 1962. "Explanation, Reduction, and Empiericism." In Feigl and Maxwell, eds. 1962, pp. 28–97.

——. 1970. "Classical Empiricism." In Butts and Davis, eds. 1970, pp. 150–70.

——. 1970a. "Against Method: Outline of an Anarchistic Theory of Knowledge." In Radner and Winokur, eds. 1970, pp. 17–130.

——. 1975. *Against Method: Outline of an Anarchistic Theory of Knowledge*. London: NLB.

——. 1999. *Conquest of Abundance: A Tale of Abstraction vs. the Richness of Being*. Ed. Bert Terpstra. Chicago: University of Chicago Press.

——. 2010. *Against Method*. 4th ed. London: Verso Books.

Feynman, Richard P. 1999. *The Pleasure of Finding Things Out*. Cambridge, MA: Perseus Books.

—— 2006. *QED: The Strange Theory of Light and Matter*. Expanded Princeton Science Library ed., with a new intro. by A. Zee. Princeton: Princeton University Press.

Ficino, Marsilio. 2001. *Platonic Theology*. Ed. J. Hankins with W. Bowen. Trans. M. Allen with J. Warden. Cambridge, MA: Harvard University Press.

Fine, Arthur. 1984. "What Is Einstein's Statistical Interpretation, or, Is it Einstein for whom Bell's Theorem Tolls?" Repr. in Fine 1996, pp. 40–63.

——. 1984a. "The Natural Ontological Attitude." Repr. in Fine 1996, pp. 112–35.

——. 1996. *The Shaky Game: Einstein, Realism and the Quantum Theory*. 2nd. ed. Chicago: University of Chicago Press.

——. 2001. "The Scientific Image Twenty Years Later." *Philosophical Studies* 106: 107–22.

——. 2007. "Relativism, Pragmatism, and the Practice of Science." In Misak, ed. 2007, pp. 50–67.

Fingarette, Herbert. 1950. "'Unconscious Behavior' and Allied Concepts: A New Approach to their Empirical Interpretation." *Journal of Philosophy* 47(18): 509–20.

——. 1951. "How Normativeness Can Be Cognitive but not Descriptive in Dewey's Theory of Valuation." *Journal of Philosophy* 48(21): 625–35.

——. 1963. *The Self in Transformation: Psychoanalysis, Philosophy, and the Life of the Spirit.* New York: Basic Books.

——. 1966. "Human Community as Holy Rite: An Interpretation of Confucius' Analects." *Harvard Theological Review* 59: 53–67.

——. 1967. *On Responsibility.* New York: Basic Books.

——. 1972. *Confucius: The Secular as Sacred.* New York: Harper.

——. 1978. "The Meaning of Law in the Book of Job." Repr. in Hauerwas and MacIntyre 1983, pp. 249–89.

——. 1979. "Following the 'One Thread' of the Analects." *Journal of the American Academy of Religion* 47(3): 373–405.

——. 1979a. "The Problem of the Self in the *Analects*." *Philosophy East and West* 29: 129–40.

——. 1988. *Heavy Drinking: The Myth of Alcoholism as a Disease.* Berkeley: University of California Press.

——. 1991. "Following an Unmapped Way: A Brief Philosophical Autobiography." In Bockover, ed. 1991, pp. xxi–xxvii.

——. 1991a. "Comment and Response." In Bockover, ed. 1991, pp. 171–20.

——. 1996. *Death: Philosophical Soundings.* La Salle, IL: Open Court.

——. 2004. *Mapping Responsibility: Explorations in Mind, Law, Myth, and Culture.* La Salle, IL: Open Court.

——. 2004a. "The Confucian Perspective: The Self." A substantially revised version of 1979a, pp. 97–103.

Fisch, Max, ed. 1996. *Classic American Philosophers: Peirce, James, Royce, Santayana, Dewey, Whitehead.* 2nd ed. Intro. Nathan Houser. New York: Fordham University Press.

Flew, Anthony and Alasdair MacIntyre, eds. 1955. *New Essays in Philosophical Theology.* London: SCM Press.

Forde, Daryll, ed. 1954. *African Worlds: Studies in the Cosmological Ideas and Social Values of African Peoples.* Oxford: Oxford University Press.

Forman, Robert K. C. 1993. "Mystical Knowledge: Knowledge by Identity." *Journal of the American Academy of Religion* 61(4): 705–38.

Fraassen, Bas van. 2002. *The Empirical Stance.* New Haven: Yale University Press.

Frankenberry, Nancy, ed. 2002. *Religion and Radical Interpretation.* Cambridge: Cambridge University Press.

Frankenberry, Nancy and Hans Penner, eds. 1999. *Language, Truth, and Religious Belief: Studies in Twentieth-Century Theory and Method in Religion.* Atlanta, GA: Scholars Press.

Frei, Hans. 1974. *The Eclipse of Biblical Narrative: A Study in Eighteenth and Nineteenth Century Hermeneutics.* New Haven: Yale University Press.

French, Peter A. Theodore E. Uehling and Howard K Wettstein, eds. 1980. *Studies in Epistemology*. Minneapolis: University of Minnesota Press.

Gager, John. 1975. *Kingdom and Community: The Social World of Early Christianity*. Englewood Cliffs, NJ: Prentice-Hall.

Gamow, George. 1966. *Thirty Years that Shook Physics: The Story of Quantum Theory*. Garden City, NY: Doubleday Anchor.

Gardner, Richard A. 1998. "Matters of Life and Death: The Middling Ways as a New Buddhist Humanism?" *Eastern Buddhist* ns 31(3): 109–24.

Geertz, Clifford. 1957. "Ethos, World View, and the Analysis of Sacred Symbols." Repr. in Geertz 1973, pp. 126–41.

———. 1964. "'Internal Conversion' in Contemporary Bali." Repr. in Geertz 1973, pp. 170–89.

———. 1966. "Religion as a Cultural System." Repr. in Geertz 1973, pp. 87–125.

———. 1968. *Islam Observed: Religious Development in Morocco and Indonesia*. Chicago: University of Chicago Press.

———. 1968a. "Thinking as a Moral Act: Ethical Dimensions of Anthropological Fieldwork in the New States." Repr. in Geertz 2000, pp. 21–41.

———. 1972. "Deep Play: Notes on the Balinese Cockfight." Repr. in Geertz 1973, pp. 412–53.

———. 1973. *The Interpretation of Cultures*. New York: Basic Books.

———. 1973a. "Thick Description: Toward an Interpretive Theory of Culture." In Geertz 1973, pp. 3–30.

———. 1975. "Common Sense as a Cultural System." Repr. in Geertz 1983, pp. 73–93.

———. 1976. "Art as a Cultural System." Repr. in Geertz 1983, pp. 94–120.

———. 1977. "Centers, Kings, and Charisma: Reflections on the Symbolics of Power." Repr. in Geertz 1983, pp. 121–46.

———. 1980. *Negara: The Theater State in Nineteenth-Century Bali*. Princeton: Princeton University Press.

———. 1983. *Local Knowledge: Further Essays in Interpretive Anthropology*. New York: Basic Books.

———. 1984. "Anti Anti-Relativism." Repr. in Geertz 2000, pp. 42–67.

———. 1988. *Works and Lives: The Anthropoligist as Author*. Stanford, CA: Stanford University Press.

———. 1995. *After the Fact: Two Countries, Four Decades, One Anthropologist*. Cambridge, MA: Harvard University Press.

———. 1999. "Passage and Accident: A Life of Leaerning." Repr. in Geertz 2000, pp. 3–20.

———. 2000. *Available Light: Anthropological Reflections on Philosophical Topics*. Princeton: Princeton University Press.

———. 2000a. "Geiger at Antioch." *Antioch Review* 58(1): 21–27.

Geiger, George R. 1944. "Can We Choose between Values?" *Journal of Philosophy* 41(11): 292–98.

——— 1949. "A Note on the Naturalistic Fallacy." *Philosophy of Science* 16(4): 336–42.

Gennep, Arnold van. 1913. "E. Durkheim—*Les Formes élémentaires de la vie religieuse. Le système totémique en Australie*." In Durkheim 1975, pp. 205–8.

——. 1961. *Rites of Passage.* Trans. M. Vizedon and G. Caffee. Chicago: University of Chicago Press.

George, Robert. 1999. "Marriage and the Liberal Imagination." In *In Defense of Natural Law.* Oxford: Oxford University Press, pp. 139–60.

Giere, Ronald and Alan Richardson, eds. 1997. *Origins of Logical Empiricism.* Minneapolis: University of Minnesota.

Gilbert, Daniel T. and Patrick S. Malone. 1995. "The Correspondence Bias." *Psychological Bulletin* 117: 21–38.

Gilder, Louisa. 2008. *The Age of Entanglement: When Quantum Physics was Reborn.* New York: Knopf.

Gillispie, Charles Coulston. 1972. "Probability and Politics: Laplace, Condorcet, and Turgot." *Proceedings of the American Philosophical Society* 116(1): 1–20.

Glatzer, Nahum. 1966. *Hillel the Elder: The Emergence of Classical Judaism.* New York: Schocken Books.

Glatzer, Nahum, ed. 1969. *The Passover Haggadah, with English Translation, Introduction, Explanations and Illustrations Based on the Haggadah Studies of E. D. Goldschmidt.* Rev. ed. New York: Schocken Books.

Godlove, Terry. 1989. *Religion, Interpretation, and Diversity of Belief: The Framework Model from Kant to Durkheim to Davidson.* Cambridge: Cambridge University Press.

Goldin, Judah. 1955. *The Fathers According to Rabbi Nathan.* Yale Judaica Series, vol. X. New Haven: Yale University Press.

——. 1957. *The Living Talmud: The Wisdom of the Fathers and its Classical Commentaries.* Chicago: University of Chicago Press.

Golding, John. 1968. *Cubism: A History and an Analysis, 1907–1914.* 2nd ed. New York: Harper and Row.

Gombrich, Ernst. 1957. "Art and Scholarship." Repr. in Gombrich 1963, pp. 106–19.

——. 1963. *Meditations on a Hobby Horse and Other Essays on the Theory of Art.* London: Phaidon Press.

——. 1970. *Aby Warburg: An Intellectual Biography.* London: Warburg Institute.

Goodman, Nelson. 1955. *Fact, Fiction, and Forecast.* Cambridge, MA: Harvard University Press.

——. 1969. "The Emperor's New Ideas." Repr. in Goodman 1972, pp. 76–9.

——. 1972. *Problems and Projects.* Indianapolis, IN: Bobbs-Merrill.

——. 1978. *Ways of Worldmaking.* Indianapolis, IN: Hackett.

Goody, Jack. 1995. *The Expansive Moment: Anthropology in Britain and Africa, 1918–1970.* Cambridge: Cambridge University Press.

Grafton, Anthony and Jeffrey Hamburger. 2010. "Save the Warburg Library!" *New York Review of Books,* September 30.

Grant, B. Rosemary and Peter R. Grant 2003. "What Darwin's Finches Can Teach Us about the Evolutionary Origin and Regulation of Biodiversity." *Bioscience* 53 (10): 965–75.

Griaule, Marcel. 1938. *Masques Dogons.* Paris: Institut D'Ethnologie.

——. 1957. *Méthode de L'Ethnographie.* Paris: Presses Universitaires de France.

——. 1965. *Conversations with Ogotemmeli: An Introduction to Dogon Religious Ideas*. Oxford: Oxford University Press.

Griaule, Marcel and Germaine Dieterlen. 1954. "The Dogon of the French Sudan." In Forde, ed. 1954, pp. 83–110

——. 1986. *The Pale Fox*. Trans. S. Infantino. Chino Valley, AZ: Continuum Foundation.

Grinker, Roy Richard. 2000. *In the Arms of Africa: The Life of Colin M. Turnbull*. New York: St. Martin's Press.

Gross, John. 1988. "Political Consequences of the Islamic Viewpoint." *New York Times*, July 8, C25.

Grundmann, Herbert. 1995. *Religious Movements in the Middle Ages*. Trans. S. Rowan. Intro. R. Lerner. Notre Dame, IN: University of Notre Dame Press.

Gura, Philip. 2007. *American Transcendentalism: A History*. New York: Hill and Wang.

Gustafson, James M. 1970. "A Protestant Ethical Approach." In Noonan, ed. 1970, pp. 101–22.

Guttenplan, Samuel, ed. 1975. *Mind and Language*. Oxford: Oxford University Press.

Haack, Susan. 1995. "Vulgar Pragmatism: An Unedifying Prospect." In Saatkamp, ed. 1995, pp. 126–47.

Hacker, P. M. S. 1996. *Wittgenstein's Place in Twentieth-Century Analytic Philosophy*. Oxford: Blackwell.

Hacking, Ian. 1975. *Why Does Language Matter to Philosophy?* Cambridge: Cambridge University Press.

Hahn, Lewis Edwin, ed. 1999. *The Philosophy of Donald Davidson*. Chicago: Open Court Press.

Halivni, David Weiss. 1986. *Midrash, Mishnah, and Gemara: The Jewish Predilection for Justified Law*. Cambridge, MA: Harvard University Press.

Hamner, M. Gail. 2003. *American Pragmatism: A Religious Genealogy*. Oxford: Oxford University Press.

Handler, Richard. 1991. "An Interview with Clifford Geertz." *Current Anthropology* 32(5): 603–13.

Hanson, N. R. 1958. *Patterns of Discovery: An Inquiry into the Conceptual Foundations of Science*. Cambridge: Cambridge University Press.

Harman, Gilbert. 1978. "Relativistic Ethics: Morality as Politics." Repr. in Harman 2000, pp. 39–57.

——. 1999. "Moral Philosophy Meets Social Psychology: Virtue Ethics and the Fundamental Attribution Error." Repr. in Harman 2000, pp. 165–78.

——. 2000. *Explaining Value, and Other Essays in Moral Philosophy*. Oxford: Oxford University Press.

Harvey, Peter. 2000. *An Introduction to Buddhist Ethics*. Cambridge: Cambridge University Press.

Haskins, Charles Homer. 1929. *Studies in Mediaeval Culture*. Oxford: Oxford University Press.

Hassett, Miranda K. 2007. *Anglican Communion in Crisis: How Episcopal Dissidents and their African Allies are Reshaping Anglicanism.* Princeton: Princeton University Press.

Hauerwas, Stanley and Alasdair MacIntyre, eds. 1983. *Revisions: Changing Perspectives in Moral Philosophy.* Notre Dame, IN: University of Notre Dame Press.

Haywood, John. 2005. *The Penguin Historical Atlas of Ancient Civilizations.* London: Penguin Books.

Heine, Bernd. 1985. "The Mountain People: Some Notes on the Ik of North-Eastern Uganda." *Africa* 55(1): 3–16.

Helm, Paul. 1971. "Manifest and Latent Functions." *Philosophical Quarterly* 21(82): 516–27.

Hempel, Carl G. 1965. *Aspects of Scientific Explanation and Other Essays in the Philosophy of Science.* New York: Free Press.

Henry, Matthew. 1706. *Commentary on the Whole Bible.* <http://www.ccel.org/ccel/henry/mhc.i.html>.

Herdt, Jennifer. 1997. *Religion and Faction in Hume's Moral Philosophy.* Cambridge: Cambridge University Press.

Hollinger, David A. 1975. *Morris Cohen and the Scientific Ideal.* Cambridge, MA: MIT Press.

——. 1980. "The Problem of Pragmatism in American History." *Journal of American History* 67(1): 88–107.

Hollis, Martin and Steven Lukes, eds. 1982. *Rationality and Relativism.* Cambridge, MA: MIT Press.

Holly, Michael Ann. 1984. *Panofsky and the Foundations of Art History.* Ithaca, NY Cornell University Press.

Holton, Gerald. 1984. "Do Scientists Need a Philosophy?" Repr. in Holton 1998, pp. 163–78.

——. 1998. *The Advancement of Science, and Its Burdens: With a New Introduction.* Cambridge, MA: Harvard University Press.

Housley, Norman. 2006. *Contesting the Crusades.* Oxford: Blackwell Publishing.

Howe, David Walker 1970. *The Unitarian Conscience: Harvard Moral Philosophy, 1805–1861.* Cambridge, MA: Harvard University Press.

Hubert, Henri and Marcel Mauss. 1964. *Sacrifice: Its Nature and Function.* Trans. W. Halls Chicago: University of Chicago Press.

Hughes, Aaron W. 2009. "Crossing, Dwelling, and a Wandering Jew." *Journal of the American Academy of Religion* 77(2): 406–12.

Hume, David. 1902. *Enquiries concerning the Human Understanding and concerning the Principles of Morals.* Ed. L. A. Selby-Bigge. 2nd ed. Oxford: Oxford University Press.

——. 1985. *Essays Moral, Political, and Literary.* Ed. Eugene Miller. Indianapolis, IN: Liberty Classics.

——. 1992. *Writings on Religion.* Ed. Anthony Flew. LaSalle, IL: Open Court Press.

——. 1992a. *Natural History of Religion.* Repr. in Hume 1992, pp. 107–82.

——. 1992b. *Dialogues concerning Natural Religion.* Repr. in Hume 1992, pp. 185–292.

Jackson, Carl T. 1982. *The Oriental Religions and American Thought: Nineteenth Century Explorations*. Westport, CT: Greenwood Press.

James, Bill. 2001. *The New Bill James Historical Baseball Abstract*. New York: Free Press.

James, William. 1902. *The Varieties of Religious Experience*. New York: Longman, Green and Co.

John Paul II. 1995. *The Gospel of Life*. New York: Times Books.

Kellner, Menahem Marc, ed. 1978. *Contemporary Jewish Ethics*. New York: Sanhedrin Press.

Kenny, Anthony. 2008. "The Beginning of Individual Human Life." In Ostnor, ed. 2008, pp. 167–75.

Kerr, Fergus. 2002. *After Aquinas: Versions of Thomism*. Oxford: Blackwell.

——. 2007. *Twentieth-Century Catholic Theologians*, Oxford: Blackwell.

——. 2008. *"Work on Oneself": Wittgenstein's Philosophical Psychology*. Washington, DC: Institute for the Psychological Sciences.

Kim, Jaegwon. 1980. "Rorty on the Possibility of Philosophy." *Journal of Philosophy* 77(10): 588–97

——. 2006. *Philosophy of Mind*. 2nd ed. Cambridge, MA: Westview Press.

Kitcher, Patricia. 1985. "Narrow Taxonomy and Wide Functionalism." *Philosophy of Science* 49(4): 78–97.

Kline, George L., ed. 1963. *Alfred North Whitehead: Essays on His Philosophy*. Englewood Cliffs, NJ: Prentice-Hall.

Knott, Kim. 2009. "Spatial Theory and Spatial Methodology, Their Relationship and Application: A Transatlantic Engagement." *Journal of the American Academy of Religion* 77(2): 413–24.

Knox, Ronald. 1950. *Enthusiasm: A Chapter in the History of Religions*. Oxford: Oxford University Press.

Koyré, Alexandre. 1957. *From the Closed World to the Infinite Universe*. Baltimore: Johns Hopkins University Press.

Krausz, Michael, ed. 1989. *Relativism: Interpretation and Confrontation*. Notre Dame, IN: University of Notre Dame Press.

Kripke, Saul. 1982. *Wittgenstein on Rules and Private Language*. Cambridge, MA: Harvard University Press.

Kuhn, Thomas. 1957. *The Copernican Revolution: Planetary Astronomy in the Development of Western Thought*. Cambridge, MA: Harvard University Press.

——. 1970. *The Structure of Scientific Revolutions*. 2nd ed. Chicago: University of Chicago Press.

——. 1977. *The Essential Tension: Selected Studies in Scientific Tradition and Change*. Chicago: University of Chicago Press.

——. 2000. *The Road since Structure: Philosophical Essays, 1970–1993, with an Autobiographical Interview*. Ed. J. Conant and J. Haugland. Chicago: University of Chicago Press.

Kuklick, Bruce. 1977. *The Rise of American Philosophy: Cambridge, Massachusetts, 1860–1930*. New Haven: Yale University Press.

——. 2001. *A History of Philosophy in America*. Oxford: Oxford University Press.

Kuper, Adam. 1973. *Anthropologists and Anthropology: The British School, 1922–1972*. New York: Pica Press.

——. 1999. *Culture: The Anthropoligists' Account*. Cambridge, MA: Harvard University Press.

LaFleur, William R. 1992. *Liquid Life: Abortion and Buddhism in Japan*. Princeton: Princeton University Press.

Lakatos, Imre. 1978. *The Methodology of Scientific Research Programmes: Philosophical Papers*. Vol. 1. Ed. J. Worrall and E. Currie. Cambridge: Cambridge University Press.

Lambert, Malcolm. 1992. *Medieval Heresy: Popular Movements from the Gregorian Reform to the Reformation*. 2nd ed. Oxford: Blackwell.

Langdale, Allan. 1999. "Aspects of the Critical Reception and Intellectual History of Baxandall's Concept of the Period Eye." In Rifkin, ed. 1999, pp. 17–35.

Lawson, E. Thomas. 1984. *Religions of Africa*. San Francisco: Harper and Row.

——. 2006. Foreword in Tremlin 2006, pp. xi–xvii.

Lawson, E. Thomas and Robert McCauley. 1990. *Rethinking Religion: Connecting Cognition and Culture*. Cambridge: Cambridge University Press.

——. 1993. "Crisis of Conscience, Riddle of Identity: Making Space for a Cognitive Approach to Religious Phenomena." *Journal of the American Academy of Religion* 61(2): 201–23.

——. 2002. *Bringing Ritual to Mind: Psychological Foundations of Cultural Forms*. Cambridge: Cambridge University Press.

Leclercq, Jean. 1961. *The Love of Learning and the Desire for God*. Trans. C. Misrahi. New York: Fordham University Press.

Leeuw, Gerardus van der. 1938. *Religion in Essence and Manifestation: A Study in Phenomenology*. Trans. J. Turner. London: George Allen and Unwin.

LePore, Ernest, ed. 1986. *Truth and Interpretation: Perspectives on the Philosophy of Donald Davidson*. Oxford: Basil Blackwell.

Levinson, Henry Samuel. 1992. *Santayana, Pragmatism, and the Spiritual Life*. Chapel Hill, NC: University of North Carolina Press.

——. 2002. "Fits, Trances, and Visions: Experiencing Religion and Explaining Experience from Wesley to James." *Journal of the American Academy of Religion* 70(1): 226–30.

Lewis, Bernard. 1988. *The Political Language of Islam*. Chicago: University of Chicago Press.

——. 1993. *Islam and the West*. Oxford: Oxford University Press.

Lewis, David. 1969. *Convention: A Philosophical Study*. Cambridge, MA: Harvard University Press.

——. 1975. "Languages and Language." Repr. in Lewis 1983, pp. 163–88.

——. 1983. *Philosophical Papers*. Vol. I. Oxford: Oxford University Press.

——. 1986. *Philosophical Papers*, Vol. II. Oxford: Oxford University Press.

——. 2000. "Causation as Influence." *Journal of Philosophy* 97(4): 182–97.

Lewontin, Richard. 1991. *Biology as Ideology: The Doctrine of DNA*. New York: Harper Collins.

——. 2000. *It Aint Necessarily So: The Dream of the Human Genome and Other Illusions*. New York: New York Review of Books.

——. 2000a. *The Triple Helix: Gene, Organism and Environment*. Cambridge, MA: Harvard University Press.

Lienhardt, R. Godfrey. 1961. *Divinity and Experience: The Religion of the Dinka*. Oxford: Oxford University Press.

Linsky, Leonard, ed. 1952. *Semantics and the Philosophy of Language*. Urbana, IL: University of Illinois Press.

Lloyd, G. E. R. 1987. *The Revolutions of Wisdom: Studies in the Claims and Practice of Ancient Greek Science*. Berkeley: University of California Press.

Lopez, Donald S. 1995. *Curators of the Buddha: The Study of Buddhism under Colonialism*. Chicago: University of Chicago Press.

Lovejoy, Arthur O. 1936. *The Great Chain of Being: A Study in the History of an Idea*. Cambridge, MA: Harvard University Press.

Lukes, Steven. 1972. *Emile Durkheim, His Life and Work: A Historical and Critical Study*. New York: Harper and Row.

——. 2008. *Moral Relativism*. New York: Picador.

Lyons, David, ed. 1979. *Rights*. Belmont, CA: Wadsworth.

McGinn, Bernard. 1979. *Visions of the End: Apocalyptic Traditions in the Middle Ages*. New York: Columbia University Press.

MacIntyre, Alasdair. 1964. "In Understanding Religion Compatible with Believing?" Repr. in Wilson ed., 1970, pp. 62–77.

——. 1966. *A Short History of Ethics*. New York: Macmillan and Co.

——. 1981. *After Virtue*. Notre Dame, IN: University of Notre Dame Press.

——. 1991. "Incommensurability, Truth, and the Conversation between Confucians and Aristotelians about the Virtues." In Deutch, ed. 1991, pp. 104–22.

——. 1998. *A Short History of Ethics*. 2nd ed. Notre Dame, IN: University of Notre Dame.

Mackie, J. L. 1974. *The Cement of the Universe: A Study in Causation*. Oxford: Oxford University Press.

Madden, Thomas F., ed. 2002. *The Crusades*. Oxford: Blackwell.

——. 2004. *Crusades: The Illustrated History*. Ann Arbor, MI: University of Michigan Press.

Malachowski, Alan, ed. 1990. *Rorty: Critical Responses to Philosophy and the Mirror of Nature (and Beyond)*. Oxford: Basil Blackwell.

Malinowski, Bronislaw. 1926. *Myth in Primitive Psychology*. New York: W. W. Norton.

Marrou, Henri I. 1956. *History of Education in Antiquity*. Trans. G. Lamb. New York: Sheed and Ward.

Maurer, Daphne and Charles Maurer. 1988. *The World of the Newborn*. New York: Basic Books.

Meiland, Jack and Michael Krausz, eds. 1982. *Relativism, Cognitive and Moral*. Notre Dame, IN: University of Notre Dame Press.

Meillassoux, Claude. 1991. "Comments on van Beek." *Current Anthropology* 32(2): 163

Mensch, Elizabeth and Alan Freeman. 1993. *The Politics of Virtue: Is Abortion Debatable?* Durham, NC: Duke University Press.

Mencius. 2004. *Mencius.* Trans. D. C. Lau. Rev. ed. London: Penguin Books.

Middeldorf, Ulrich. 1975. "Michael Baxandall, *Painting and Experience in Fifteenth Century Italy.*" *Art Bulletin* 57(2): 284–5.

Milgram, Stanley. 1963. "Behavioral Study of Obedience." *Journal of Psychology* 67: 371–78.

Miller, Richard B. 1991. *Interpretations of Conflict.* Chicago: University of Chicago Press.

——. 2002. "Aquinas and the Presumption against Killing and War." *Journal of Religion* 82(2): 173–204.

Mills, C. Wright. 1959. *The Sociological Imagination.* Oxford: Oxford University Press.

Misak, Cheryl. 2004. *Truth and the End of Inquiry: A Peircean Account of Truth.* Rev. ed. Oxford: Oxford University Press.

——. 2004a. "C. S. Peirce on Vital Matters." In Misak, ed. 2004, pp. 150–74.

——. 2010. "Richard Rorty's Place in the Pragmatist Pantheon." In Auxier and Hahn, eds. 2010, pp. 27–43.

Misak, Cheryl, ed. 2004. *The Cambridge Companion to Peirce.* Cambridge: Cambridge University Press.

——. ed. 2007. *The New Pragmatists.* Oxford: Oxford University Press.

Momigliano, Arnaldo. 1994. *Studies on Modern Scholarship.* Ed. and trans. G. Bowersock and T. Cornell. Berkeley: University of California Press.

Monk, Ray. 1990. *Ludwig Wittgenstein: The Duty of Genius.* New York: Free Press.

Moore, R. I. 2007. *The Formation of a Persecuting Society.* 2nd ed. Oxford: Blackwell.

Morris, Donald R. 1965. *The Washing of the Spears: A History of the Rise of the Zulu Nation under Shaka and its Fall in the Zulu War of 1879.* New York: Simon and Schuster.

Mossner, Ernest C. 1954. *The Life of David Hume.* Austin, TX: University of Texas Press.

Motolinía, Toribio de Benevente. 1985. *Historia de los Indios de la Nueva España.* Ed. Georges Baudot. Madrid: Editorial Castalia.

Muller, Joseph-Emile. 1967. *Fauvism.* New York: Frederick A. Praeger.

Mure, Geoffrey R. E. 1940. *An Introduction to Hegel.* Oxford: Oxford University Press.

——. 1958. *Retreat from Truth.* Oxford: Basil Blackwell.

Nagel, Ernest. 1933. "Charles Peirce's Guesses at the Riddle." *Journal of Philosophy* 30(14): 365–86.

——. 1936. "Impressions and Appraisals of Analytic Philosophy in Europe, I." *Journal of Philosophy* 33(1): 5–24.

——. 1936a. "Impressions and Appraisals of Analytic Philosophy in Europe, II." *Journal of Philosophy* 33(2): 29–53.

——. 1940. "Charles S. Pierce, Pioneer of Modern Empiricism." *Philosophy of Science* 7: 69–80.

Nagel, Thomas. 1979, *Mortal Questions*. Cambridge: Cambridge University Press.

Neurath, Otto. 1931. "Sociology and Physicalism." Repr. in Ayer 1959, pp. 282–317.

Nicolas, A. T. de. 1977. "Cultural Lobotomy: The Failure of Philosophy." *Philosophy East and West*, 27: 97–113.

Noonan, John T. 1965. *Contraception*. Cambridge, MA: Harvard University Press.

———. 1970. "An Almost Absolute Value in History." In Noonan, ed. 1970, pp. 1–59.

———. 1972. *Power to Dissolve: Lawyers and Marriages in the Courts of the Roman Curia*. Cambridge, MA: Harvard University Press.

Noonan, John T., ed. 1970. *The Morality of Abortion: Legal and Historical Perspectives*. Cambridge, MA: Harvard University Press.

Novak, David. 1974. "A Jewish View of Abortion." Repr, in Novak 2008, pp. 266–78.

———. 2008. *Tradition in the Public Square: A David Novak Reader*. Ed. R. Rashkover and M. Kavka. Grand Rapids, MI: Eerdmans.

Nystrom, Derek and Kent Puckett, eds. 1998. *Against Bosses, Against Oligarchies: A Conversation with Richard Rorty*. Charlottesville, VA: Prickly Pear Pamphlets.

Oliver, Roland and Anthony Atmore. 2001. *Medieval Africa, 1250–1800*. Cambridge: Cambridge University Press.

———. 2005. *Africa since 1800*. 5th ed. Cambridge: Cambridge University Press.

Oliver, Roland and Gervase Mathew, eds. 1963 *History of East Africa*. Vol. I. Oxford: Oxford University Press.

Ostnor, Lars, ed. 2008. *Stem Cells, Human Embryos and Ethics*. Dordrecht: Springer.

Otto, Rudolf. 1950. *The Idea of the Holy*. Trans. Harvey. 2nd ed. Oxford: Oxford University Press.

Pataux, Agnès. 2004. *Dogon: People of the Cliffs*. Milan: Five Continents.

Peirce, Charles Sanders. 1868. "Questions Concerning Certain Faculties Claimed for Man." Repr. in Peirce 1992, pp. 11–27.

———. 1868a. "The Consequences of Four Incapacities." Repr. in Peirce 1992, pp. 28–55.

———. 1869. "Grounds of Validity of the Laws of Logic: Further Consequences of Four Incapacities." Repr. in Peirce 1992, pp. 56–82.

———. 1871. "Fraser's *The Works of George Berkeley*." Repr. in Peirce 1992, pp. 83–105.

———. 1877. "The Fixation of Belief." Repr. in Peirce 1992, pp. 109–23.

———. 1878. "How to Make Our Ideas Clear." Repr. in Peirce 1992, pp. 124–41.

———. 1878a. "Deduction, Induction, and Hypothesis." Repr. in Peirce 1992, pp. 186–99.

———. 1891. "The Architecture of Theories." Repr. in Peirce 1992, pp. 285–97.

———. 1892. "The Doctrine of Necessity Examined." Repr. in Peirce 1992, pp. 298–11.

———. 1892a. "Man's Glassy Essence." Repr. in Peirce 1992, pp. 334–51.

———. 1893. "Evolutionary Love." Repr. in Peirce 1992, pp. 352–71.

———. 1898. "The First Rule of Logic." Repr. in Peirce 1998, pp. 42–56.

———. 1901. "Pearson's *Grammar of Science*." Repr. in Peirce 1998, pp. 57–66.

———. 1903. "The Categories Undefended". Repr. in Peirce 1998, pp. 161–78.

———. 1905. "What Pragmatism Is." Repr. in Peirce 1998, pp. 331–45.

———. 1906. "The Basis of Pragmaticism in Phaneroscopy." Repr. in Peirce 1998, pp. 360–70.

——. 1906a. "The Basis of Pragmaticism in the Normative Sciences." Repr. in Peirce 1998, pp. 371–97.

——. 1913. "An Essay towards Improving our Reasoning in Security and in Uberty." Repr. in Peirce 1998, pp. 463–74.

——. 1923. *Chance, Love, and Logic.* Ed. Morris R. Cohen. New York: Harcourt, Brace and Co.

——. 1992. *The Essential Peirce*, Vol. 1: *1867–1893.* Ed. N. Houser and C. Klousel. Bloomington, IN: Indiana University Press.

——. 1998. *The Essential Peirce*, Vol. 2: *1893–1913.* Ed. by the Peirce Edition Project. Bloomington, IN: Indiana University Press.

Penner, Hans. 1989. "What's Wrong with Functional Explanations?" Repr. in Frankenberry and Penner 1999, pp. 246–72.

——. 1995. "Why Does Semantics Matter to the Study of Religion?" Repr. in Frankenberry and Penner 1999, pp. 473–506.

——. 2002. "You Don't Read a Myth for Information." In Frankenberry, ed. 2002, pp. 153–70.

Perry, John, ed. 1975. *Personal Identity.* Berkeley: University of California Press.

Phillips, D. Z. 1976. *Religion without Explanation.* Oxford: Basil Blackwell.

Phillips, D. Z. and Mario von der Ruhr, eds. 2008. *Religion and the End of Metaphysics.* Tubingen: Mohr Siebeck.

Pinckaers, Servais. 1993. "Dominican Moral Theology in the 20th Century." Repr. in Pinckaers 2005, pp. 73–89.

——. 1995. *The Sources of Christian Ethics.* Trans. from the 3rd ed by Mary Thomas Noble. Washington, DC: Catholic University of America Press.

——. 2005. *The Pinckaers Reader: Renewing Thomistic Moral Theology.* Ed. J. Berkman and C. Titus. Trans. M.T. Noble Washington, DC: Catholic University of America Press.

Pitcher, George, ed. 1966. *Wittgenstein, The Philosophical Investigations: A Collection of Critical Essays.* Notre Dame, IN: University of Notre Dame Press.

Plantinga, Alvin. 1967. *God and Other Minds: A Study of the Rational Justification of Belief in God.* Ithaca, NY: Cornell University Press.

——. 1983. "Reason and Belief in God." In Plantinga and Wolterstorff, eds. 1983, pp. 16–93.

Plantinga, Alvin and Nicholas Wolterstorff, eds. 1983. *Faith and Rationality: Reason and Belief in God.* Notre Dame, IN: University of Notre Dame Press.

Polkinghorne, John. 2002. *Quantum Physics: A Very Short Introduction.* Oxford: Oxford University Press.

Pols, Edward. 1958. "To Live at Ease Ever After." *Sewanee Review* 66(2): 229–51.

——. 1975. *Meditation on a Prisoner: Towards Understanding Action and Mind.* Carbondale, IL: Southern Illinois University Press.

——. 1992. *Radical Realism: Direct Knowing in Science and Philosophy.* Ithaca, NY: Cornell University Press.

Pope, Stephen J., ed. 2002. *The Ethics of Aquinas.* Washington, DC: Georgetown University Press.

Prebish, Charles and Kenneth Tanaka, eds. 1998. *The Faces of Buddhism in America.* Berkeley: University of California Press.

Preziosi, Donald. 2009. *The Art of Art History: A Critical Anthology*. Oxford: Oxford University Press.

Proudfoot, Wayne. 1976. "Mysticism, the Numinous, and the Moral." *Journal of Religious Ethics* 4(1): 3–28.

———. 1985. *Religious Experience*. Berkeley: University of California Press.

———. 1993. "Explaining the Unexplainable response." *Journal of American Academy of Religion* 61(4): 793–803.

Pruitt, Roy W. 1985. "The Boddhisattva Paradox." *Philosophy East and West* 35.

Putnam, Hilary Press. 1974. "Language and Reality." Repr. in Putnam 1975b, pp. 272–90.

———. 1975. "The Meaning of 'Meaning.'" Repr. in Putnam 1975b, pp. 215–71.

———. 1975a. *Mathematics, Matter, and Method: Philosophical Papers*. Vol. I. Cambridge: Cambridge University.

———. 1975b. *Mind, Language, and Reality: Philosophical Papers*. Vol. 2. Cambridge: Cambridge University Press.

———. 1983. *Reason, Truth and History*. Cambridge: Cambridge University Press.

———. 1991. "Reichenbach's Metaphysical Picture." Repr. in Putnam 1994, pp. 99–114.

———. "The Question of Realism." Repr. in Putnam 1994, pp. 294–312.

———. 1994. *Words and Life*. Ed. James Conant. Cambridge, MA: Harvard University Press.

———. 1997. "A Half Century of Philosophy, Viewed from Within." *Daedalus* 126(1): 175–208.

Quine, Willard van Orman. 1951. "Two Dogmas of Empiricim". Repr. in Quine 1961, pp. 20–46.

———. 1960. *Word and Object*. Cambridge, MA: MIT Press.

———. 1961. *From a Logical Point of View*. 2nd rev. ed. Cambridge, MA: Harvard University Press.

———. 1968. "Reply to Chomsky." In Davidson and Hintikka, eds. 1968, pp. 302–11.

———. 1976. *The Ways of Paradox and Other Essays*. Rev. ed. Cambridge, MA: Harvard University Press.

———. 1981. *Theories and Things*. Cambridge, MA: Harvard University Press.

Rabinow, Paul. 1986. "Representations Are Social Facts: Modernity and Post-Modernity in Anthropology." In Clifford and Marcus, eds. 1986, pp. 7234–61.

Radner, Michael and Stephen Winokur, eds. 1970. *Analyses of Theories and Methods of Physics and Psychology: Minnesota Studies in the Philosophy of Science*, Vol. IV. Minneapolis: University of Minnesota Press.

Randall, John Herman. 1960. *Aristotle*. New York: Columbia University Press.

Rappaport, Roy A. 1984. *Pigs for the Ancestors: Ritual in the Ecology of a New Guinea People*. Rev. ed. New Haven: Yale University Press.

Rashdall, Hastings. 1936. *The Universities of Europe in the Middle Ages*. Ed. F. Powicke and A. Emden, 3 vols. Oxford: Oxford University Press.

Rawls, John. 1997. "The Idea of Public Reason Revisited." Repr. in Rawls 1999, pp. 573–615.

——. 1999. *Collected Papers*. Ed. S. Freeman Cambridge, MA: Harvard University Press.

Ray, Benjamin. 1991. *Myth, Ritual, and Kingship in Buganda*. Oxford: Oxford University Press.

Reichenbach, Hans. 1951. *The Rise of Scientific Philosophy*. Berkeley: University of California Press.

Reichler, Joseph L. 1982. *The Baseball Encyclopedia*. 5th ed. New York: MacMillan and Co.

Renou, Louis. 1964. *Indian Literature*. Trans. P. Evans. New York: Walker and Co.

Rescher, Nicholas. 1980. "Conceptual Schemes." In French et al., eds. 1980, pp. 323–45.

Rewald, John. 1973. *The History of Impressionism*. 4th ed., New York: Metropolitan Museum of Art.

Richardson, Cyril C., ed. 1953. *Early Christian Fathers*. Philadelphia: Westminster Press.

Richter, Gisela. 1974. *A Handbook of Greek Art*. 7th ed. London: Phaidon Books.

Richter, Hans. 1965. *Dada: Art and Anti-Art*. New York: Abrams Books.

Rifaat, Alifa. 1987. *Distant View of a Minaret*. Trans. D. Johnson-Davies. London: Heinemann Educational Books.

Rifkin, Adrian, ed. 1999. *About Michael Baxandall*. Oxford: Blackwell.

Riley-Smith, Jonathan. 1980. "Crusading as an Act of Love." Repr. in Madden 2002, pp. 32–50.

Rishel, Joseph and Katherine Sachs, eds. 2009. *Cezanne and Beyond*. Philadelphia: Philadelphia Museum of Art.

Roberts, Adam and Richard Guelff, eds. 2000. *Documents on the Laws of War*. 3rd ed. Oxford: Oxford University Press.

Rorty, Amelie, ed. 1980. *The Identity of Persons*. Berkeley: University of California Press.

Rorty, Richard M. 1959. *"Experience and the Analytic: A Reconsideration of Empiricism* by Alan Pasch." *Ethics* 70(1): 75–7.

——. 1961. "Pragmatism, Categories, and Language." *Philosophical Review* 70(2): 197–223.

——. 1962. "Realism, Categories, and the 'Linguistic Turn'. [trs.].'" *International Philosophical Quarterly* 2(2): 307–22.

——. 1963. "The Subjectivist Principle and the Linguistic Turn." In Kline, ed. 1963, pp. 134–57.

——. 1972. "The World Well Lost." Repr. in Rorty 1982, pp. 3–18.

——. 1976. "Realism and Reference." *The Monist* 59(3): 321–40.

——. 1976a. "Realism and Necessity: Milton Fisk's *Nature and Necessity*." *Nous* 10 (3): 345–54.

——. 1976b. "Professionalized Philosophy and Transcendentalist Culture." Repr. in Rorty 1982, pp. 60–71.

———. 1977. "*Why Does Language Matter to Philosophy?* by Ian Hacking." *Journal of Philosophy* 74(7): 416–32.

———. 1979. *Philosophy and the Mirror of Nature.* Princeton: Princeton University Press.

———. 1979a. "On Worldmaking." *Yale Review* 69(2): 276–9.

———. 1982. *Consequences of Pragmatism: Essays 1972–1980.* Minneapolis: University of Minnesota Press.

———. 1982a. "Philosophy in America Today." Repr. in Rorty 1982, pp. 211–30.

———. 1982b. "Introduction: Pragmatism and Philosophy." In Rorty 1982, pp. xiii–xlvii.

———. 1984. "The Historiography of Philosophy: Four Genres." Repr. in Rorty 1998a, pp. 247–3.

———. 1986. "Pragmatism, Davidson and Truth." Repr. in Rorty 1991, pp. 126–50.

———. 1987. "Non-Reductive Physicalism." Repr. in Rorty 1991, pp. 113–25.

———. 1991. *Objectivity, Relativism, and Truth: Philosophical Papers.* Vol. 1. Cambridge: Cambridge University Press.

———. 1991a. "Inquiry as Recontextualization." In Rorty 1991, pp. 93–110.

———. 1993. "Trotsky and the Wild Orchids." Repr. in Rorty 1999, pp. 3–20.

———. 1993a. "Hilary Putnam and the Relativist Menace." Repr. in Rorty 1998a, pp. 43–83.

———. 1993b. "Human Rights, Rationality, and Sentimentality." Repr. in Rorty 1998a, pp. 167–85.

———. 1994. "Feminism and Pragmatism." Repr. in Rorty 1998a, pp. 202–27.

———. 1994a. "Religion As Conversation-stopper." Repr. in Rorty 1999, pp. 168–74.

———. 1995. "Response to Haack." In Saatkamp, ed. 1995, pp. 148–53.

———. 1997. "Justice as a Larger Loyalty." Repr. in Rorty 2007, pp. 42–55.

———. 1998. *Achieving Our Country: Leftist Thought in Twentieth-Century America.* Cambridge, MA: Harvard University Press.

———. 1998a. *Truth and Progress: Philosophical Papers.* Vol. 3. Cambridge: Cambridge University Press.

———. 1998b. "Antisceptical Weapons: Michael Williams versus Donald Davidson." In Rorty 1998a, pp. 153–63.

———. 1999. *Philosophy and Social Hope.* Harmondsworth: Penguin Books.

———. 1999a. "Davidson's Mental-Physical Distinction." In Hahn, ed. 1999, pp. 575–94.

———. 2000. "Universality and Truth." In Brandom, ed. 2000, pp. 1–30.

———. 2000a. "Response to Williams." In Brandom, ed. 2000, pp. 213–19.

———. 2003. "Religion in the Public Square: A Reconsideration." *Journal of Religious Ethics* 31(1): 141–9.

———. 2007. *Philosophy as Cultural Politics: Philosophical Papers.* Vol. 4. Cambridge: Cambridge University Press.

———. 2009. "The Philosopher as Expert." In the 30th anniversary ed. of Rorty 1979, pp. 395–421.

———. 2010. "Intellectual Biography." In Auxier and Hahn, eds. 2010, pp. 3–24.

Rorty, Richard, ed. 1967. *The Linguistic Turn: Recent Essays in Philosophical Method.* Chicago: University of Chicago Press.

Rosen, Stanley (S.R.). 1980 "Rorty, R. *Philosophy and the Mirror of Nature.*" *Review of Metaphysics* 33(4): 799–802.

Rosner, Fred. 1968. "The Jewish Attitude toward Abortion." Repr. in Kellner 1978, pp. 257–69.

Royce, Josiah. 1908. *The Philosophy of Loyalty.* New York: MacMillan.

——. 1982. *The Philosophy of Josiah Royce.* Ed. J. Roth. Indianapolis, IN: Hackett.

Rubio, Julie Hanlon. 2010. *Family Ethics: Practices for Christians.* Washington, DC: Georgetown University Press.

Runciman, Steven. 1951. *A History of the Crusades.* Vol. I: *The First Crusade and the Foundation of the Kingdom of Jerusalem.* Cambridge: Cambridge University Press.

Ruse, Michael. 2006. *Darwinism and its Discontents.* Cambridge: Cambridge University Press.

Russell, Jeffrey Burton. 1991. *Inventing the Flat Earth: Columbus and Modern Historians.* Westport, CT: Praeger.

Saatkamp, Herman J., ed. 1995. *Rorty and Pragmatism: The Philosopher Responds to his Critics.* Nashville, TN: Vanderbilt University Press.

Sacks, Oliver. 1985. *The Man Who Mistook his Wife for a Hat and Other Clinical Tales.* New York: Simon and Schuster.

Said, Edward. 1978. *Orientalism.* New York: Pantheon Books.

Schapiro, Meyer. 1956. "Freud and Leonardo: An Art Historical Study." Repr. in Schapiro 1998, pp. 153–92.

——. 1978. *Modern Art: 19th and 20th centuries.* New York: George Braziller.

——. 1998. *Theory and Philosophy of Art: Style, Artist, and Society.* New York: George Braziller.

Schauss, Hayyim. 1938. *The Jewish Festivals: History and Observance.* New York: Schocken Books.

Schleiermacher, Friedrich. 1996. *On Religion: Speeches to its Cultured Despisers.* Trans. R, Crouter. 2nd ed. Cambridge: Cambridge University Press.

Schwartz, Benjamin. 1985. *The World of Thought in Ancient China.* Cambridge, MA: Harvard University Press.

Schwartz, Robert. 1983. "*Philosophy and the Mirror of Nature.* Richard Rorty." *Journal of Philosophy* 80(1): 651–677.

Scott, John D. and Tony Pawson. 2000. "Cell Communication: The Inside Story." *Scientific American* 282(6): 72–9.

Segal, Robert. 2010. "Functionalism since Hempel." *Method and Theory in the Study of Religion* 22(4): 340–53.

Segal, Robert, ed. 2006. *Blackwell Companion to the Study of Religion.* Oxford: Blackwell.

Sellars, Wilfrid. 1948. "Realism and the New Way of Words." Repr. in Feigl and Sellars 1949, pp. 424–56.

——. 1956. "Empiricism and the Philosophy of Mind." Repr. in Sellars 1963, pp. 127–96.

——. 1960. "Being and Being Known." Repr. in Sellars 1963, pp. 41–59.

——. 1962. "Truth and 'Correspondence.'" Repr. in Sellars 1963, pp. 321–58.

——. 1963. *Science, Perception, and Reality*. London: Routledge and Kegan Paul.

——. 1968. *Science and Metaphysics: Variations on Kantian Themes*. London: Routledge and Kegan Paul.

——. 1997. *Empiricism and the Philosophy of Mind*. ed. R. Brandom. Cambridge, MA: Harvard University Press.

Sellars, Wilfrid and John Hospers, eds. 1952. *Readings in Ethical Theory*. New York: Appleton, Century, Crofts.

Shapin, Steven. 1996. *The Scientific Revolution*. Chicago: University of Chicago Press.

Shapiro, Ian, ed. 1995. *Abortion: The Surpeme Court Decisions*. Indianapolis: Hackett Books.

Sharf, Robert H. 1993. "Zen and Japanese Nationalism." *History of Religions* 33(1), pp. 1–43.

Shook, John R. and Joseph Margolis, eds. 2009. *A Companion to Pragmatism*. Oxford: Blackwell.

Shute, Stephen and Susan Hurley, eds. 1993. *On Human Rights*. New York: Basic Books.

Sinith, Heng. 2009. "Cambodian village worships calf that had reptilian skin." *Richmond Times-Dispatch*, 22 August, p. A2.

Skinner, Quentin. 2002. *Visions of Politics*. Vol. I: *Regarding Method*. Cambridge: Cambridge University Press.

Skinner, Quentin, ed. 1985. *The Return of Grand Theory in the Human Sciences*, Cambridge: Cambridge University Press.

Slingerland, Edward. 2008. "Who's Afraid of Reductionism? The Study of Religion in the Age of Cognitive Science." *Journal of the American Academy of Religion* 76 (2): 375–411.

Smith, Jonathan Z. 1987. *To Take Place: Toward Theory in Ritual*. Chicago: University of Chicago Press.

——. 2001. "A Twice-Told Tale: The History of the History of Religions' History." *Numen* 48(2): 131–46.

——. 2002. "Manna, mana, everywhere and /_/_/_." In Frankenberry, ed. 2002, pp. 188–212.

Smith, Quentin. 1999. "George Geiger, 1903–1998." *Proceedings and Addresses of the American Philosophical Association* 72(5): 204–6.

Soames, Scott. 2003. *Philosophical Analysis in the Twentieth Century*. 2 vols. Princeton: Princeton University Press.

Solomon, Norman. 1996. *Judaism: A Very Short Introduction*. Oxford: Oxford University Press.

Solomon, Robert C. 1974. "Freud's Neurological Theory of Mind." In Wollheim, ed. 1974, pp. 25–52.

Sosa, Ernest, ed. 1975. *Causation and Conditionals*. Oxford: Oxford University Press.

Spickard, James V. 1989. "A Guide to Mary Douglas's Three Versions of Grid/Group Theory." *Sociological Analysis* 50(2): 151–70.

——. 1991. "A Revised Functionalism in the Sociology of Religion: Mary Douglas's Recent Work." *Religion* 21(2): 141–64.

——. 1999. "Missing Persons: A Critique of Personhood in the Social Sciences." *Sociology of Religion* 60(3): 337–9.

Staal, Frits. 1974. "Review: *Mysticism and Morality.*" *Journal of Philosophy* 71(7): 174–81.

Stocking, George W. 1983. "The Ethnographer's Magic: Fieldwork in British Anthropology from Tylor to Malinowski." In Stocking, ed. 1983, 70–120.

Stocking, George, ed. 1983. *Observers Observed: Essays on Ethnographic Fieldwork.* Madison, WI: University of Wisconsin Press.

Stout, Jeffrey. 1981. *The Flight from Authority: Religion, Morality, and the Quest for Autonomy.* South Bend, IN: University of Notre Dame Press.

——. 1983. "Holism and Comparative Ethics: A Response to Little." *Journal of Religious Ethics* 11(2): 301–16.

——. 2002. "Radical Interpretation and Pragmatism: Davidson, Rorty, and Brandom on Truth." In Frankenberry, ed. 2002, pp. 25–52.

——. 2004. *Democracy and Tradition.* Princeton: Princeton University Press.

Stout, Jeffrey and Robert MacSwain, eds. 2004. *Grammar and Grace: Reformulations of Aquinas and Wittgenstein.* London: SCM Press.

Strack, Hermann L. 1931. *Introduction to the Talmud and Midrash.* New York: Atheneum.

Stroud, Barry. 1965. "Wittgenstein and Logical Necessity." Repr. in Pitcher 1966, pp. 477–96.

Suppe, Frederick, ed. 1977. *The Structure of Scientific Theories.* 2nd ed. Urbana IL: University of Illinois Press.

Tarski, Alfred. 1944. "The Semantic Conception of Truth and the Foundations of Semantics." Repr. in Feigl and Sellars 1949, pp. 52–84.

——. 1956. *Logic, Semantics, Metamathematics: Papers from 1923–1938.* Ed. J. H. Woodger. Oxford: Oxford University Press.

Taves, Ann. 1999. *Fits, Trances, and Visions: Experiencing Religion and Explaining Experience from Wesley to James.* Princeton: Princeton University Press.

——. 2009. *Religious Experience Reconsidered: A Building-Block Approach to the Study of Religion and Other Special Things.* Princeton: Princeton University Press.

Taylor, Charles. 1973. "Peaceful Coexistence in Psychology." Repr. in Taylor 1985, pp. 117–38.

——. 1985. *Human Agency and Language: Philosophical Papers.* Vol. 1. Cambridge: Cambridge University Press.

Taylor, Joshua. 1957. *Learning to Look: A Handbook for the Visual Arts.* Chicago: University of Chicago Press.

Taylor, Mark C., ed. 1998. *Critical Terms for Religious Studies.* Chicago: University of Chicago Press.

Thayer, H. S. 1968. *Meaning and Action: A Critical History of Pragmatism.* Indianapolis, IN: Bobbs-Merrill.

Toorn, Karel van der. 2007. *Scribal Culture and the Making of the Hebrew Bible.* Cambridge, MA: Harvard University Press.

Torrell, Jean-Pierre. 1996. *Saint Thomas Aquinas.* Vol. 1: *The Person and His Work.* Trans. Royal. Washington, DC: Catholic University of America Press.

——. 2005. *Aquinas's Summa: Background, Structure, and Reception*. Washington, DC: Catholic University of America Press.

Tremlin, Todd. 2006. *Minds and Gods: The Cognitive Foundations of Religion*. Cambridge: Cambridge University Press.

Tsuji, Shizuo. 2006. *Japanese Cooking: A Simple Art*. Rev. ed. Tokyo: Kodansha International.

Tugwell, Simon. 1982. *Early Dominicans, Selected Writings*. Ramsey, NJ: Paulist Press.

Tugwell, Simon, ed. and trans. 1988. *Albert and Thomas, Selected Writings*. Mahwah, NJ: Paulist Press.

Turnbull, Colin M. 1972. *The Mountain People*. New York: Simon and Schuster.

Turner, Victor. 1969. *The Ritual Process: Structure and Anti-Structure*. Chicago: Aldine Publishing.

Tweed, Thomas A. 1992. *The American Encounter with Buddhism, 1844–1912: Victorian Culture and the Limits of Dissent*. Bloomington, IN: Indiana University Press.

——. 1997. *Our Lady of the Exile: Diasporic Religion at a Cuban Catholic Shrine in Miami*. Oxford: Oxford University Press.

——. 2000. "Preface." In *The American Encounter with Buddhism, 1844–1912: Victorian Culture and the Limits of Dissent*. Paperback ed. Chapel Hill, NC: University of North Carolina Press.

——. 2006. *Crossing and Dwelling: A Theory of Religion*. Cambridge, MA: Harvard University Press.

——. 2009. "Crabs, Crustaceans, Crabiness, and Outrage: A Response." *Journal of the American Academy of Religion* 77(2): 445–59.

Tweed, Thomas A. and Stephen Prothero, eds. 1999. *Asian Religions in America: A Documentary History*. Oxford: Oxford University Press.

Tyerman, Christopher. 2004. *The Crusades: A Very Short Introduction*. Oxford: Oxford University Press.

——. 2006. *God's War: A New History of the Crusades*. Cambridge, MA: Harvard University Press.

Tyler, Stephen A. 1986. "Post-Modern Ethnography: From Document of the Occult to Occult Document." In Clifford and Marcus, eds. 1986, 122–40.

Upton, Candace L. 2009. "Virtue Ethics and Moral Psychology: The Situationism Debate." *Journal of Ethics* 13: 103–115.

Urmson, J. O. 1956. *Philosophical Analysis: Its Development between the Two World Wars*. Oxford: Oxford University Press.

Vásquez, Manuel A. 2009. "The Limits of the Hydrodynamics of Religion." *Journal of the American Academy of Religion* 77(2): 434–45.

Vries, S. J. de. 1962. "Biblical Criticism." In *The Interpreter's Dictionary of the Bible*. Nashville, TN: Abingdon Press.

Warburg, Aby. 1995. *Images from the Region of the Pueblo Indians of North America*. Trans. Michael Steinberg. Ithaca, NY: Cornell University Press.

Weinberg, Steven. 1993. *The First Three Minutes: A Modern View of the Origin of the Universe*. Rev. ed. New York: Basic Books.

Werblowsky, R. J. Zwi. 1991. "*Mizuko kuyo*: Notulae on the Most Important 'New Religion' of Japan." *Japanese Journal of Religious Studies* 18(4): 295–354.

White, Morton. 1956. *Toward Reunion in Philosophy.* Cambridge, MA: Harvard University Press.

Whitehouse, Harvey. 1995. *Inside the Cult: Religious Innovation and Transmission in Papua New Guinea.* Oxford: Oxford University Press.

Whitehouse, Harvey and Luther Martin, eds. 2004. *Theorizing Religions Past: Archaeology, History, and Cognition.* Walnut Creek, CA: Altamira Press.

Wiener, Philip P. 1949. *Evolution and the Founders of Pragmatism.* Cambridge, MA: Harvard University Press.

——. 1952. "Peirce's Evolutionary Interpretation of the History of Science." In Wiener and Young, eds. 1952, pp. 143–52.

Wiener, Philip P. and Frederic H. Young, eds. 1952. *Studies in the Philosophy of Charles Sanders Peirce.* Cambridge, MA: Harvard University Press.

Wiggins, David. 2004. "Reflections on Inquiry and Truth Arising from Peirce's Method for the Fixation of Belief." In Misak, ed. 2004, pp. 87–126.

Willett, Frank. 1971. *African Art: An Introduction.* Oxford: Oxford University Press.

Williams, Michael. 1991. *Unnatural Doubts.* Oxford: Blackwell.

——. 2009. "Introduction." 30th anniversary ed. of Rorty 1979, pp. xiii–xxix.

Williams, Peter W. 1990. *America's Religions: Traditions and Cultures.* New York: MacMillan.

Wilson, Bryan, ed. 1970. *Rationality.* Oxford: Basil Blackwell.

Woiak, Joanne. 2004. "Pearson, Karl." *Dictionary of National Biography.* Oxford: Oxford University Press.

Wolff, Kurt H., ed. 1960. *Emile Durkheim, 1858–1917: A Collection of Essays, with Translations and a Bibliography.* Columbus, OH: Ohio State University Press.

Wollheim, Richard. 1971. *Freud.* London: Fontana/Collins.

Wollheim, Richard, ed. 1974. *Freud: A Collection of Critical Essays.* Garden City, NY: Doubleday Anchor Books.

Wolterstorff, Nicholas. 1983. "Can Belief in God Be Rational if It Has No Foundations?" In Plantinga and Wolterstorff, eds. 1983, pp. 135–86.

Woodfield, Richard, ed. 2001. *Art History as Cultural History: Aby Warburg's Projects.* Amsterdam: G and B Arts International.

Worsley, Peter. 1957. *The Trumpet Shall Sound: A Study of 'Cargo' Cults in Melanesia.* London: Macgibbon and Kee.

Yearley, Lee. 1990. *Mencius and Aquinas: Theories of Virtue and Conceptions of Courage.* Albany, NY: State University of New York Press.

Yourgrau, Palle. 2005. *A World without Time: The Forgotten Legacy of Gödel and Einstein.* New York: Basic Books.

Zaehner, Robert Charles. 1957. *Mysticism Sacred and Profane: An Inquiry into Some Varieties of Praeter-Natural Experience.* Oxford: Oxford University Press.

Zimmer, Carl. 2006. "Humans May Have Limiting Effect on the Origin of (New) Species." *New York Times,* May 23, p. F2.

Zumwalt, Rosemary. 1982. "Arnold van Gennep: The Hermit of Bourg-la-Reine." *American Anthropologist* NS 84(2): 299–313.

Index

abduction 41, 43, 44 n.14
abortion 7, 180–91
  American public opinion 189
  Christian tradition and 187–9
  Hyde Amendment 195–7
  Japanese Buddhism and 182–5, 187
  Kenny on 180–1
  rabbinic texts on 181–2, 187
advocacy 5, 6, 7, 197
African art 18 n.6
Alberti, Leon Battista 153, 155, 161
Alberts et al. 104
algebra 134
Allen, Michael 128
American Reformed Judaism 115
Anagni enactment (1265) 169
analytic-synthetic distinction 86, 88
anthropology 18 n.6, 19, 72, 102, 120,
  123–46, 193
Apel-Habermas notion 88
apostolic life 166
Appleman, Philip 13 n.4
Aquinas, Thomas 7, 119, 163–72,
  179–80, 194
Archimedes' law 65
Aristotle 33, 35, 57, 79, 84, 129, 191
arithmetic 133
Arnold, John 72
art criticism, inferential 152–62, 186
art world 5–7, 18 n.6, 59, 97, 149–61, 185–6
Asad, Talal 137 n.3
astronomy 129, 133
attributional approach 11, 100
authentication 72
authority 32, 36, 59–60, 67, 91, 123–4
Ayer, A. J. 50, 57

Bacon, Francis 186
Baker, Benjamin 159
Bambrough, Renford 44 n.13
bar mitzvah 115
Barnard, William 94, 95, 100, 101
Barth, Fredrik 10 n.1, 144–5

Baxandall, Michael 153–62, 164, 172–4,
  185, 186
Bede 192, 194–5
behaviorism 108–9
Bell, John 41 n.8
Berkeley, George 50, 80
Bernoulli, Daniel 33
biochemistry 15
biology 13, 65, 97, 99, 100, 105
Blackmun, Justice 188
blame 57–8, 70, 148
Bohr, Niels 120
Boodin, John 49
Bowler, Peter 11
Boyer, Pascal 10, 101–2
Boyer et al. 122
Boyle, Leonard 33, 168, 169
brain 10, 41–2, 101–4, 112, 173
Brandom, Robert 75 n.1, 83
bridges 158–9
Brundage, James A. 176–7 n.2
Buckley, William 84
Buddhism 21, 55, 58, 59, 94, 132, 148–9,
  157, 182–5
Burgess, John 110
Butterfield, Herbert 11 n.2

calculus 134
Cantor, Georg 38
Carlyle, Thomas 84
Carnap, Rudolph 49 n.1, 79
Carrasco, Davíd 135
categories 10, 46, 62, 78, 86, 87, 89, 115,
  138, 149
Catholicism 97, 166, 177, 180, 181
causal feedback loop 67, 69
ceremony 61–2, 184
Cezanne, Paul 5, 150–1
chance 37, 42, 106
character traits 177–9
charity 170–1
Chenu, M.-D. 164–7
Childress, James 162–6, 194

China 71, 147
Chinese Buddhism 21
Chomsky, Noam 10, 108–9, 112
Christian, William 18
Christianity 4, 10, 93, 132, 166, 168–70, 177, 180, 185, 195
Churchland, Paul 102–3
Churchland, Paul and Churchland, Patricia 10
church law 165, 168, 188, 191
Cicero 153
Cladis, Mark 17
Clifford, James 139
cognitions 24–5, 27, 94
cognitive science of religion 10–15, 17, 99–122, 194
Cohen, Morris Raphael 32 n.2, 42–3
collective action 63–4, 70
collective good 64
colonialism 9, 139
common agreement 60
common-sense realism 31, 53, 56, 79, 80–3, 89–90, 120–1, 123, 139
conceptual schemes 82–3, 126–35, 137 n.3, 139, 141, 145, 151
"conditions of trade" 154, 158, 159–60
Confucius 59–60, 61, 62, 63, 71, 93, 127
consciousness 14, 25, 27, 31, 100–1
Constable, Giles 117
contextualist-attributional theory 100–1
contraception 183, 184
conventions 68–70
Copernicanism 129, 132–3, 173
correspondence bias 177–8
cosmology 38, 40, 41, 71, 131, 141–2
Courbet, Gustave 5
creation, independent 11–13
creationism 131
creation stories 141, 145
Creel, H. G. 59
Crusaders 117
culture 8–9, 71, 84, 90, 115, 133, 138, 142, 143, 144, 145, 160, 162, 173, 184
Cummins, Robert 66–7
Cuvillier, Armand 45–6

Dante, Alighieri, *Inferno* 24–5
Danto, Arthur 147–53, 149–53, 156–7, 183, 185–6
Darwin, Charles 17, 40
Darwinism 11–13, 14, 42
Davidson, Donald 28, 145–6, 173, 186
  conceptual schemes 82–3, 126–35, 137 n.3, 139, 141, 145, 151
  criticized by Rescher 131–4, 145

critique of Pinker 122
dismissal of truth theories 33–4
on language 82, 109–14, 119, 120, 136, 193–4
limits of relativism 126–31
mental/physical events 105–6, 107–8
primacy of the idiolect 112, 114–15, 119, 126, 137 n.3, 160, 187, 193
Rorty on 81–3, 84, 85, 86, 89, 90, 97
shared beliefs 138
deduction 29, 33, 36
deductive-nomological approach 19
defense mechanism 51, 53
Dennett, Daniel 105
Descartes, René 24–31, 33, 76, 78, 85, 134
determinism 13, 38, 39, 41, 43, 104–5
Dewey, John 20, 46, 47, 53–4, 55, 84, 85, 90, 173
Dieterlen, Germaine 141, 142
disciplinary matrix 84–6, 119
Dogon people 121, 141–3, 144, 145
Donagan, Alan 49
Dorf, Elliot 182 n.4
Doris, John 177, 178
doubt 26, 29, 31, 33, 34, 34 n.3, 36, 120, 152, 167, 172, 173
Douglas, Justice 176
Douglas, Mary 4, 19, 67–71, 72–3, 87, 98, 123, 186
  How Institutions Think 62, 70
  Purity and Danger 62–3, 67, 73, 193
dreams 14, 15, 16, 25
Dummett, Michael A. E. 85
Dürer, Albrecht 158
Durkheim, Emile 4, 16–17, 18–19, 20, 45–8, 64, 73, 87
Durkheim-Fleck program 63 n.3, 64
Dworkin, Ronald 124

Eckhardt, Meister 59
economics 72, 148, 158, 182
Edelman, Gerald 40, 41, 103, 105
ego 26, 57
Einstein, Albert 41, 44, 45, 120
Eliade, Mircea 10
Elster, Jon 67–8
embodied rationality 9
Emerson, Ralph Waldo 84, 85
emotions 64, 91, 94–5, 95, 189
emotivism 50, 51, 54, 55, 56, 61, 191
empiricism 32, 46, 47, 56, 73, 75, 82, 87, 129
  first dogma of 86, 88
  human behavior 72
  limits of 50–5

second dogma of 76, 88, 93, 94
third dogma of 82–3, 126–35, 137 n.3,
    139, 141, 145, 151
epistemology 24–31, 45–8, 78, 85, 90, 138
Erhart, Michael 158
ethics 2, 5, 7, 48, 124
    Danto on 148, 156
    Fingarette on 53–5, 61, 174, *see also*
        abortion
ethnography 72, 93, 126, 135, 137–8,
    141–2, 193
Euler, Leonhard 38
Evans-Pritchard, E. E. 64, 65, 67
evolution 37, 42, 108
exegesis 144 n.6, 145
experience 11, 29, 33, 80, 89, 91–3,
    100–1, 149
experiments 33, 37, 41, 141, 161, 179
EXREL Project 99, 100, 114

fallacy 33, 50, 65–6, 155, 157, 193
fallibilism 32, 36, 42, 47, 72, 88, 124, 152
feelings 51–2, 56, 89, 94, 193
Feldman, David 181, 182
feminism 17
Feuer, Lewis 37, 40
Feyerabend, Paul 84, 87, 88, 123,
    126, 129
Feynman, Richard P. 41 n.8
Ficino's *Platonic Theology* 127–8
fieldwork 19, 136, 140, 141–6, 176, 193
Fine, Arthur 44–5, 75 n.1, 119, 120, 125
Fingarette, Herbert 49, 50, 69, 70, 71,
    160, 191
    art appreciation analogy 59
    collective action 63
    Confucianism 59–60, 61, 62
    on ethics 53–5, 61, 174
    game analogy 55–7
    on logic and morality 86
    notion of 'blame' 57–8
    responsibility 55–9
    on unconscious behavior 51–3
Finnis, John 176
Fleck, Ludwik 63 n.3
Fodor, Jerry 112
Forman, Robert 95–6
formulae 14, 20–1, 37, 81
Forth Bridge 158–9
Foucault, Michel 137 n.3, 138, 139, 173
foundationalism 94, 96
Fraassen, Bas van 44
free-rider problems 63–4
Freud, Sigmund 17, 52, 136, 193, 194
functionalism 16, 62–8, 109, 118, 193

Galapagos Islands 12
Galileo 127, 134
game-playing 55–7, 58
game theory 3, 161
Gamow, George 41 n.8
Gardner, Richard 182, 183
Geertz, Clifford 4, 98, 123, 135–41
Gell-Mann, Murray 128
Gennep, Arnold van 18–19, 20
geometry 133, 134
George, Robert 176–7
Gerhoh of Reichersberg 166
Gilder, Louisa 120
Goethe, Johann Wolfgang von 84
Gombrich, Ernst 155, 156, 157
Goodman, Nelson 72, 113 n.4
Goody, Jack 18 n.6
Greek drama 59
Greek philosophy 180
Griaule, Marcel 141–6
Grisez, Germain 176
Grove, Maxwell 112 n.3
guilt 54, 55, 58, 66, 145 n.7, 182
Gustafson, James 189

Haack, Susan 86, 88
Haacke, Hans 185–6
habits 36, 37, 38–9, 52, 53, 69, 73, 76, 89,
    92, 95, 105, 113, 178, 179
Hacking, Ian 84, 126
HADD (hyperactive agency detection
    device) 15
Halivni, David Weiss 143–4
Hanson, N. R. 44, 87
Harman, Gilbert 83, 85, 90, 175, 177,
    178–9, 191
Harris v. McRae case 196
Harvey, Steve 152
Hawking, Stephen 131
Hebrew Bible 71
Hehir, Bryan 165
Heidegger, Martin 85
Hempel, Carl 65–6
Henry, Matthew 122
Herdt, Gilbert 139–40
hermeneutics 85, 91
Hinduism 58, 59, 93, 94
historical inquiry 162
historical narrative 3, 60–1, 143–4, 151–2
historical predictability 96
historical reconstruction 72, 125, 155, 163
history 72–3, 93, 117–19, 124, 126, 135,
    151–2, 155, 193
Holton, Gerald 43, 48
Hook, Sidney 85

human behavior 4, 21, 52, 53, 54, 72, 94, 97, 106, 107, 110, 112–13, 177–8, *see also* anthropology; ethnography
humanism 153–4
human mind 24, 38–9, 101
human rights 140
Humbert of Romans 168
Hume, David 17, 50, 73, 91, 119, 172
Huxley, T. H. 166
Hyde Amendment 196–7
hypotheses 20–1, 31, 33, 36, 53, 73

ideal-language theory 78–9
idiolect, primacy of the 112, 114–15, 119, 126, 137 n.3, 160, 187, 193
incapacities 26, 27–8, 29
independent creation 11–13
India 147
Indonesia 135
induction 31, 33
induction (ritual) 116
ineffability 27, 91, 92, 93, 95
infallibility 86–7
infant imitation 102
infant language acquisition 25–6, 109, 112, 113–14
inferences 25, 26, 29–30, 31, 33, 36, 43, 77, 102
inferential criticism 153–62, 186
innateness 10, 109, 112
innatism 62, 73, 87
innovation 36, 69, 97, 111, 115–16
inquiry 40–1, 53–4, 72, 73
    Fingarette 54–5, 174
    Peirce 3, 21, 22, 28, 31–6, 41, 43, 72, 73, 76, 120, 124, 173, 198
    Rorty 90, 124
institutions 62, 68, 69–71, 73, 97, 120, 123, 142, 144, 147, 160, 183
intentionality 81, 102, 164, 188
intentional language 82, 86, 94, 97, 103–4, 105, 110, 118
intentional visual interest 158–61
intention(s) 14, 15, 21, 27, 68, 106, 107, 117, 128
introspection 27, 28, 32, 52, 95
intuition(s) 24–6, 27, 29, 32, 50, 73, 76, 77, 95
Islam 135–6

James, William 17, 23–4, 32 n.2, 46, 47, 49, 90, 91, 105, 106, 107, 173
Jameson, Fredric 139
Japanese Buddhism 7, 21–2, 182–5, 187

Jewish diaspora 18, 71
Jews 60–1, 115, 143–4, 145, 181–2
Job, Book of 59, 62, 71
Johns, Jasper 150
Johnson, James 166
Johnson, Paul 140
Joyce, James 128
Judaism 18, 115
judgments 28–9, 31, 36, 52–6, 93, 97, 115, 119, 144, 151, 155, 175
Julius Caesar 132–3
justice 123, 148, 163, 165, 170, 171
justification 29, 50, 72–3, 77, 86, 87, 90, 144, 146, 175
just-war doctrine 162–72

Kandinsky, Wassily 6
Kant, Immanuel 35, 76, 78, 85
karma, doctrine of 55, 58, 147, 183
Katz, Steven 91
Kenny, Anthony 180–1, 187, 191
Kim, Jaegwon 85
Kitaro, Nishida 21
knowledge 23, 24, 25, 27, 31, 46, 48, 54, 61, 80–1, 85, 86, 89, 90, 108, 132–5, 141–2, 145, 168
knowledge claims 27–9, 34, 78
Kuhn, Thomas 44, 72, 82, 85, 87, 88, 129
Kulik, Buzz 189
Kuper, Adam 18 n.6

Ladd-Franklin, Christine 37
LaFleur, William 182, 183–5
Lakatos, Imre 22
Landino, Cristoforo 155–6
language 10, 32, 70, 97, 146, 192–3
    acquisition 25–6, 108–9, 109, 112, 113–14
    art criticism 153, 155
    conceptual scheme 126–31
    Davidson on 82, 109–14, 119, 120, 136, 193–4
    first meanings 110–11
    ideal-language theory 78–9
    intentional 82, 86, 94, 97, 103–4, 105, 110, 118
    "linguistic consensus" 78
    linguistic division of labor 118–19
    natural 108–14
    ordinary 78–80, 91
    religious 90–3
    Rorty on 78–9
    translations 127–8, 130
    truth of sentences 124, 126–31

Laplace, Pierre-Simon 13, 42
law 69, 71, 125, 143–4, 171, 176, 182, 184,
    188, 189, 196
laws of nature 38
Lawson, E. Thomas 116
Lawson, E. Thomas and McCauley,
    Robert 10, 108, 109, 115, 145 n.7
Leeuw, Gerardus van der 172
legal process 54–5
Leibniz, Gottfried 134
Leonardo da Vinci 156, 193
Leviticus, Book of 62, 71, 193
Lewis, David 68, 69, 109–10, 111
Lewontin, Richard 14, 104
Lichtenstein, Roy 150
Liguori, Alfonso de' 188
linguistic habits 73, 95, 107, 178,
    see also language
Lippi, Filippo 153, 156
Little, Rich 102
Lobachevsky, Nicolai 36
Locke, John 80, 85
logic 30, 44, 86–8
logical positivism 19, 75
logic of science 31–6
Lovejoy, Arthur O. 11 n.2
Lukes, Steven 19 n.7, 124–5, 139, 140

MacIntyre, Alasdair 195
magic 61, 194
Maimonides 189
Malachowski, Alan 75 n.1
malapropisms 110, 111
maleficence 162–3
Malinowski, Bronislaw 66
Mantegna, Andrea 161
Marquis, Don 136
marriage 176–7
Marrou, Henri I. 133
Martino de Fano 167 n.2
Marx, Karl 194
Marxism 136
Masaccio 156
Masao, Abe 21
masturbation 176, 180
Masuzawa, Tomoko 8, 9
mathematics 133, 134
Maurer, Daphne and Maurer, Charles 113
medical materialism 40 n.6, 106, 107,
    147, 193
mentalese 102, 112
metaphysics 39, 76, 78–80, 83, 90, 97, 141,
    157, 187
Metropolitan Museum of Art, New York 5–6
Middeldorf, Ulrich 153

Midrash 144–5
Milgram, Stanley 177 n.3, 179
Mill, J. S. 30, 76, 191
Miller, Richard 162–7, 170, 172, 174, 194
MINDlab 99
miracle plays 158
Misak, Cheryl 35, 75
Mishnah 143–4, 181–2
mizuko kuyo 182–3, 184
Mondrian, Piet 5–7
Moore, G. E. 43, 50, 55
morality 84, 86, 124, 148–9, 175
moral psychology 50
moral relativism 124–5, 191
Mozart, Wolfgang Amadeus 112 n.3
Müller, Max 4
Mu Qi 150, 151
Muslims 92, 93, 136
mystical experience 91–2, 100–1, 149
mysticism 59, 91, 95, 147, 149
'myth of the given' 88–9, 94, 101

Nagel, Ernest 43–4
Nagel, Thomas 75, 85, 90, 95
narrative, historical 3, 60–1, 143–4, 151–2
natural language 108–14
natural law 37
natural sciences 2, 3, 11, 13, 22, 36, 72, 82,
    83, 84, 97, 105, 120, 123, 141
natural selection 12, 37
Neurath, Otto 50
neurobiology 14–15
neurochemistry 15, 42, 107
neuroscience 11, 15, 16, 17, 40 n.6, 194
Newcomb, Simon 36
Newton, Sir Isaac 133–4
Nguni tribe 116
nirvana 148
NOA (natural ontological attitude) 45
nominalism 35, 37, 76
nomological approach 19, 65, 108
Noonan, John 187–8
Nussbaum, Martha 140

objectification 80
objectivity 86, 87, 109, 160
Oliver, Roland and Atmore, Anthony
    115–16
Olson, Mancur 64
ordinary language 78–80, 91
Otto, Rudolf 10

pacifism 162, 165, 166
Pap, Arthur 52
Parsons, Charles 136

Passover Seder 60–1
Pataux, Agnès 121
PCE (the pure consciousness event) 95–6
Peirce, C. S. 3, 19–24, 72, 73, 80, 83, 90,
    105, 106, 124, 172
    Collected Papers 37–43
    critique of Cartesianism 24–31, 77
    on doubts 34 n.3, 152
    Durkheim and 45–8
    fallibilism 32, 36, 42, 47, 88
    Firstness, Secondness and Thirdness 76,
        77, 87, 88, 89
    fixation of belief 32, 34, 36, 38–9, 123,
        167, 173, 191
    ideal-language approach 79
    Illustrations of the Logic of Science 31–6
    inquiry 3, 21, 22, 28, 31–6, 41, 43, 72, 73,
        76, 120, 124, 173, 198
    legacy of pragmatism 42–5
    on logic 86, 87
    The Monist essays 37–42
    Rorty on 75–9
    on theories 161–2
    and Wittgenstein 42, 44 n.13, 75–9
Penner, Hans 64–5
"period eye" 154–5, 156, 158, 160, 174
Pfeiffer, Paul 186
Phillips, D. Z. 93–4, 122
philology 7, 93
philosophy 4, 24, 26–7, 43–4, 49, 83–90,
    142, 180, 195
philosophy of science 43–5, 82, 119, 120,
    126, 127
physics 37, 41, 134
    quantum 41, 44, 106, 120, 134
physiognomic fallacy 155, 157
Picasso, Pablo 97, 159, 160, 161
Piero della Francesca 161, 168, 173
Pinker, Steven 102, 112, 122
Pliny 155
Plutarch 133
politics 3, 4, 59, 67, 72, 84, 131, 135, 136,
    138–41, 143, 146, 180, 186, 188,
    190, 197
Pols, Edward 78 n.2
Popper, Karl 44, 119
positivism 19, 49 n.1, 61, 75
power relations 137–8
pragmatism 3, 19–20, 22, 23–4, 28–9, 32
    n.2, 44, 49, 135, 175–9
    Durkheim on 45–8
    ethics of abortion 185–98
    Fingarette on 50
    Rorty on 75

and the study of religion 90–8,
    see also Peirce; James; Dewey
Prebish, Charles and Tanaka, Kenneth 22
predictions 3, 53, 54
probability 31, 42, 76, 109
professionalization of philosophy 84
prolegomena 49, 51
propositions 30–1, 32, 35–6, 54
Protestantism 4, 172
Proudfoot, Wayne 4, 90–4, 100–1, 120,
    122, 149
psychoanalysis 50–5, 58–9
psychology 51, 58, 65, 87, 89
Putnam, Hilary 20, 49 n.1, 85, 87, 88, 90,
    118 n.7, 119

quantum physics 41, 44, 106, 120, 134
Quine, W. V. O. 72, 82, 83, 84, 85, 90
    on the analytic-synthetic distinction 86
    on language 112–13

Rabbinic Jews 143–4, 145
rabbinic texts 7, 115, 180, 181–2, 187
Rabinow, Paul 138–9, 145 n.7, 146
Radcliffe-Brown, Alfred 66
Ramsey, Frank 42, 44 n.13
rape 125, 188, 189, 190, 196
Rappaport, Roy 20
rationalism 46, 47–8, 72, 127
rationality 8, 9, 17, 23, 45, 56, 82, 119–20,
    127, 140, 141, 146, 191, 192
rational reconstruction 163–4
Rauschenburg, Robert 150
Rawls, John 162, 180
reaction-sensation 89
realism, *see* common-sense realism
reasonableness 192–8
reasoning 24, 27, 28, 29, 30, 31, 38, 89, 148,
    163, 164, 180
reductionism 76, 88, 93, 94
regularity 1–2, 11, 30–1, 38–9, 105
Reichenbach, Hans 49, 51
relativism 23, 76, 82, 88, 123–35, 137,
    139–41, 140, 145, 151, 191
religion 2, 3, 4, 8, 16, 51, 67, 114–22, 136,
    162, 173, 185, 193, 194–5, 198
    cognitive science and study of 9–11, 99,
        101–2, 194
    Durkheim on 18, 20
    Fingarette on 59
    pragmatism and study of 19–22, 90–8
religious belief 46, 101, 117, 131, 143, 147
repression 51, 53, 185
Rescher, Nicholas 131–4, 145

responsibility 56–7, 58–9, 61
Rieber, Charles 49
Riemann, Bernhard 36
rites of passage 19
ritual 10, 18, 115–17
Roe v. Wade case 189, 197
Romans 132–4
Rorty, Richard 123, 140, 145 n.7, 146, 164
  common-sense realism 31, 53, 56, 79,
    80–3, 89–90, 120–1, 123, 139
  criticism of 87, 90
  and Davidson 81–3, 84, 85, 86, 89, 90, 97
  disciplinary matrix 84–6
  and epistemology 90, 138
  Haack on 86–7
  on Peirce and Wittgenstein 75–9, 80, 81,
    83, 84, 86–91, 95, 97
  Philosophy and the Mirror of Nature 75, 83,
    85–90
  professionalization of philosophy 84–5
  and Quine 85, 86, 87–8, 90
  and Sellars 80–1, 82, 83, 85, 86,
    88–9, 91
  on Whitehead 79–80
Rosner, Fred 181
Royce, Josiah 42, 49, 85, 124
Rubio, Julie 177
Runciman, Steven 117
Rupert, abbot of Deutz 167
Ruse, Michael 13, 14
Russell, Bertrand 50, 55
Ryle, Gilbert 85

Sacks, Oliver 106–7
Said, Edward 173
St Alban 192, 194–5
St Bernard of Clairvaux 96
St John Chrysostom 177
Samkhya system 91
sampling 72, 73
samsara 148
Sankara, Adi 92, 93
Santayana, George 84
Schapiro, Meyer 6–7, 193
Schiller, Friedrich 46
Schleiermacher, Friedrich 9, 91, 172
Schwartz, Robert 86
science 65, 76, 87–9, 97, 105, 123, 138
  Peirce on 27, 28, 31–8, 43–5
  philosophy of 43–5, 82, 119, 120,
    126, 127
  Roman curriculum 133, *see also* cognitive
    science; natural sciences; neuroscience;
    social sciences
Scientific American (June 2000) 103

Scott, John D. and Pawson, Tony 103–4
Segal, Robert 66–7
self-consciousness 25, 26, 77
Sellars, Wilfrid 79, 80–1, 82, 83, 85, 86,
  88–9, 91, 101
semantics 80–1, 112, 114
sense-data 88–9, 95
sexuality 139–40, 176
Shaka (Zulu ruler) 116
Shapiro, Ian 188
Sharf, Robert 8, 21–2
signaling 103–4
skepticism 90, 140
Skinner, Quentin 4, 108, 109
Slater, Steve 63
Slingerland, Edward 11, 14
Smith, Jonathan 8, 9, 18
social anthropology 63 n.3
social contract 60
social division of labor 118–19
social sciences 7, 22, 45–8, 51, 65, 73, 84,
  94, 119–20
sociology 45–8, 51, 72
sociology of science 63 n.3
Sontag, Susan 84
Soviet Union 60
Spanish Catholics 18
Spickard, James V. 71 n.5
Stevenson, C. L. 51
Stewart, Justice 196
Stoller, Paul 9
Stout, Jeff 4
Strathern, Marilyn 139
subjectivist principle 79–80
sub-routines 1–2, 67
Suetonius 133
Sukarno, President of Indonesia 135–6
superego 57
superintuition 77
Suzuki, D. T. 21
synechism 38
syntax 112, 114

Tacitus 60
Tarski, Alfred 33, 83, 129
Taves, Ann 9–11, 14–15, 16, 17, 19, 21,
  99, 100–1
TAVS (threat activation system) 15
Taylor, Mark 7, 17, 19, 21
technical terms 128
tenacity 32, 36, 123
theories 2–3, 7–17, 28–30, 119, 126, 129,
  136–7, 161–2
theory of truth 23, 33, 34–5, 45, 47, 48, 56,
  90, 130

Thompson, Robert 18
threat vigilance system 15
To Find a Man (1972) 189
Tolkien, J. R. R. 7
Toorn, Karel van der 71
Torah 71
Torrell, Jean-Pierre 171
Tourette, Gilles de la 106
Transcendental Meditation 96
troc 158, 159–60
truth 17, 20, 76, 87, 90, 96, 137–41
    and belief 114
    historical 72, 151–2
    intentional language and 82
    logic of science 32–6
    pragmatism and 23–4
    radical change and 45
    of sentences 124, 126–31
    theory of 23, 33, 34–5, 45, 47, 48, 56,
        90, 130
Tugwell, Simon 166
Turner, Victor 19, 98
Tweed, Thomas 17–18, 19, 20,
    21, 22
Tyler, Stephen 137–8, 139
Tylor, E. B. 93

UCLA (University of California, Los
    Angeles) 49
"unconscious behavior" 51, 53, 54
universal doubt 26, 31
Upton, Candace 177 n.3

value judgments 50, 51, 54–5, 56, 61
Van Beek, W. E. A. 141–3
Vienna Circle 44
Viola, Franca 125

virtues and vices 61, 148, 169–70, 171, 177,
    178–9, 194

Warburg, Aby 155
Warhol, Andy 149, 150, 152
Warnock Committee (1984) 180
Weber, Max 4, 17, 136
Weinberg, Steven 40, 41, 42
Werblowsky, R. J. Zwi 182–3, 185
Whitehead, Alfred North 79–80
Whitehouse, Harvey 99
Whitney Biennial 2000 185
Wiggins, David 34
William of Conches 166
Williams, Bernard 88
Williams, Michael 75 n.1, 90
Wills, Garry 84
Wilson, Bryan 119
Wisdom, John 44 n.13, 119
Wittgenstein, Ludwig 50, 84, 85, 95,
    119, 123, 127, 146
    Davidson on 28
    debunking approach 83
    Douglas and 72
    Fingarette and 55, 61
    historicity of categories 89
    Nagel on 43–4
    and Peirce 42, 44 n.13, 75–9
    Rorty on 75–9
    Tractatus 44, 97
Wolterstorff, Nicholas 195

Yeats, W. B. 151–2

Zaehner, Richard 92, 93
Zen doctrine 21
Zulus 115–16